SCREENING STEPHEN KING

D1610141

SCREENING STEPHEN KING

Adaptation and the Horror Genre in Film and Television

SIMON BROWN

University of Texas Press

AUSTIN

All box-office figures in this book are from www.boxofficemojo.com.

Requests for permission to reproduce material
from this work should be sent to:
Permissions
University of Texas Press
P.O. Box 7819
Austin, TX 78713-7819
utpress.utexas.edu/rp-form

♾ The paper used in this book meets the minimum requirements of
ANSI/NISO Z39.48-1992 (R1997) (Permanence of Paper).

LIBRARY OF CONGRESS CATALOGING-IN-PUBLICATION DATA
Names: Brown, Simon (Simon David), author.
Title: Screening Stephen King : adaptation
and the horror genre in film and television / Simon Brown.
Description: First edition. | Austin : University of Texas Press, 2018. |
Includes bibliographical references and index. | Filmography.
Identifiers: LCCN 2017037706
ISBN 978-1-4773-1491-3 (cloth : alk. paper)
ISBN 978-1-4773-1492-0 (pbk. : alk. paper)
ISBN 978-1-4773-1493-7 (library e-book)
ISBN 978-1-4773-1494-4 (nonlibrary e-book)
Subjects: LCSH: King, Stephen, 1947—Criticism and interpretation. |
King, Stephen, 1947—Film adaptations. | King, Stephen, 1947—
Television adaptations. | American fiction—20th century—Film
adaptations. | Horror films—United States—History and criticism. |
Horror television programs—United States—History and criticism. |
Motion pictures—United States—History and criticism.
Classification: LCC PS3561.I483 Z6223 2018 | DDC 813/.54—dc23
LC record available at https://lccn.loc.gov/2017037706

doi:10.7560/314913

CONTENTS

ACKNOWLEDGMENTS

THIS BOOK HAS BEEN TWO YEARS IN THE WRITING, BUT thirty-four years in the making. I've been a Constant Reader of King since first reading *Christine* in 1983, and over the following years, I have acquired first editions of all his books. I've also seen most of the adaptations, although in preparing for this book, I realized I'd missed a few. King has been my companion for more than three decades, and I am delighted to have finally acquired the knowledge, skills, and opportunity to say something about him in print.

A lot of people have helped me in this task. First, I'd like to offer a very big thank you to Desiree Butterfield-Nagy and the staff of the Fogler Library at the University of Maine in Orono, for making the Stephen King collection available and for making me so welcome. I'd also like to thank Jim Burr at the University of Texas Press for taking a chance on this book. I am delighted my work has found a home there. I'd also like to thank all the staff at the BFI Reuben Library who, as usual, have been extremely helpful. They run a collection the quality of which is unparalleled. Special thanks also go to Hannah Priest for her extraordinary help and support.

I've been encouraged on this project along the way by a lot of good and smart people, and I'd particularly like to thank Regina Hansen, Erin Giannini, Sorcha ní Fhlainn, Matthew Pateman, Rebecca Williams, Catherine Spooner, and Bethan Jones for being my kind of academics: interested, supportive, fiercely smart, and ego free. It's a perfect way to be in this life.

Finally, I have as always to thank my family: my dogs, Max and Lily, and my wife, Stacey. Stacey is my Tabitha. She reads all my stuff before anyone else and knows instinctively if it works. She's talked through ideas on our daily walks and sat through a large number of King adaptations. (I spared her some of the really bad ones. I'll let you decide for yourself what they are.) A far better scholar than I can ever hope to be, she inspires me every day to

INTRODUCTION

I write for only two reasons: to please myself and to please others.

STEPHEN KING, *THE STAND*

AT THE TIME OF THIS WRITING IN JANUARY 2017, STEPHEN King has published forty-nine novels (plus seven as Richard Bachman), eleven short story or novella collections, eight nonfiction books, one original screenplay, and a number of eBooks and limited editions. In addition, his work has so far spawned thirty-eight theatrical films adapted from his writing (along with a number of sequels that, besides their connection to the original feature, have nothing to do with King), and twenty small-screen adaptations, encompassing TV movies, miniseries, episodes within anthologies, and three long-running dramas. Excluding sequels, there have therefore been fifty-eight adaptations of his work since Brian De Palma's *Carrie* (1976). These adaptations span both the big and small screen, over a period of more than forty years. In addition, King has written four original screenplays for film or TV.

Almost all these adaptations are connected to the horror genre in some way, although not all are horror. In some cases, the connection comes through the content—for example, storylines and/or visuals that draw upon existing tropes of the genre, such as supernatural elements (the haunted house in *The Shining*, 1980 and 1997, or vampires in *Salem's Lot*, 1979 and 2004); imagery showing the abject body or the body in disarray (*The Dead Zone*, 1983; *Children of the Corn*, 1984); or the use of a genre-specific visual style, as in *Carrie*. The connections to horror can also be extratextual via a director associated with the genre—such as John Carpenter (*Christine*, 1983), David Cronenberg (*The Dead Zone*), and Mick Garris (*Sleepwalkers*, 1992; *The Stand*, 1994; plus others)—or even the extent to which the adaptations are discussed in magazines specifically devoted to horror, such as *Fangoria* or *The Dark Side*. For many of the films, the categorization as horror comes not just from the film itself but also through marketing that emphasizes an association with King as a horror writer, tying the films to the genre sometimes regardless of content. Another type of film, such as *Stand by Me* (1986), *The Running Man* (1987), and *The Shawshank Redemption* (1994), is specifically not horror, containing few horror tropes in the content and also shunning any references to King's name in the publicity. These films thus avoid ties to horror through that association. Nevertheless, in light of the sheer number of films and TV programs based on his work, alongside the fact that the majority of these are linked to horror and span a period of more than forty years, King offers a rich and fascinating case study of one author's work being adapted within or around a single genre and across a variety of media with differing industrial and cultural contexts over a considerable period of time.

The aim of this book is to present such a study in order to examine the relationship that these King adaptations have had to the horror genre and to assess the impact of these works on the genre in film and on TV since the mid-1970s. For the purposes of my argument, I approach the concept of horror not from a philosophical position (for such an analysis, see, for example, Carroll 1990, Jancovich 1992, and Hills 2005), but rather in genre terms as a series of cinematic, televisual, and literary conventions that together identify an individual piece of work—be it film, book, or TV show—as belonging to the horror genre as it is defined within its respective medium. As James Naremore has pointed out, a genre not only consists of a series of textual artifacts, but is also "a discourse . . . helping to shape commercial strategies and aesthetic ideologies" (1995–1996, 14). In other words, the horror genre is defined not only by what is found in the films/books/TV shows attributed to it, but also by the ways in which these texts are marketed to and talked about and consumed by society at large. This is particularly relevant to Stephen King since his works are defined as horror as much by the manner in which they have been promoted as by the intention of King's narratives. While there is no doubt that many of his novels and short stories use elements of the supernatural or contain scenes of violence, many others do not and yet still fall under the banner of works by the so-called master of the macabre. In this book, I use horror as a genre concept that encompasses either texts that evidence engagement with established generic tropes or those that are discussed and defined as horror through marketing and/or critical discourses.

Over the years, the film and TV projects taken from King's stories have inspired a forest of printed commentary, mainly in film magazines and fanzines, but also in some scholarly works, notably those by Michael R. Collings (2006), Tony Magistrale (2003, 2012), and Mark Browning (2009, 2011). However, these adaptations have rarely been considered in the broader context of the horror genre and, more often than not, are principally related either to other King adaptations or to the original literary works. In addition, the majority of these discussions of the film and TV works have originated not in film and TV studies, but in literature. Collings and Magistrale are primarily literature scholars, making Browning one of the few film academics to date who have addressed King's work on the big and small screen.

The reasons for this seem obvious. King's ability to transcend the apparent perception of literary horror as a niche market to achieve significant mainstream popularity has prompted a handful of literature specialists— like Magistrale, Collings, and also Gary Hoppenstand and Ray B. Browne (1987)—to take his work seriously, associating King with the recognized tradition of American Gothic writing alongside the likes of Edgar Allen Poe and H. P. Lovecraft. Some of these scholars have explored both his body of work and the films taken from it. Both Magistrale and Collings, for example, have written books about King and his literature in addition to the films.

In contrast, the adaptations have failed to rouse similar interest among film and TV academics. This may be due to the variable quality of the works. As we shall see, some have been hailed by critics and audiences as classics of American cinema (*The Shining*, *The Shawshank Redemption*), others as poor examples not just of the horror genre, but also of film or TV in general (*Maximum Overdrive*, 1986; *Kingdom Hospital*, 2004). As Don Herron suggests, King is "hot stuff in B. Dalton, Crown and Waldenbooks, but his name doesn't mean much to that larger audience of horror-moviegoers, who would rather see Freddy Krueger than Stephen King" (1988, 224). While a negative critical and audience reaction does not preclude any film from serious study, the perceived lack of quality across this oeuvre does mean that it has not stood as a useful starting point for discussions of the horror genre, which has itself been deemed, at times, barely worthy of critical acknowledgment. Robin Wood refers to the horror film as "one of the most popular and, at the same time, the most disreputable of Hollywood genres" (1986, 77), while Ernest Mathijs and Jamie Sexton say that "horror cinema in general remains reviled by moral majorities, eschewed by policymakers, and dismissed by critics" (2011, 202). Philip Simpson agrees, stating that "the horror genre is regarded with deep suspicion by many social commentators and critics who proclaim themselves to be guardians of the public morality" (2011, 42).

Furthermore, the films and TV projects adapted from King's work are often atypical of the horror genre. This is mainly due to the fact that as a horror writer and, more importantly, as a horror brand, King is, above all, a popular author whose books regularly make, and for the most part top, lists of best-selling books in both hardcover and paperback. His work is primarily of mass-market appeal, and his best-seller status is seemingly at odds with a perception of the horror genre as niche, especially in cinematic and television terms. Mathijs and Sexton, for example, explore the horror genre through the concepts of cult and fandom, ideas that lean toward specific subcategories of the cinematic horror market, and King's very popularity precludes the adaptations of his work from such discussions. He may work in a niche genre, but in trying to tap into the market represented by his huge number of "Constant Readers," the adapted works are arguably too popularist to be beloved by horror audiences or taken seriously by horror critics. Tony Magistrale suggests that "perhaps King's extraordinary popular reputation has spilled over to defray efforts to treat these films as serious works of cinematic art" (2012, 5), and I would argue that this same popularity has also affected their being considered as serious works of cinematic and televisual horror.

As a result, few of the vast number of books exploring the cinematic and televisual horror genres make more than passing mention of King adaptations. Mark Jancovich offers a rare case study, and even he does not specifically discuss the relationship of King adaptations to the film/TV horror genres. Rather, he more generally considers King's significance as a proliferator of horror conventions to a wide audience before delving into King's thematic preoccupations (1992, 98–104). Barry Keith Grant's two volumes on horror, *The Dread of Difference* and *Planks of Reason* (1996a and b) barely mention King adaptations, except for an analysis of *The Shining* (1996b, 93–94). Gregory Waller in his introduction to *American Horrors* refers only generally to what he calls "the spate" of King adaptations as being indicative of a movement among Hollywood studios in the 1970s and 1980s to turn to horror literature for inspiration (1987a, 10). In his cultural history of horror, David J. Skal devotes several pages to King's novels and also to the Broadway version of *Carrie*, but only one page to the films, which he merely describes as having "a jinx-like aura," highlighting the general sense that these films have a poor reputation (1993, 366).

This dearth of serious critical analysis of adapted King works also extends to adaptation studies, where his name barely appears, despite the fact that the majority of films and shows are adaptations, some relatively faithful (*The Dead Zone*; *Firestarter*, 1984; *The Green Mile*, 1999), others so altered as to be barely recognizable (*The Running Man*, *The Lawnmower Man*, 1992). Forrest Wickman used writer credits in IMDb to produce a list of the most adapted authors of all time; King tied with Georges Simenon at eighteenth (2011). King is the only living author in the top twenty-four, yet important works on adaptation by the likes of Brian McFarlane (1996), James Naremore (2000), Robert Stam (2005), Linda Hutcheon (2006), and Simone Murray (2012) rarely mention King, and when they do, it is, as in the case with Barry Keith Grant, almost exclusively in relation to Stanley Kubrick's film of *The Shining*.

Arguably, this is because that film is famous for the way in which it di-

each concept. His name on a poster represents a stamp of authorship, even though he often has little or nothing to do with the script or the production. Equally, King's name also represents a genre, ostensibly a subgenre of horror, which is itself problematic since King films are not always horror films nor indeed are King's novels. The reality is that in filmic terms, Stephen King is, more than anything, a brand, and one of the key challenges of any examination of his work is to define exactly what that concept means in relation to both King and cinema.

King acknowledges this in a 1980 piece titled "On Becoming a Brand Name," reprinted in *Secret Windows* (2000). In it, King recounts how he came to be both published and successful, but also offers thoughts on what being a brand name actually means. He writes, "I would describe a 'brand name author' as one who is known for a certain genre of the popular novel . . . . I, perhaps, am the Green Giant of what is called the 'modern horror story.'" He also describes it as being "not much different than Hollywood typecasting" (2000c, 39, 56). His suggestion is that his output is immediately recognizable because of his name and that his name is associated with horror, arguing that by the time his third book, *The Shining* (1977), came out, "it could be neatly categorized by this time as 'a Stephen King novel' (just as when you say Hellman's, most everyone knows you're talking about mayonnaise)" (66).

Yet, horror author and King collaborator Peter Straub suggested in 2000 that King "moved on from writing immediately classifiable horror fiction two decades ago, with *The Dead Zone* . . . of course every one of [his] novels was categorized as horror immediately upon publication, because that is what reviewers are like: they think in terms of categories and straight lines, and once they have you labeled, you might as well be branded, because you will wear that label forever" (2000, ix). It is important to note here that claiming that any piece of work is immediately classifiable within a certain genre implies that genre has a finite and unequivocal set of characteristic components, something that Steve Neale suggests can only lead to definitions that are, at best, banal or tautological (1995, 171). However, Straub is not alone in suggesting that by the time *The Dead Zone* came out, King had shifted away from "straight" horror. Douglas E. Winter describes *The Stand*, published before *The Dead Zone*, as being the first of his novels to break the barriers of the traditions of horror and enter the territory of "epic fantasy" (1989, 66). Equally, Alan Warren notes that "*Christine* was trumpeted as a return to the purely supernatural horror tale—following such science-fictional excursions as *The Stand*, *The Dead Zone*, *Firestarter*, *The Dark Tower: The Gunslinger* [1982], and the non-supernatural *Cujo* and *Different Seasons*" (1985, 19). Finally, Philip Simpson suggests that it was slightly later, with *Different Seasons*, that King "moved away from the kind of supernatural horror tales . . . into realistic fiction" (2011, 41). Since *Christine*, one could argue that *Pet Sematary* (1983), *IT* (1986), *The Dark Half* (1989), *Needful Things* (1991), and *Cell* (2006) fall under the category of "immediately classifiable horror fiction," not least because of their featuring classic horror monsters such as zombies, doppelgangers, and the devil himself. But King's work also contains titles that do not fit into this category, such as *The Tommyknockers* (1987), *Lisey's Story* (2006), *Duma Key* (2008), *Under the Dome* (2009), and *11/22/63* (2011). The implication from both King and Straub is that a Stephen King book is labeled as horror whether he, or indeed anyone else, considers it so or not and with little consideration as to what a horror novel actually is. Here the element of branding becomes key in that while a King book may be synonymous with horror, it is equally part of an authorial canon that transcends that genre as being part of a body of work that is recognizably King's take on its inherent tropes.

While some of his books may be "immediately classifiable horror fiction" and others are not horror at all, consistent elements run throughout King's work, notably his use of language, visual description of places, and brand names, plus the way in which he draws his characters. These elements clearly identify a book as being "by Stephen King" and stem not primarily from the story or the events, but from the writing style. This, in turn, is necessarily often absent from the films taken from his books. They may retain some of his dialogue, but his descriptive prose must be transformed into visual terms. For example, in *Christine*, King describes Will Darnell, owner of the garage in which Arnie Cunningham works on his 1958 Plymouth Fury, through the first-person view of Arnie's friend, Dennis Guilder:

> Darnell turned to me. He was wearing a sail-like white shirt and brown khaki pants. Great rolls of fat bulged out his neck and hung in dewlaps from below his chin. . . . Darnell walked with the graceful, almost feminine movements of a man who has been fat for a long time and sees a long future of fathood ahead of him. . . . I guess you could say he was a man who hadn't let his infirmities get him down. (1983, 54)

In Carpenter's film, this description is visualized in the form of actor Robert Prosky. Sporting a white shirt but also a tie and waistcoat, Prosky's Darnell is visually nowhere near as fat as King's, and so the focus of the characterization becomes one of an unkempt appearance, slovenly habits, and an irascible nature. Much of the latter comes through in dialogue, often directly lifted from King—for example, his observation to Dennis: "Kiddo, if you sold him that piece of shit you ought to be fucking ashamed of yourself" ("fucking" is added in the film). But the descriptive prose is reconfigured in visual terms through costume, makeup, and performance.

Robert Prosky as Will Darnell in Christine *(1983).*

Thus, while within literature the notion of a Stephen King brand can be discussed in relation to horror, to mainstream popular success, and to a consistency of style, in cinema, this concept becomes more ephemeral. Not only is King's prose style or dialogue not always present, but also not all the films are successful, as evidenced by the often indifferent responses to many of them. Indeed, Michael Collings went so far as to suggest in 1987, a year in which the cinematic Brand Stephen King was particularly struggling, that "associating King's name with a film almost automatically endangers the project" (63). In shifting King's work from page to screen, his brand somehow transforms from being bankable and popular to being, for all intents and purposes, a liability.

LOST IN TRANSLATION?

Thus, to analyze the films made from King's work, the concept of his status as a brand and as a mainstream popular author within a niche genre must be explored in relation to the process of moving his work from page to screen. As discussed above, and as Linda Hutcheon points out, the traditional approach of adaptation theory has been for many years a largely comparative one in which "the source text is granted an axiomatic primacy and authority, and the rhetoric of comparison has often been that of faithfulness and equivalence" (2006, 16).

Certainly, debates about King on film in academic texts, reviews, and magazine and online articles have tended to adopt this comparative approach, often finding the films to be pale imitations of the books. It is, however, a testament to the perception of King as a mass-market writer that, in some cases, the situation is reversed and the adaptations are seen as transcending the limitations of King's own work. As Daniel Cziraky points out, "as bankable as King's name has become in the publishing world, the poor performance of past films based on his works was most likely a very big factor in Columbia's releasing the film *Stand by Me* [1986] as 'A Rob Reiner Film' instead of Stephen King's *The Body*" (Collings 1987, 65). Don Herron is far blunter in his opinion regarding the awfulness of *Maximum Overdrive*, the film version of King's short story "Trucks," which he both wrote and directed: "It's easy to understand why someone making a serious film might ease King's name out of the pre-release publicity. . . . A 'Stephen King movie,' as now we all know, looks exactly like *Maximum Overdrive*" (1988, 229, 233).

Comparisons between *Stand by Me* and *Maximum Overdrive*, released around the same time, highlight the difficulties in discussing adaptations, which transform King's works from a single voice into multiple voices across different media with different contexts and syntax. As Eliza Pezzotta points out, "adapting a novel to screen is like translating . . . from one set of conventions into another" (2013, 5–6). Pezzotta takes this further:

> A cinematic adaptation is not only the child of its two parents, which is to say, its director and its source novel, but also of its mode and context of production and of the cinematic tradition that precedes it. In a perennial exchange among the filmmakers' style, the cinematic conventions and genres, fluctuating meanings and stories about our world and imaginary ones are continually re-actualized in different sociocultural contexts, subjected to different audiences' demands, industry's and censorship's regulations, and technological discoveries. (2013, 6)

To address this issue, Pezzotta proposes that a "synchronic, ahistoric comparison between a book and its adaptation should be substituted by a diachronic, historic discussion of the dialogical exchange among different media and different texts of the same media" (2013, 6). Lawrence Venuti further suggests that "[a] film adaptation . . . [detaches] its prior materials from their contexts." He goes on to argue that "the source text is not only decontextualized but *recontextualized*" and that "the recontextualizing process entails the creation of another network of intertextual relations established by and within the translation" (2012, 93). Simone Murray similarly argues that what is required is not so much a focus on the texts themselves (be they literary, cinematic, or "other"), but rather an analysis that asks how "the mechanisms by which adaptations are produced influence the kind of adaptations released, how certain audiences become aware of adapted properties, and how the success of an adaptation may impact differently upon various industry stakeholders" (2012, 4). She suggests that "adapted texts may be interesting, in short, not so much for their intricate ideological encodings, but for the way they illuminate the contexts of their own production" (5).

Pezzotta, Venuti, and Murray are saying that focusing primarily on the comparisons to the source material makes it impossible to construct this new context. This links back to the issues of de-contextualization that arise from the work on King films by Tony Magistrale and Mark Browning. If, as Pezzotta suggests, an adaptation is the child of the author and the director, plus the mode and context of production, Magistrale and Browning take King the author as their primary focus, paying less attention to the influence of the other elements. Pezzotta and Venuti recommend that adaptations be explored within their own set of intertextual and industrial relations, which is the approach that I take here. In this specific case, this means detaching King films from the "prior materials" of their source texts and instead focusing upon the new contexts that emerge.

This is not to suggest that I do not consider King himself to be of any significance in the discussion to come. Indeed, he lies at the heart of every page of this book. But it is nevertheless important to acknowledge that while to a significantly variable degree the films and TV dramas I discuss draw from and reflect the literary source material, King's original ideas are nevertheless filtered through a new set of thematic and industrial preoccupations being imposed by the screenwriters, directors, studios, and networks. My approach doesn't consider the films in relation to the novels, instead looking at them in terms of a specifically cinematic/televisual form of Stephen King, one constructed in cinemas and on TV by an increasing number of King films/shows designed to appeal to particular types of audiences. These are related to the novels, and to King himself, but they are also different, often in terms of narrative but, more importantly, in their relationship to a cinematic or televisual horror genre that is itself different from the literary genre in which King writes. My approach embraces the fact that horror in film, TV, and literature is often different in terms of its themes, preoccupations, and audiences. Furthermore, across these different media, these elements are not fixed and consistent but also change over time.

Therefore, through considering King as a popular author and a brand name and exploring the films taken from his work in the context of the horror genre, this book has two interlinking aims. The first is to examine the films through an exploration of the different industrial contexts that are brought to bear on them. This will encompass the financing and target audience (is this a big-budget film aimed at mainstream audiences or a low-budget film aimed specifically at horror fans?); the concept of authorship (is *Christine* a John Carpenter film rather than a Stephen King film?); and an examination of the notion of genre style. I will examine what occurs when King's consistent prose is replaced by the very different aesthetic requirements of the cinema/TV mediums in general and the horror genre in particular. My second aim is to situate these Stephen King adaptations within the context of developments in the cinematic horror genre in order to both locate these films within that genre over the past forty years and to assess to what extent a cinematic or televisual Brand Stephen King has affected changes and advancements in cinematic horror. Is there a televisual or cinematic Brand Stephen King at all, beyond a name on a poster, and if there is, has it had an impact on the cinematic horror genre?

STRUCTURE

The first chapter sets out the key concepts that underpin this discussion. It establishes King as a best-selling author of horror for a mass readership and defines his success within the context of a particularly mainstream form of horror. It then explores the reasons for his unique success within that genre by examining his works as hybrid forms of horror, looking at both story and style and focusing in particular on the latter and the various stylistic tropes that can be traced across King's body of work. These include his use of language, his characterization, his sense of place, his use of brand names, and the interplay within his writing between reality and fantasy. In doing so, it uses the concept of hybridity to establish both the literary brand Stephen King and a hypothesis as to why King achieved such a notable breakthrough into mainstream popular culture. It then takes the elements that make up this hypothesis and discusses them in relation to the adaptations to identify the cinematic and televisual Brand Stephen King and how it both relates to and differs from the literary brand.

With the notions of the mainstream and the Stephen King brand established as parameters for the discussion, the rest of the book focuses on the film and television versions of his stories. In keeping with Pezzotta's recommendation, I propose to take a largely diachronic approach, albeit one that is neither strictly chronological nor periodic. Chapter 2 focuses on the early adaptations, from *Carrie* through *Cat's Eye*. Following the contextual, rather than the purely thematic or textual approach established above, this chapter examines the films in terms of their industrial and sociopolitical contexts: as horror films within a transitional period for both American cinema and the horror genre. I discuss the political and industrial underpinnings of both books and films and consider how the attitudinal shifts in American politics and American cinema between the 1970s and 1980s are reflected in these works. An exploration of the relationships between the directors, the studios, and King's work as a mainstream horror project relative to their previous work forms a key part of this chapter.

Having established an early relationship between King films and the mainstream, chapter 3 takes this further by exploring the bigger-budget, studio-based King adaptations of the late 1980s to the 2000s, looking at a selection of film versions of King's work since 1986, notably *Pet Sematary*, *Misery*, *Needful Things* (1993), *Dolores Claiborne*, *Apt Pupil* (1998), *Dreamcatcher* (2003), *Secret Window*, *1408* (2007), and *The Mist* (2007). This analysis expands the definition of Stephen King as a mainstream brand within the cinematic horror genre. The chapter considers how, post-1986, the cinematic Brand Stephen King was tainted by critical failures, such as *Maximum Overdrive*, and looks at how the Brand attempted to reassert itself in the 1990s via a number of different strands, including reworking King's material to fit into pre-existing genres such as the science-fiction action blockbuster (*The Running Man*, *The Lawnmower Man*), downplaying horror elements in order to present the work as psychological thriller (*Dolores Claiborne*), and presenting the work as serious horror films distinct from the then-current standard cinematic horror movies (*Pet Sematary*, *The Dark Half*).

Chapter 3 also examines the non-horror films *Stand by Me*, *The Shawshank Redemption*, *The Green Mile*, and *Hearts in Atlantis* (2001). With the exception of *Hearts in Atlantis*, in terms of box-office receipts and/or critical acclaim, these represent the pinnacle of King adaptations. According to the website Box Office Mojo, *The Green Mile* is the largest-grossing King film to date, adjusted for inflation, with *Stand by Me* at number six. At the same time, *The Shawshank Redemption*, a much bigger success on home video than in cinemas, was voted number four in the *Empire* magazine survey of the five hundred greatest movies of all time, behind *The Empire Strikes Back* (1980), *Raiders of the Lost Ark* (1981), and *The Godfather* (1972) (Anon. 2008). These three King films are prestige productions with significant actors (Morgan Freeman, Tim Robbins, Tom Hanks, Anthony Hopkins, Richard Dreyfuss) and directors not associated with horror (Scott Hicks, Rob Reiner, and Frank Darabont, although Darabont later filmed King's *The Mist* and co-created the critically acclaimed AMC horror series, *The Walking Dead*, 2010–). The analysis of these films plays a vital role in unlocking some of the hybrid themes beneath the surface of King's horror associations that, I argue, simultaneously explain his popular appeal and go some way in explaining the problems of adapting King as horror.

With the mainstream credentials of King films established over the previous chapters, chapter 4 looks at the opposite end of the market and the low-budget horrors derived from his work, such as *Graveyard Shift* (1990). It also examines the many unauthorized sequels to King adaptations that emerged in the 1990s, including the *Children of the Corn, Mangler,* and *Sometimes They Come Back* franchises. Each was produced outside or on the periphery of the Hollywood mainstream, and none have the kind of high-profile actors or directors connected to those films discussed in the previous chapter. On the contrary, many of the people involved in these films have stronger appeal to predominantly horror audiences or to fans of Stephen King as a horror writer. *The Mangler* was directed by Tobe Hooper, who was established by that time as a director of low-budget horror films after a brief flirtation with mainstream, big-budget horror. *Graveyard Shift* was produced in part in association with the Maine Film Commission and, unlike the majority of King adaptations, was actually shot in the author's home state, which lent the film an element of authenticity and authorization.

The casting of these films also drew on horror films for appeal—notably, the appearance of Robert Englund from the *Nightmare on Elm Street* series in *The Mangler* and Brad Dourif from *Child's Play* (1988) and *The Exorcist III* (1990) in *Graveyard Shift*. Such credentials, using familiar horror actors, writers, and directors, alongside the closer ties to King himself in the case of *Graveyard Shift* and *The Mangler*, not only place these films more firmly within horror in its more traditional guise as a niche genre, but also suggest that in some way perhaps these are more "authentic" King films, much more interested in, as King alludes to in the trailer for *Maximum Overdrive*, "scaring the hell" out of the audience. As such, they offer a counterpoint to what has previously been discussed, being more focused on the horror elements of King's hybridity.

The final chapter draws upon all the preceding arguments, but shifts the focus from film to television, looking at King adaptations from *Salem's Lot* to *Under the Dome* (2013–2015). It considers different television formats—the miniseries, the TV movie, and the serial narrative—and takes the idea of King as a mainstream, branded writer into the televisual medium. The unique nature of television's relationship to horror, and to King in particular, makes it ideally suited to both develop and focus the themes and ideas discussed throughout.

While TV horror is, at the time of writing, flourishing with series like *The Walking Dead, American Horror Story* (2011–), and *True Blood* (2008–2014), television's relationship with horror has always been, as Jowett and Abbott point out, "fraught with tension and potential" (2013, xiii). Far more stringent restrictions on content historically problematized the depiction of horror on the small screen. Although cable and subscription channels, such as AMC and HBO, have pushed the boundaries of acceptability, network television, where King adaptations mainly make their home, still operates under cautious parameters. Networks such as ABC—which broadcast, among others, *IT* (1990), *The Stand*, and *The Shining*—are still beholden to the advertising revenues brought in by large audiences and so are still bound to produce quality material that has a broad mainstream appeal. In this regard, King's affiliation with the major networks is significant, as it cements the idea of King as a popular brand and an author of mainstream fiction, as opposed to a niche horror writer.

King has generally taken a far more hands-on approach to his work on TV, adapting *The Stand* and *The Shining*, writing original teleplays for *Storm of the Century* (1999) and *Rose Red* (2002) and developing and writing much of *Golden Years* (1991) and *Kingdom Hospital*. In addition, although King has remained largely hands-off with the series *Haven* (2010–2015), loosely adapted from his novel *The Colorado Kid* (2005), he has been more involved in the writing and production of *Under the Dome*. Furthermore, he has developed more long-standing creative partnerships on television than in film, notably with ABC and with director Mick Garris, who first directed *Sleepwalkers* for cinema but went on to direct *The Stand*, *The Shining*, *Desperation* (2006), *Quicksilver Highway* (1997), and *Bag of Bones* (2011) for TV. The chapter concludes with an analysis of *Under the Dome*, an adaptation of King's substantial novel into a long-running TV series that diverges significantly from his original story. I argue that *Under the Dome* represents a new, symbiotic relationship between Stephen King as brand and *Under the Dome* as a series, transcending its source material to become, perhaps like Stanley Kubrick's film of *The Shining*, an entity in its own right.

The conclusion examines what is a clear contemporary resurgence of interest in King's work. In 2016, following the 2015 cancellation of *Under the Dome*, J. J. Abrams produced an eight-part adaptation of the time travel story *11/22/63* for the streaming service Hulu. That year also saw the belated release of the film of King's zombie horror novel, *Cell*. These were followed in 2017 by the ten-episode reimagining of *The Mist* for the network Spike and, in cinemas, part one of a remake of *IT* and *The Dark Tower*. I argue that the revival of interest in King takes two forms: one nostalgic and including new versions of previously adapted and identifiably horror-genre stories, like *The Mist* and *IT*, and the other following King's own literary preoccupations and moving away from horror toward fantasy, as in *The Dark Tower*, and thrillers, such as *Big Driver* (2014), *A Good Marriage* (2014), *11/22/63* (2016), and the TV adaptation of his *Mr. Mercedes* trilogy (2017). As he approaches his seventieth year, King has transcended his niche horror branding as the "master of the macabre." And, finally, the adaptations have begun to do the same, taking the cinematic and televisual Brand Stephen King in new directions. At the same time, another strand harks nostalgically back to the heyday of classic film and TV horror.

In the audio commentary on the DVD version of *The Shining* (1997), King says that he prefers to work with network television rather than with cable because, simply enough, more people will see the show. He doesn't see the point, he says, in putting all this work into something that few people will get the chance to watch. Network TV is available to anyone. No expensive cable subscriptions are needed, just a TV set and an aerial. There is something fundamentally democratic and non-elitist about network TV in the United States. This again is consistent with King's worldview and blue-collar roots. Yet, his affiliation with the networks, and the reasons behind it, also betray his basic desire that as many people as possible are exposed to his work. As a writer, King is, but also wants to be, popular.

This reflects the conflicting desire at the heart of his work. On the one hand, he wants to, as he says in the trailer for *Maximum Overdrive*, scare the hell out of people, but on the other, he wants to scare the hell out of as many people as possible. Furthermore, as noted earlier, on the one hand, King believes that horror should be, as in the case of *The Boogens*, a "shitty movie" that is "*fun*, dammit, *fun*," yet, at the same time, the majority of the adaptations of his work across film and TV are aimed at a mass audience and carry with them large budgets, high-quality actors and directors, and an approach to the genre that often downplays violence and gore. Given that horror, in particular on film and TV, is associated generally with smaller niche and even cult audiences, the question must be asked, what kind of horror does King represent and what relationship has he had to the horror genre at large on cinema and television screens over the last forty years? To begin this discussion, it is first necessary to explore the reasons for King's uncommon literary success.

1 / MAINSTREAM HORROR
AND BRAND STEPHEN KING

Book buyers want a good story . . . . This happens,
I think, when readers recognize the people in a book,
their behaviors, their surroundings, and their talk.

STEPHEN KING, *ON WRITING*

PART OF THE PURPOSE OF THIS BOOK IS TO CONSIDER King's literary works, and the films deriving from them, as a particularly mainstream form of horror. In order to do so, it is first necessary to try to define the mainstream, and the starting point for this must be King's phenomenal success. After all, from the early to mid-1980s, King was the most commercially successful living writer. In 1987, Michael Collings published a survey of King's appearances on three key US weekly best-seller lists, the *New York Times Book Review*, *LA Times Book Review*, and *Publishers Weekly*. He noted that, across these three lists, "during the 520 weeks from August 1976 through July 1986, King's name appears at least 545 times" and further, that "for 141 weeks . . . King was represented by at least two titles." In 1981, King became the first American author to have three titles on the list simultaneously, a record he broke in October 1985 with four titles, and then again in November 1985 with five (1987, 37–38). Collings also surveyed the steadily increasing print runs of each book during this period. After King's first novel *Carrie* sold, as Douglas Winter points out, "a modest thirteen thousand copies" and *Salem's Lot* "a respectable twenty-six thousand," *The Dead Zone*, published in August 1979, had an initial hardcover print run of 110,000 copies (1989, 41, 43). A year later, *Firestarter* was in its fifth reprinting, with 275,000 copies, after only seventeen weeks. *Cujo* was in its third reprinting, totaling 300,000 copies, by the time it was officially released in September 1981. And the list goes on: *Christine* had an initial printing of 325,000 copies in hardcover; *Pet Sematary*, 350,000; and *IT* reached an initial US run of

860,000. Furthermore, while King was breaking records in hardcover, his paperbacks were selling in the millions. By July 1980, *The Shining*, for example, was in its twenty-first printing for a total paperback circulation of 4.4 million copies (Collings 1987, 40–42).

KING AS MAINSTREAM HORROR

Who was buying all these books? Anyone and everyone it appears, giving King a broad-based appeal. In 1985, Gary William Crawford suggested that "King is read by construction workers, railroad men, college coeds, housewives, doctors and lawyers" (1985, 42). Mark Jancovich similarly notes that King "is accessible to both the poorly and the highly educated. He has been able to engage young readers and old, popular readers and academics" (1992, 98). His status as a writer with mainstream success therefore derives first from the fact that he sold substantially more books than any writer in the horror genre in the late 1970s and early 1980s, and second, that for a time he sold more books than any other author alive, regardless of genre. The argument as to how he was able to sell in such huge numbers seems to be, according to Crawford and Jancovich, that his writing crossed boundaries of class, gender, age, and intellect.

Certainly large sales numbers are considered at least one of the benchmarks for defining a book, or indeed a film, as mainstream. Matt Hills has suggested that mainstream texts are "highly commercial and culturally omnipresent" (2010, 68), while Jancovich and Nathan Hunt refer to the mainstream in terms of "consumerism . . . adherence to the profit motive and interest in numbers" (2004, 31). Both Hills and Jancovich and Hunt are writing about the mainstream in relation to cult television, which exhibits very different economic criteria from that of literature. Nevertheless, the adherence to commercialism and consumerism as a definition of the mainstream is useful since they point to the concept of mainstream as being associated with large-scale financial success, or at least the desire for such. It is not my intention to suggest that the two are mutually exclusive or that King as an author has sought commercial success over artistic integrity. King flatly denies this, saying in the afterword to *Full Dark, No Stars* that "money was a side effect. Never the goal. Writing fiction for money is a mug's game" (2010, 338). Rather, I wish to use this to demonstrate that, at least in part, the very fact of his commercial success, of producing something that appeals to many people, carries with it the connotations of mainstream.

But King is also a writer of horror stories, which makes his categorization as a mainstream author all the more unusual. The horror market is a traditionally niche literary genre that exists largely on the periphery of popular culture due to its "social unacceptability" (Jancovich 1992, 8). So part of King's success involves attracting a readership from outside the genre fan base, which again ties into his wide appeal across class and gender. As Gary Hoppenstand and Ray B. Browne point out, King has been able to tap into a vast audience that "otherwise would never choose a horror novel" (1987, 5), so it is necessary to consider him as the writer and, cinematically speaking, as the creator not just of mainstream fiction but also of specifically mainstream horror tales.

Notions of niche or mainstream are, in Matt Hills's term, "relational," so that any labeled status depends upon the position from which it is viewed (2010, 67). To fans of a relatively graphic horror writer such as James Herbert, King may seem popularist in his avoidance of the kind of explicit depictions of violence or sex for which Herbert is known. Conversely, to readers who would never touch a horror novel, King is, as Hoppenstand and Browne put it, both niche and despised as "a critically unpopular author writing in a critically unpopular genre" (1987, 2).

If breakout financial success is straightforward evidence that King is part of the literary mainstream, it is far more challenging to determine how the author managed to achieve this, given that horror is niche and King has been labeled a horror writer throughout his career. A useful starting point for this discussion, especially given the focus of this book on adaptations, is to look at another moment in which horror broke into the mainstream. As Stacey Abbott has pointed out, in the 1990s, a number of cinematic adaptations within the horror genre—including *Silence of the Lambs* (1991), *Bram Stoker's Dracula* (1992), and *Mary Shelley's Frankenstein* (1994)—were packaged and sold as blockbuster films. Abbott's analysis of these films, discussed in more detail in chapter 3, demonstrates that for all that horror is niche, the genre nevertheless includes projects that are mainstream. It is, however, important to note one crucial difference, which is that, while King denies writing horror tales for financial success, Abbott points out that these blockbuster horrors of the early 1990s were specifically conceived as moneymakers through their deliberate presentation as a special type of horror picture (2010a, 29). *Mary Shelley's Frankenstein* and *Bram Stoker's Dracula* were sold as faithful renditions of the literary source texts, a fact embedded in the titles themselves. This isn't *Dracula*, it's *Bram Stoker's Dracula*. Significantly, these source texts have themselves transcended their generic connections to become, as Abbott notes, classic tales that "extend well beyond the traditional audiences for horror" (29). For the adaptations to "extend well beyond" horror audiences, the films embrace conventions outside the genre, meaning they are horror movies but also, in Abbott's words, "so much more" (30). In the case of *Bram Stoker's Dracula*, this involved reframing the narrative as an epic gothic love story with the tagline, "Love Never Dies." In addition, it meant casting actors such as Gary Oldman and Anthony Hopkins, who brought with them "the respectability of a tradition of classical acting," and the foregrounding of director Francis Ford Coppola, whose reputation, like that of Kubrick with *The Shining*, "lent the film critical prestige" (30). The same is true of *Mary Shelley's Frankenstein*, which again highlighted its literary heritage in the title and was directed by and starred the classically trained British Shakespearian actor Kenneth Branagh alongside American acting royalty Robert De Niro. Abbott concludes that in manufacturing these products as films that "moved out of niche markets and pushed into the mainstream . . . horror [could] only be one of many genre influences" (41). In other words, in order to achieve a broad appeal, these films embraced their horror elements and origins, but presented them as one ingredient within a hybrid text that offered scares, but also gothic romance, sumptuous visuals and design, and quality acting.

When analyzing King's own writing with a view to explaining his broad appeal, it is possible to see that it too evidences a form of hybridity, in which horror exists alongside a number of other, equally significant, thematic and stylistic elements. As Carl Sederholm points out, King is "seen as the master of horror, but (is) the master of creating his own hybrid genre" (2015, 154). Together, these various features work to formulate the literary brand that is Stephen King. Furthermore, it is the manner in which these elements are de- and re-constructed in the process of adaption that forms the very different cinematic Brand Stephen King. But before considering how this hybridity contributed to King's mainstream success, it is first relevant to examine how he managed to build his writing career and readership.

THE ERA OF MODERN HORROR AND THE MAKING OF STEPHEN KING

King became a published novelist in 1974, a time when horror was undergoing a renaissance across literature, film, and television. In literary terms, as King himself says, three books "kicked off a new horror 'wave' in the seventies—those three, of course, being *Rosemary's Baby*, *The Exorcist*, and *The Other*. The fact that these three books, all published within five years of each other, enjoyed such wide popularity helped to convince (or reconvince) publishers that horror fiction has a commercial potential" (King 1981b, 284). (Gary Hoppenstand suggests that Shirley Jackson should be added to this list, but while her work, notably *The Haunting of Hill House* [1959] and its adaptation *The Haunting* [1963], are acknowledged by King as an influence, they predate this particular wave of new horror writers [2011, 2]). For all the impact the three works had on literary horror fiction, two arguably had a stronger influence on horror cinema. Ira Levin's second novel, *Rosemary's Baby*, was published in 1967 and William Peter Blatty's *The Exorcist* came out in 1971, as did Thomas Tryon's *The Other*. In 1968, Roman Polanski directed the film version of *Rosemary's Baby*. *The Other*, directed by Robert Mulligan and adapted by Tryon himself, came out in 1972 and *The Exorcist*, directed by William Friedkin, in 1973. The film version of *The Other* largely failed on its initial release, but *Rosemary's Baby* and, in particular, *The Exorcist* proved enormously popular.

These two films played a key role in the renaissance of the American horror film in the late 1960s through the 1970s, their success inspiring a type of big-budget, studio-produced horror film that Gregory Waller describes as "highly professional [and] much-publicized" (1987a, 5). As with *Bram Stoker's Dracula* and *Mary Shelley's Frankenstein*, both *Rosemary's Baby* and *The Exorcist* were literary adaptations, but from popular books rather than literary classics. In addition, they were serious, challenging, and adult horror films at a time when the cinematic horror genre, best exemplified by Hammer Film Productions in the United Kingdom and Roger Corman's Edgar Allan Poe adaptations in the United States, was moving increasingly toward camp. Set in the real and contemporary world rather than in a quasi-mythic nineteenth-century past, *Rosemary's Baby* and *The Exorcist* emphasized realism over gothic excess. It was this seriousness of tone, the large budgets, the studio backing, and the box-office success—particularly in the case of *The Exorcist*—that marked both as being a type of horror film aimed at general audiences. Waller describes these films as "mainstream" forms of horror and asserts that this label signaled that they were "somehow acceptable and authorized" and therefore suitable for general cinemagoers (5). These associations meant that they were in some ways more respectable than their genre, as indicated by Jancovich's observation that the novel of *Rosemary's Baby* "is usually unfavorably compared with the film version, probably because the film was directed by the respected 'auteur' director Roman Polanski" (1992, 87).

Yet, this horror renaissance did not take place just in the respectable confines of studio-based American cinema. It also occurred in low-budget horror outside the studio system, similarly beginning in 1968 when alongside *Rosemary's Baby* came George A. Romero's independent zombie film, *Night of the Living Dead* (1968). Between them, these two films shepherded in what Waller calls the era of the "modern horror film" (1987a, 2). The success of *Rosemary's Baby* led to Warner Bros. making *The Exorcist*, while Romero's work, shot guerrilla-style on a tiny budget, inspired a number of young would-be filmmakers who would use the horror genre to show their despair at the state of America.

The destruction of the family unit in Night of the Living Dead *(1968).*

Thematically, *Rosemary's Baby* and *The Exorcist* focused on a comfortable middle-class milieu and took as their main theme the "desecration of everything that was considered wholesome and good about the fading American Dream—the home, the family, the church and, most shockingly, the child" (Kermode 1997, 9). Romero's film offered an even bleaker assessment of the state of the country at the end of the decade. In it, the family unit, the basis of America's vision of itself in the 1950s, is shattered, as indeed it is in *The Exorcist*. Yet, while *The Exorcist* ends with an albeit shaky return to a form of equilibrium in which the broken family unit of mother, daughter, and absent father is restored and the demon (apparently) defeated, the family in Romero's film destructs to the extent that the daughter is zombiefied and eats her own father before killing her mother with a trowel.

Rosemary's Baby, The Exorcist, and *Night of the Living Dead* all address the breakdown of the family, but Romero's film is more political. It has been argued that the casting of a black central character, Ben, who is shot by Southern militia at the end of the film, comments explicitly on the civil rights movement that was tearing American society apart in the late 1960s. Romero denies this was the intention, but, as Ben Hervey points out, the review of the film in the French film journal *Cahiers du Cinema* stated that "the real subject of the film is not the living dead, but racism" (2008, 115).

Thus, while *The Exorcist* and *Rosemary's Baby* adopt an enclosed familial setting in which to explore the disintegration of the American family and the American Dream, *Night of the Living Dead* opens its analysis to a broader political canvas. As Robin Wood noted, "the film continually counterpoints the disintegration of the social microcosm, the patriarchal family, with the cultural disintegration of the nation" (1986, 115). While the ending of *Rosemary's Baby*, in which Rosemary embraces her offspring despite knowing that the devil is the father, remains ambiguous, Romero's denouement, featuring the burning of Ben's body, is nihilistic and offers neither solution nor resolution. *Night of the Living Dead* presents no answers, only a bleak future in which America is unable to overcome its differences to combat the menace that it faces.

This pessimistic vision of the disintegration of family and society, along with the bleak, unresolved, and ambiguous ending, was picked up by Wes Craven in *The Last House on the Left* (1972) and by Tobe Hooper in *The Texas Chainsaw Massacre* (1974), both of which, again, are political films. In the latter, a perverted form of the nuclear family terrorizes a group of teenagers, but the source of their perversion is largely economic. The slaughterhouse that sustained them financially has closed and so they simply use their skillset to survive—in this case, by killing and eating those they come across. In another reflection of the grim economics of the early 1970s, the 1973 oil crisis, the teenagers are stranded because they ran out of gas. Craven's film draws on his own disgust at the brutality of the Vietnam War to present a series of atrocities that blur and ultimately break the boundaries between good and evil behavior. The reactions of the parents to the rape and murder of their daughter by the sadistic Krug Stillo and his gang—an allusion to the Manson family—are just as brutal as the events that spawned them. Between them, the studio-based and low-budget horrors came to represent what Robin Wood referred to as "The American Nightmare," a series of films that reflected the darker side of American society (70).

Both the studio-based and the low-budget films took horror away from the historical and often European settings of horror cinema in the 1960s under the auspices of Hammer and Corman, placing it instead in a contemporary world, which was largely rural and political in the low-budget films, but more urban and social in terms of critique in the bigger-budget literary adaptations of Levin and Blatty. As Tony Magistrale points out, "several critics . . . have reminded us of King's debt to the book and the film successes of *Rosemary's Baby* and *The Exorcist*. In the early 1970s these publications revitalized public fascination with the horror genre by focusing upon its urban possibilities [and] the horror potential in the everyday world" (1988, 15). Stacey Abbott has noted that in the 1970s, "the horror genre began to turn inward . . . the mythic European villages and cities . . . were gradually replaced by familiar American settings and locations" (2007, 80). Horror films were abandoning the traditional gothic tropes that had been their staple first in the 1930s and then in the late 1950s and early 1960s.

Television meanwhile was returning to and revitalizing these same gothic classics, partly through the launch of the TV movie in 1968 with ABC's *Movie of the Week*, which aired in a prime-time Sunday evening slot. While TV movies encompassed many genres, horror found a home there, and in the United States during the 1970s, "over 100 made for television horror movies . . . premiered on prime-time network television" (Waller 1987b, 146), including adaptations of *Frankenstein* (1973), *Dracula* (1973), and Henry James's *Turn of the Screw* (1974). Two modern dramas, *The Night Stalker* (1972) and *The Night Strangler* (1973), eventually led ABC to produce *Kolchak: The Night Stalker* in 1974. In this short-lived series, journalist Carl Kolchak investigated supernatural phenomena. *Kolchak* would later influence *The X-Files* (1993–2002, 2016), for which King would contribute an episode and which would itself influence TV's relationship to horror in the twenty-first century.

With horror appearing on network TV on Sunday night and films like *The Exorcist* drawing huge audiences, the early 1970s saw a renewed public fascination for the genre. This was also reflected in a proliferation of new horror novels and novelists alongside King, including James Herbert (first novel, *The Rats*, 1974); Guy N. Smith (first novel, *Werewolf by Moonlight*, 1974); Frank De Felitta (first horror novel, *Audrey Rose*, 1975); Anne Rice (first novel, *Interview with the Vampire*, 1976); Graham Masterton (first novel, *The Manitou*, 1976); John Saul (first novel, *Suffer the Children*, 1977); Peter Straub (first horror novel, *Julia*, 1977); and Virginia Andrews (first novel, *Flowers in the Attic*, 1979).

King's initial three novels, *Carrie* (1974), *Salem's Lot* (1975), and *The Shining* (1977), were part of this new wave of horror literature and were earmarked for that genre from the outset. As recounted by Douglas Winter, once *Carrie* was accepted by New York publishing house Doubleday, King began to discuss his next book with his editor. He had two novels in the works at that time. The first, *Blaze*, drew on John Steinbeck's *Of Mice and Men* (1937) in its story about a physically strong but mentally disabled character who kidnaps a young girl. The other, *Second Coming*, was about vampires taking over a small Maine town. Doubleday chose the latter, which would eventually be retitled *Salem's Lot*. King mothballed *Blaze*, which would not be published until 2007. Upon reading the manuscript of King's proposed third novel, a tale of a haunted hotel, which at that point had the title *The Shine*, his editor, Bill Thompson, expressed concern that King would become pigeonholed as a horror writer. Winter gives King's response:

[A]nd then I thought about all the people who have been typed as horror writers . . . Lovecraft, Clark Ashton Smith, . . . Robert Bloch, Richard Matheson and Shirley Jackson . . . and I decided . . . "That's okay, Bill,"
I said. "I'll be a horror writer if that's what people want. That's just fine."
(1989, 42)

In the essay "On Becoming a Brand Name," King tells a slightly different
story. In this version, when he presented his second novel, *Salem's Lot*, to his
publishers, they were delighted because "horror was big . . . and I had showed
no signs with my second book of exchanging my fright wig and Lon Chaney
makeup for a pipe and tweed jacket and writing something Deep and Meaningful" (2000c, 59). According to Winter's telling, it was King who made the
conscious decision to be a horror writer. In King's version, produced around
the same time, he positions his labeling as a horror writer as something determined by outside forces—in this case, his publisher's delight that King was
continuing to work in a money-spinning genre.

Certainly, *Carrie*, *Salem's Lot*, and *The Shining* drew upon circulating, if not
always traditional, horror tropes. *Carrie* tied into the trend for horror stories
that articulated a fear of the young, which included the books and the film adaptations of *Rosemary's Baby* and *The Exorcist*. By the time Brian De Palma's
film version of *Carrie* was released in 1976, 20th Century Fox had added to
this subgenre with *The Omen* (1976), in which the child to be feared was literally the son of the devil. The script was also turned into a best-selling book by
the film's screenwriter, David Seltzer. *Salem's Lot* was a vampire story with an
acknowledged debt to Stoker's *Dracula* (1897) by way of Thornton Wilder's
Our Town (1938) and the TV soap *Peyton Place* (1964–1969) (Earnshaw 2013,
31). As for the Overlook Hotel in *The Shining*, it is, more than anything, a
very large haunted house—in King's phrase, a "Bad Place"—that was influenced in part by Shirley Jackson's Hill House from her 1959 novel *The Haunting of Hill House* (King 1981b, 254–255). These were obviously horror novels.

Yet, as noted above, *Carrie* and *Salem's Lot* in particular achieved only
modest hardcover success, and King's sales were demonstrably boosted by
De Palma's film version of *Carrie*, which was released in November 1976, became a major box-office hit in 1976–1977, and secured Oscar nominations for
Sissy Spacek and Piper Laurie as Carrie and her mother. Collings's analysis
of King's publication record indicates that in February 1977, *The Shining* became the first of King's books to make the best-seller lists in hardcover because of the successful run of the movie tie-in paperback of *Carrie*, which had
been on the lists since December 1976, the month after the film was released
(1987, 40, 45). *Salem's Lot* had reached number one in paperback in 1976 (see
Palko 2011, 29). More importantly, like *The Exorcist* and *Rosemary's Baby* be-

fore it, *Carrie* was a studio-financed and therefore, in Waller's words, "main-stream . . . acceptable and authorized" horror film, and moreover was very popular (1987a, 5). As discussed in more detail in chapter 2, it was therefore partly thanks to the success of De Palma's cinematic adaptation that King was not only thrust to the forefront of the new horror writers of the 1970s, but was also the only one to transition into mainstream success both cinematically and, as a direct result of the film, in bookstores.

"HORROR IN DISGUISE": KING AND HYBRID HORROR

Thus, from the outset, there is a link between this cinematic/televisual version of his work aimed at mainstream cinema audiences and King's own breakout from the pack of horror writers emerging in the 1970s. But while *Carrie* the film contributed toward making King a household name, his book sales continued to grow and by 1985, showed no signs of slowing. Given the fact that, as discussed in chapter 2, between *Carrie* in 1976 and *Cujo* in 1983, there were only two adaptations of King's work, the TV miniseries *Salem's Lot* and Kubrick's *The Shining*, and also given the fact that the film adaptations that followed *Cujo* between 1983 and 1985 achieved inconsistent results with audiences and critics, it is evident that King's sustained literary success did not similarly rely upon cinematic exposure, but rather on the books themselves. At least some of the people who bought and presumably read the tie-in paperback of *Carrie* after seeing the film did not then discard King, but stayed around to see what else he had to say, and then liked it enough to keep coming back.

Like *Rosemary's Baby* and *The Exorcist* before it, and indeed *Bram Stoker's Dracula* and *Mary Shelley's Frankenstein* after, *Carrie* was a studio-funded picture aimed at a mainstream audience, featured an experienced cast of quality actors, and had a story that was horrific but also something more than horror. As De Palma says, "I sort of put everything into *Carrie*: I had the romantic story between Tommy Ross and Carrie White; I had all the visual suspense elements, and the terror elements" (Magistrale 2003, 25). In De Palma, the film also had a director who could manage the material so that both the horror and the non-horror elements, especially the pathos of the plight of the central character, were genuinely effective.

De Palma's *Carrie* therefore had crossover appeal by being a hybrid of horror and non-horror elements, as indeed was King's novel. For King, *Carrie* was part horror, part metaphor. He describes the book on one level as being about "the loneliness of one girl, her desperate effort to become a part of the peer society in which she must exist, and how her effort fails" and on another level, about "how women largely find their own channels of power, and what men fear about women and women's sexuality" (1981b, 198). Discussing the origins of the story in *On Writing*, King recounts his memories of two girls he knew in high school, both loners and both bullied by the other students, one because she was from an ultra-religious household and the other because she wore the same clothes to school every day. This memory, he says, helped to shape the character of Carrie, but the story developed while he was cleaning the girls' shower room at Brunswick High school, where he worked briefly. He imagined a girl suddenly having her period, being humiliated by other girls, and fighting back against her tormentors. Trying to work out how she would do this, he remembered an article he had read in *Life* magazine about telekinesis and "two unrelated ideas, adolescent cruelty and telekinesis, came together, and I had an idea" (2000b, 52–58).

The origins of the book therefore lie in both the supernatural and the natural world. It is part horror story and part high school drama. This hybrid balancing of horror and non-horror elements is also visible in the novels *Salem's Lot* and *The Shining*. As noted above, *Salem's Lot* mixes vampires with *Peyton Place*, America's first primetime soap opera, while *The Shining*, like *Carrie*, introduces a supernatural element—in this case, the haunted house—but also draws upon the very real horrors of addiction and spousal and child abuse. As noted in the introduction, King's next major work, *The Stand*, is even more ambiguous in terms of its generic identity: it is less of a horror novel than the first three despite the fact that the world's population is wiped out in the opening pages. Douglas Winter's description of the book as "an epic fantasy" (1989, 66) connects to the fact that the journey undertaken by lead characters Stu Redman, Glenn Bateman, Larry Underwood, and Ralph Brenter from the safety of Boulder to the enemy territory of Las Vegas recalls Sam and Frodo's journey into Mordor in J. R. R. Tolkien's *Lord of the Rings* (1954–1955). Another echo can be found in the depiction of Las Vegas as being separated from the world of light by mountains—in this case, the Rockies—and ruled by a dark figure who has an all-seeing eye and draws the forces of evil toward him.

Yet, for all Winter asserts the fantasy elements of the story, he notes that in both hardcover and paperback, *The Stand* was sold, as were *Carrie*, *Salem's Lot*, and *The Shining*, as a horror novel (66). The dust jacket of the first US hardcover edition declares that this is "a new novel by the author of *The Shining*." The flap copy describes the book as "a story of dark wonders and irresistible terror" and brings out a few horror elements, referring to "the dance of death about to begin" and to "Randy Flagg, the Walkin' dude . . . the living image of Satan. His hour come round again." These words by Elizabeth Levine connect to horror, but they seem restrained in comparison to the hyperbole to be found on the jacket of the UK first edition, published by New

English Library (NEL). On the rear flap, King is described as "the world's foremost living horror writer," while the front blurb begins:

> One by one the people were dying. In houses and hotel rooms, in cafes, nightclubs and cinemas, down in the subway and along the highway, the plague had spread, leaving cities of rotting corpses. (1978)

The horror angle is played up far more in the NEL edition than in Double-day's American hardcover, the British volume featuring a brooding cover showing the title of the book and the name of the author being shattered by lightning. However, although Doubleday's jacket is more restrained than that of NEL, the first American paperback, published by Signet, ramped up the horror angle by featuring a black cover with a shadowed face and the tagline "a novel of ultimate horror." Despite the fact that *The Stand* marked a shift away from using the kind of horror tropes that formed the backbone of King's first three novels, by 1978 when the book was released, the horror writer label about which Bill Thompson had warned him was squarely in place. While the US hardcover, which by virtue of price was aimed at a more specialist market, attempted at least partly to show *The Stand* as something other than horror, the mass-market paperback ignored the hybrid complexities of King's story and went straight for the horror vein.

At this point in King's publishing career, the machinery of expectation took over, the horror label being routinely applied despite the fact that his next novels, *The Dead Zone*, *Firestarter*, and *Cujo*, moved even further away from the likes of haunted houses and vampires. All three novels contain echoes both of King's earlier works and of traditional horror tropes, although in each case, the horror elements are secondary to other preoccupations. While both *The Dead Zone* and *Firestarter* feature main characters gifted/afflicted with some form of mental powers, as is Carrie, these books are primarily political anti-government narratives. In *Firestarter*, the main plot concerns Charlie's persecution by the government, not her pyrokinetic ability. The story of Johnny Smith's developing precognitive "gift" in *The Dead Zone* is interrupted by a parallel narrative charting the rise of amoral politician Greg Stillson, with whom Johnny is on a collision course. In both cases, there is more to fear from corrupt government than from characters with supernatural powers, and indeed, one could argue that for much of the novel, Carrie's religious fanatic mother and the high school students that pick on her are far more terrifying than she.

Cujo, meanwhile, focuses on family drama. Ostensibly, the eponymous dog draws upon the trope of nature fighting back, a common thread within horror and science fiction since the 1950s in films like *Them* (1954), *Godzilla*

(1954), and *Night of the Lepus* (1972). But while giant ants, mutated dinosaurs, and killer bunnies presented a warning to humans about environmental meddling, the source of Cujo's rage is natural, and even tragic. In both book and film, humans do not particularly mistreat Cujo, and his aggression is due to his infection with rabies. This is not a tale about nature fighting back, but rather one in which Cujo's largely unrelated disease serves to highlight a broken family unit similar to that of the Torrances in *The Shining*: father and mother have a fractured relationship (due to suspicion over Jack's drinking in *The Shining* and owing to Donna's affair in *Cujo*), and in both cases, this leads to mother and son being in peril. Both stories contain elements of the supernatural, but these are more overt in *The Shining* with the menacing ghosts and spirits in the Overlook Hotel. In *Cujo*, the supernatural is downplayed, only existing in the hints that the dog may be possessed by the spirit of Frank Dodd, the Castle Rock Killer from *The Dead Zone*, and in the links made between the rabid St. Bernard and Tad Trenton's fear that a monster hides in his closet. When Vic Trenton returns home to try and establish what happened to his wife and son, he goes into Tad's bedroom:

> Heart thumping heavily in his throat, Vic got up and went to the closet. He could smell something in there, something heavy and unpleasant. Perhaps it was only mothballs—that smell was certainly part of it—but it smelled . . . savage. . . .
> He closed the closet door and watched, as wide-eyed as a child, as the latch lifted and popped free of its notch. The door began to swing open again.
> *I didn't see that. I won't believe I saw that.* (1981a, 296)

Yet, for all that this hints at something outside the natural order, by the end of the novel, King closes down any supernatural possibilities and also absolves Cujo of all blame: "he had always tried to be a good dog . . . he had been struck by something, possibly destiny, or fate, or only a degenerative nerve disease called rabies. Free will was not a factor" (1981a, 318). The horror elements in *Cujo* are therefore very different from those in the otherwise-similar *The Shining*, where it is explicit that the ghosts of the Overlook are both real and returning. Ultimately, both are stories of a family in crisis, whose problems are exacerbated by forces beyond their control. In *The Shining*, these are paranormal—the forces of the Overlook attacking Jack's fragile grip on sobriety. In *Cujo*, they are natural in the form of a catalogue of unfortunate coincidences: the extreme hot weather, Cujo being bitten by a bat infected with rabies, Charity Camber's unlikely lottery win that takes her and her son out of town, the sudden disastrous turn taken by Vic's advertising campaign for

Sharp's Red Zingers breakfast cereal, and, above all, the mechanical problems affecting Donna's Pinto. Thus, while *The Shining*, with its haunted hotel, is more clearly linked to traditions of the horror genre than the very different take on the avenging monster trope in *Cujo*, both tales are as much, or indeed more, about families in crisis as they are about the supernatural.

The implication is that even though King is identified as a writer of horror, the horrific elements in his stories are usually a mixture of real world and supernatural horror and blend generic tropes with other elements. This has formed a significant strand in academic discussions of King's work. Michael Collings, for example, calls King's stories "horror in disguise" and suggests that the writer "consistently combines horror with other genres" (1985, 17). If De Palma's *Carrie*, reaching wide audiences with its hybridized mixture of human drama and horror, provided the spark that drove King to the forefront of the new horror writers of the 1970s, this similarly hybrid form of horror in King's own writing is one of the reasons for keeping the readers constant.

There are many elements to this hybridity, but the principal one is reality. Tom Newhouse argues that King's novels "evoke the troubled atmosphere of contemporary America, one harried as much by the realities of corrupt government . . . as by monsters" (1987, 49). Although the monsters—by which Newhouse means the horror elements—are always there for, as King says, "sooner or later my mind always seems to turn back in that direction," his writing is as much about the modern world as it is about vampires, werewolves, or other phenomena (Winter 1989, 124). As Heidi Strengell suggests, King's work represents a fusion of the supernatural and the natural in the form of what she describes as "literary naturalism" (2007, 22). Naturalism, she argues, "lends the worldview implicit in King's multiverse" (23), and it is this fusion of the supernatural and the natural that has been cited by a number of commentators on King's work as a key reason for his success. Strengell again, for example, refers to his "contrast of realism and fantasy" and his "balance between the supernatural and the rational" (181, 182). Hoppenstand and Browne concur, suggesting that, as noted above, "*The Shining* is a soap opera that just happens to be a haunted house novel" (1987, 5), while Burton Hatlen says that King's work is a "blend of gritty social realism and supernatural horror" (1988, 20). Ben Indick suggests that "the basic groundwork of [his] stories is their intense realism, rooted in genuine small towns as a rule, and quite average individuals, with all the familiar settings of their lives" (1985, 9) and argues that King introduces the horror only after this groundwork is established.

Indick doesn't necessarily mean that horror or supernatural elements are not present from the start of the story, but rather that it takes time for them to become the main focus. Before that happens, these elements are either subordinate to or, in rare cases, equal with, the aspects of realism that focus on contemporary American life. For example, it is eighty pages into *Salem's Lot* before Ralphie Glick disappears, taken by the vampire Kurt Barlow's familiar, Richard Straker. Ralphie's brother Danny is found dead on page 116 and it is not until page 158 that Barlow makes his first appearance, meaning that the opening third of the book, while imbued with events that prefigure the annihilation of the town, is principally about Salem's Lot, its inhabitants, and their lives (King 1975). Looming over these events is the ominous shadow of the Marsten House, where lead character Ben Mears underwent a traumatic childhood experience that prompts him to return to Salem's Lot to write about the nature of evil. Yet, while Mears and other characters discuss and dissect the nebulous potential threat of the creepy and looming old house, they fail to recognize the real evil that lurks there in the form of the vampire Barlow.

Similarly in *Christine*, it takes more than a third of the book before Arnie Cunningham's '58 Plymouth Fury is on the road again and almost half before it becomes clear to Dennis Guilder, Arnie's friend and the book's narrator, that Arnie is becoming possessed by the spirit of the car's former owner, Roland D. LeBay. It is only at this point that the car, named "Christine," takes on autonomous life and begins to kill (King 1983a). Although the opening third of the book touches on Dennis's increasing unease about the car, the story is propelled forward more through the mundane minutiae of high school loser life; Arnie's purchase of the car and his efforts to find somewhere to keep it; his altercations with the school bully, Buddy Repperton, and garage boss, Will Darnell; his attempts to repair Christine; and his increasingly strained relationship with his parents. Dennis has dreams and visions about Christine that hint at her menace, and his meeting with LeBay's brother George outlines some of the unpleasant history between the car and its former owner. However, until the book shifts from Dennis's first-person narration to third-person narration for the section covering Christine's nocturnal murders, it is far more about a bullied and nerdy young teenager making the transition to manhood through the right of passage that is the buying of one's first car than it is about the evil spirit that possesses this vehicle. Like Mears's mistaken focus on the Marsten House, Dennis's sense that something is wrong coalesces around Christine without really understanding just how bad things will be until it is too late.

Thus, the openings of both books exhibit an unfocused sense of menace that invokes the supernatural but is really an exploration of the horrors of everyday life. The main incidents in the first half of *Salem's Lot* revolve around the petty issues that divide the "good" townsfolk: Ben's burgeoning relationship with Susan Norton sets up a love triangle with her current boyfriend, Floyd Tibbets; seventeen-year-old Sandy McDougall punches her infant son because he won't stop crying; mean-spirited Korean War vet Charles Rhodes throws two young kids off his school bus for passing notes; Mark Petrie is bullied at school; and Bonnie Sawyer enjoys an extramarital affair. In the case of *Christine*, as with *Carrie*, those horrors revolve around teenage isolation and desperation as Arnie pours what's left of his self-esteem and dreams into the wreck of Christine, only to find himself met with derision and opposition. First, his parents refuse to allow him to keep the car at home, and then, while driving it to Darnell's garage, Arnie gets a flat, leaving him parked outside the house of an unpleasant family. Dennis arrives with a spare to find Arnie squaring off with the man of the house, Ralph:

> "I'm not going to drive it on the rim," Arnie said. "I told you that. You wouldn't do it if it was yours."
>
> "I'll drive you on the rim, Pizza-Face," Daddy said, apparently intent on showing his children how big people solve their problems in the Real World. "You ain't parking your cruddy hotrod in front of my house." (1983a, 47)

Although with an adult, this confrontation is couched in the terms of high-school bullying. Dennis notes that "[t]en years younger [Ralph] would have been one of the guys at school who thought it was terribly amusing to slam Arnie's books out of his arms when he was on the way to class" and that Arnie knew that "there was something about him, God knew what, that made a certain type of guy want to pound the living shit out of him" (48). The same theme occurs when Arnie meets Darnell. "Like the kids in the smoking area at school, like Ralph on Basin Drive, like Buddy Repperton . . . [Darnell] had taken an instant dislike to Arnie—it was a case of hate at first sight" (54). Thus, the events in the first half of the book derive, as they do in *Carrie*, from the treatment Arnie receives from those around him responding to his status as a loser, a nerd, a picked-upon teenager, and Arnie's gradual emergence from this fate. In both *Salem's Lot* and *Christine*, the focus, as Indick suggests, is on realism, revolving around average individuals and familiar settings, and the horrors on display (poverty, the responsibility of bringing up a child, the misery of a loveless marriage, bullying) are the kind that real people face in the real world.

The idea of holding back the supernatural in order to first establish the world in which it is to be unleashed is not unique to King. Nevertheless, many commentators have suggested that an important part of his appeal is the type of world that he creates and the manner in which he does so, focusing upon, as Indick suggests, average individuals, familiar settings, and genuine small towns. Jonathan P. Davis, for example, comments that "King writes about ordinary individuals with whom his readers can identify" (1994, 23). For King, this focus on ordinary people comes from his background and "has to do with knowing what most Americans know, as opposed to people who know the head waiter at the Four Seasons. I haven't lived anywhere else; never had any pretensions; never associated with people who have money. I know about housing developments, TV dinners and McDonalds—the American iconography" (2000c, 332). The second reason for having ordinary folk as his protagonists has to do with the importance of character and identification. For King, "if . . . the audience has come to like and understand—or even just to appreciate—the characters . . . as real people . . . blood can fly everywhere and the audience *cannot* remain unimpressed" (1981b, 186). Douglas Winter quotes King saying, "You've got to love the people . . . because the more you love . . . then that allows the horror to be possible. There is no horror without love and feeling . . . without a concept of normality there is no horror" (1989, 56).

Therefore, even though King is considered a horror novelist, this emphasis on character and realism is a key element of his popular appeal. Collings states, "King's power depends on his ability to put ordinary people into extraordinary situations" and that "the situations bring the readers into the text, while the realistically drawn characters keep the readers there" (2006, 92). Jancovich takes this idea further by highlighting the interiority of King's character writing, noting that his works are "highly personal and interior novels in which we watch his characters' thought processes. The drama of the novels takes place as much within these thought processes as within the moments of action and violence" (1992, 99). Thus, before plunging his readers into the extraordinary situation of haunting and possession in *Christine*, King draws them into Arnie's life through the ordinary and identifiable issue of bullying and through Dennis's pity for, and love of, Arnie. Likewise, the reader is drawn into Johnny Smith's painful, lonely recovery and difficult semi-reintegration into society long before his date with destiny and Greg Stillson in *The Dead Zone*.

Alongside this emphasis on ordinary people is King's use of the trappings of Americana. His characters don't drink a soda, they have a Coke or Pepsi. They smoke Luckies or Camels or Tareytons, and they relax with a Pabst or a Narragansett. Alain Silver and James Ursini argue that in King stories, "geography and brand names are used to evoke a sense of the everyday" (1994, 162), an idea echoed by Tony Magistrale, who notes that "King's landscapes are littered with the well-known brand names of corporate America . . . . he seeks to reproduce a detailed and highly visual sense of the real world—in order to subvert it" (1988, 54). King's characters are therefore, at least initially, drawn in a realistic way from familiar walks of life, are preoccupied by real issues, are often open to the reader emotionally either through first- or third-person narration, and are rooted in a very real world.

Interlinking these elements brings these characters to life. For example, when neighbor Jud Crandall is introduced in *Pet Sematary*, his smoking habits are highlighted through the point of view of the novel's protagonist, Louis Creed:

> [Louis] turned and saw an old man of perhaps seventy . . . . He wore biballs over a blue chambray shirt . . . . His face was sunburned, and he was smoking an unfiltered cigarette. . . . Crandall pulled out a deck of Chesterfield Kings, poked one into the seamed corner of his mouth, nodded at them pleasantly as they laughed . . . and popped a wooden match alight with his thumbnail. *The old have their tricks,* Louis thought. *Small ones, but some of them are good ones.* (1983b, 13, 14)

The description of the unfiltered cigarette—the Chesterfield brand popular in the United States, particularly in the first half of the twentieth century—and the wooden match connects with that of the seamed mouth, biballs, and chambray shirt to give an impression of a man from a bygone era. One could imagine that if King described Crandall as he looked in the 1940s, the author would use exactly the same words, except for the seamed mouth. Crandall is therefore perfectly suited to introduce Louis to the atavistic and mystical burial ground that will be his undoing. There is an element of grandfatherliness to Crandall in this description, to which Louis warmly responds. Still, the emphasis on Crandall's unhealthy smoking habit—especially in comparison to Louis, who is a doctor—hints toward a darker side, someone who knows something is bad, but does it anyway. The Chesterfield brand here not only places Crandall in the real world, but, along with the other elements of this description, it also brands *him* as a particular type of character.

King uses language as a short cut to character identification in a similar fashion. He liberally uses profanity in both his books and his written interviews (he tends to be more discreet on TV), tapping into the vernacular of the everyday. As Peter Tremayne puts it, "King talks American," as do his characters (1988, 107). In *Christine*, Buddy Repperton is introduced as "one of those guys who spend their high school time majoring in Smoking Area" (1983a, 76). Once he begins to have run-ins with Arnie at Darnell's, Buddy "was swerving out of his way to give Arnie a whistling clap on the back, accompanied by a bellowed 'How ya doin, Cuntface'" (78–79). Even though Dennis and Arnie, and in particular Darnell and LeBay, swear throughout the novel, the word "cunt" is owned by Repperton, setting his vernacular, and himself, apart from the other characters in order to identify him as Arnie's primary antagonist. Later, Dennis attempts to contact LeBay's brother via the secretary of the Libertyville American Legion, Richard McCandless, a World War II veteran who works in a furniture store. McCandless's brief appearance is peppered with swearing, including references to fighting in the South Pacific ("two fucking million Japs coming at us," 414) and to Roland LeBay ("He loved that fucking car," 414), prompting Dennis to wonder about his sales patter:

> I could see him showing some smart young lady around, saying, *Here's one fuck of a nice couch, ma'am, and look at this goddam settee, we sure didn't have nothing like that on Guadalcanal when those fucking stoned-out Japs came at us with their Maxwell House swords.* I grinned a little. (415–416)

Here an incidental character is brought humorously to life via a commentary on his use of language, and, as with Louis's reaction to Crandall, prompts a warm response in Dennis that is transmitted to the reader via the identification and trust that his narration has built up through the novel. In this case, that warmth comes through this emphasis on what McCandless says, how he says it, and how it makes Dennis feel.

Indeed, King, like McCandless, is an earthy, often vulgar but fundamentally good-natured storyteller, using identifiable characters, settings, and language to create a familiar world in which his stories then unfold. Collings suggests that "the references to brand names and contemporary consumer goods helps [to ensure that] readers do not notice King's narrative style . . . instead they move directly through a transparent style to engage the narrative head on" (2006, 14). Strengell agrees, citing the writer's "simple style and vernacular," which serves to "make King's realism so effective" and thus "contrast . . . realism and fantasy" in such a way that "the supernatural intrudes on our everyday awareness of contemporary culture and morals" (2007, 181, 182–183). Magistrale also refers to King's prose style as being "deceptively simple and accessible" (1988, 13). King's style therefore does two things: it creates a real world with which the readers can engage and to which is added the supernatural element, and by replicating patterns of everyday life, it allows for a focus on story. As Collings suggests, "His writing subsumes considerations of style to considerations of story," stories that "move through break-neck narrative and powerful episodes" (2006, 14, 93).

Furthermore, the emphasis on the real world enables King to "employ the supernatural . . . as a narrative device that allows him to explore the darkest corners of the human condition" (Hoppenstand 2011, 4). As Jennifer Jenkins puts it, "fantasy acts not necessarily as narrative, but the gateway to it" (2014, 11). Just as Cujo is simultaneously an unfortunate rabid dog and, in some unformed way, the monster in Tad's closet and the Castle Rock killer, so Douglas Winter suggests that he is also "a personification, a culmination, of our everyday fears . . . decaying marriages, economic woes, malfunctioning automobiles" (1989, 115–116). All those elements with which the Trenton family is dealing—Donna's infidelity and isolation, the crisis in Vic's advertising business—coalesce in Cujo's relentless onslaught. They are the things that put Donna and Tad in their broken car in the Cambers' empty yard, and they reflect many of the "broad range of social problems that face Americans daily" that, Jonathan P. Davis argues, King explores in his work, including "the question of moral choice, technology, religion, government, capitalism" (1994, 25).

King therefore writes stories that reflect upon the issues that face contemporary America. *Cujo* and *The Shining* use monsters and ghosts to investigate the breakdown of the American family. The vampires of *Salem's Lot* expose the petty sins and hatred that lurk behind the façade of the small American town. *Carrie*, *The Dead Zone*, and *Firestarter* use innocents with telekinetic powers to illuminate the real world horrors of high-school life (in the case of *Carrie*) and political corruption, secrecy, and power (in the case of *The Dead Zone* and *Firestarter*). The haunted car in *Christine* also reveals the terrors of high-school life. Similarly, the book considers the investment in material goods as a form of self-identification, as well as the post-1970s death of the American love affair with the automobile, as rising gas prices and shrinking wages replaced design with practicality.

Furthermore, in writing about these issues and how they are to be faced, King takes what Strengell refers to as a "strong moral tone" (2007, 263). Davis concurs, arguing that "the true horrors stem from human misconduct: child abuse, alcoholism, self-serving governments, immoral sexual behavior, repressive societal organizations" (1994, 4). For Davis, King's work revolves around these key themes, and what separates good characters from evil ones is how they relate to them. In *Firestarter*, the good characters are Andy and Charlie McGee, the father and daughter with psychic powers who are being pursued or persecuted by the shady government organization known as "The Shop." The bad characters are the ones who work for The Shop. Yet, within these black and white categories, King differentiates between Cap Hollister, leader of The Shop, who wishes to harness or contain Charlie's power and is just doing his job, and John Rainbird, the psychotic assassin who wishes to kill Charlie and absorb her power. Cap is the better person, but ultimately, both men are bad and are punished for their crimes. In *Carrie*, Sue Snell feels guilt after taking part in the humiliation of Carrie, pelting her with tampons in the shower, and attempts to make amends by having her boyfriend Tommy take Carrie to the prom. Sue is spared at the end of the book and the film, unlike Chris Hargensen and those who are complicit in dumping pig's blood on Carrie. In *The Stand*, one of the most morally polarized of all King's works, the characters drawn to Randall Flagg and Las Vegas are destroyed at the end of the book, while those who follow kindly mother Abigail in Boulder are permitted to live, or at least to die in service of others. In *Christine*, Arnie Cunningham dies having finally found the courage to battle the spirit of LeBay that possesses him, while Johnny Smith in *The Dead Zone* sacrifices himself for the world after having a vision implying that Greg Stillson will turn the Earth into a wasteland. Even the alcoholic Jack Torrance, a man guilty of many things, including abuse, eventually turns, at least partially, against the Overlook that possesses him before finally receiving redemption and reconciliation with Danny in *Doctor Sleep* (2013), the sequel to *The Shining*. Louis Creed in *Pet Sematary* is somewhat of an anomaly, being ultimately punished for selfishly denying the natural laws and burying both his child and wife in the Micmac burial ground. Creed stands out because he is unable to differentiate between good and evil through his inability to accept the finality and randomness of death. He cannot make the correct moral choice, and in this respect, he is similar to sixteen-year-old Harold Lauder in *The Stand*. Jealous of Frannie Goldsmith's relationship with Stu Redman, Harold is seduced by Nadine Cross, erstwhile wife of Randall Flagg, into betraying the Boulder community and ultimately is left in the wilderness to die for his poor choices and lack of moral fiber.

Although good individuals do not always survive in King's world, good almost always triumphs over evil, be it natural, supernatural, or part of a diseased American society. As Deborah Notkin suggests, "King is one of the few writers . . . whose primary theme is one of hope and survival, despite the odds. In this light his popularity is predictable, and perhaps his large audience is in itself a small portent of hope for the future" (1990, 142). The ultimate message is that ordinary people can defeat evil in all its forms by maintaining "a sound sense of morality, cherishing childhood memories, controlling the thirst for technological advance, abstaining from a selfish interpretation of capitalist ideology and establishing a balance between individuality and societal conformity" (Davis 1994, 102).

The essence of King's mainstream success is therefore this hybridity in his works, comprising a straightforward writing style and an emphasis on narrative that allows for a focus on everyday characters, settings, locations, and language. Into these settings are placed extraordinary events, which in some manner reflect contemporary concerns and which the characters must overcome through making moral and selfless decisions, leading ultimately to the defeat of evil. Together, the interplay of an everyday world that is as instantly recognizable and decidedly blue-collar as the bulk of his characters with a series of monsters that act as both literal threat and metaphor helps to explain the mainstream success that King achieved in the first ten years of his writing career. As many of the scholars discussed above have argued, this focus on ordinary people and the everyday trappings of ordinary lives, along with the use of monsters, brings to King's work an appeal far beyond vampires, ghosts, and murderous technologies and so encouraged viewers of De Palma's film version of *Carrie* to buy and read the book and then keep coming back for more. But between 1975 and 1985, his consistent style, his hybrid approach to horror, the marketing of his books as horror regardless of actual content, and his mainstream success and subsequent fame led to King becoming something more than an author. He became a brand.

BRAND STEPHEN KING ON FILM AND TV

If the literary King brand is marked by a hybridity of realism and horror tropes, cinematically and televisually speaking, the situation is more polarized. A superficial reading suggests that King adaptations tend to be either designated as horror or as not-horror and that audiences and critics have generally reacted more positively to King adaptations that focus more on character development and story than those that foreground horror elements. Indeed, the evidence further suggests that the less a film is specifically connected to King, the less connected to the horror genre it is and, in many cases, the better it is consequently received.

Taking two extremes, Michael Collings offers a comparison of the critical reaction to *Maximum Overdrive*, written and directed by King, and *Stand by Me*, released a month later. *Maximum Overdrive* was specifically branded as a Stephen King horror project. The trailer features King himself, looking decidedly crazed, saying, "a lot of people have directed Stephen King novels and stories, and I finally decided, if you want something done right, you oughta do it yourself. . . . I just wanted someone to do Stephen King right." In contrast, *Stand by Me* was adapted by Ray Gideon and Bruce Evans from King's novella, *The Body*, and directed by Rob Reiner. Unlike *Maximum Overdrive*, *Stand by Me* made no mention of its connection to King in its marketing and was not sold as a horror film. Collings quotes a number of positive reviews, such as that of Kevin Lally, who "insists that the underlying narrative is atypical of King, improved by strong direction from Reiner, and equally strong writing" (1987, 66). The result is that, "according to several early reviewers, where the film succeeds it shows Reiner's hand, where it fails, it shows King's," which, coupled with the decision not to use King's name in the marketing, means that *Stand by Me* "has the unfortunate side effect of distancing King from the finest film adaptation of his works yet produced" (65). The opportunity for comparisons offered by the proximity of the releases of the two films did not help, with critic Richard Freeman saying that "Reiner [is] as skilled behind the camera as King is a seemingly hopeless duffer" (67). Ultimately, Collings can only conclude that "[i]n the cases of *Maximum Overdrive* and *Stand by Me*, King's reputation is an almost impossible barrier to overcome. One film apparently failed because of King, the other succeeded in spite of him" (68).

Certainly, *Stand by Me* was more appreciated by audiences. In the Box Office Mojo list of domestic box-office successes of films adapted from King's work, adjusted for inflation, as of 1 May 2017, *Stand by Me* comes in at sixth place with an overall gross of $124.5 million, while *Maximum Overdrive* manages only number thirty-four with just $17.5 million. The simplistic interpretation of this comparison suggests that *Maximum Overdrive* was less successful than *Stand by Me* because it was not as good, which is admittedly true. Yet, the situation is more complex than simply "good" and "bad." Neither *The Shawshank Redemption* nor *The Green Mile*, both considered among the best and most admired adaptations of his work, used King's name in the marketing, so it is significant that his name was also not used in marketing *Stand by Me*. Yet, it is not true to say that all the non-horror, non-King-branded films, like *Stand by Me*, were more popular than the branded products, like *Maximum Overdrive*. While *The Green Mile*, sold as a magical realist tale, is the biggest-grossing King adaptation to date with almost $231 million, the four films that separate it and *Stand by Me* were tied to the horror genre and to King—namely, *The Shining*, *Carrie*, *Misery*, and *Pet Sematary*. King scripted *Pet Sematary* and his name featured prominently in the promotional campaign. While the others did not necessarily sell themselves on King's name, they avoided specifically downplaying his involvement as the source material, as did *Stand by Me*, *The Shawshank Redemption*, and, to a lesser extent, *The Green Mile*. Furthermore, the Box Office Mojo listings of King adaptations in terms of revenue shows *Maximum Overdrive* ranked directly above Bryan Singer's adaptation of *Apt Pupil*, which is significant because the latter is the third of the three tales—along with the novellas *The Body* and *The Shawshank Redemption*—so far adapted from King's collection *Different Seasons*, described by Debra Stump as being recognized as "King's non-horror effort" (1985, 131). While *Stand by Me* and *The Shawshank Redemption* are both popular and beloved, *Apt Pupil*, drawn from the same collection, is not.

Another factor to consider is the relationship of the adaptations to the source material. Both *Stand by Me* and *Maximum Overdrive* are faithful to King's original stories as compared to, say, *The Shining* or *The Lawnmower Man*, both of which also performed well at the box office. So it therefore cannot be concluded that the benchmark for success depends upon whether or not a film is a "bad" adaptation of King's work, even if it was a simple thing to define just what exactly a bad adaptation is. As discussed in chapter 2, for example, *Firestarter* is a very faithful adaptation of King's novel, jettisoning very few sequences and using much of King's dialogue verbatim, yet this seems to have had little impact in terms of improving its box office or critical reception.

The evidence does not therefore imply that when an adaptation is promoted as a horror film and is trying to, again quoting King in the *Maximum Overdrive* trailer, "scare the hell out of you," cinema audiences stay away. As a result, it is not possible to accept the kind of polar positions implied by the comparisons between *Maximum Overdrive* and *Stand by Me*. It cannot be asserted absolutely that an adaptation of King's work that positions itself within the horror genre is less popular than one that is specifically non-horror, nor that films with which King was heavily involved and that acknowledge his contribution are less successful than ones with which he was not associated.

Similarly, it is not possible to say that an adaptation is more accepted by audiences and critics when it connects more closely to the original story. The box-office figures also suggest that there is little discernible correlation between the popularity of King's books and that of the films. In the period from 1975 to 1985, each of King's fiction books (or, in the case of compilations, several of the stories within those books) was adapted to the big or small screen. Yet, aside from *Carrie* and *The Shining*, the films that came out during the same period met with varying degrees of success. Returning to the box-office rankings of King adaptations, *Creepshow* (1982), *Cujo*, *The Dead Zone*, *Christine*, and *Firestarter* appear at 12, 13, 15, 16, and 19, respectively, with *Children of the Corn*, *Cat's Eye*, and *Silver Bullet* bringing up the rear at 21, 26, and 29. The films all made money, but did not achieve the kind of breakout performance of the ever-increasing success of the corresponding books.

It is notable that the three films that performed worst were based upon short stories, rather than novels. This does not necessarily suggest that King's short stories are less fruitful territory for adaptation, but the titles would most likely be less familiar to general audiences than those of the novels, which would have been in wide circulation in bookstores. Even without picking up a King book, a regular reader would be more likely to be familiar with the title *The Dead Zone*, having seen it on the shelves, than with "Children of the Corn," one of the stories within *Night Shift*. Title awareness therefore seems significant, yet both *The Body* and *The Shawshank Redemption* were similarly within a collection. Here, arguably, the lack of title awareness proved to be to the films' advantage, since they were less likely to be connected to King.

While it is therefore possible to argue that King's literary brand of hybrid horrors and accessible writing style led to a consistent and growing readership and to popular success (aided by De Palma's film version of *Carrie*), no clear explanation emerges as to why a particular adaptation or set of adaptations succeeded or failed. The reasons for this are obvious: the adaptations are films, not books, and are (for the most part) not written by King, who therefore has little or no creative control. As Simone Murray points out, cinemagoers and book readers aren't necessarily the same people (2012, 157). Furthermore, these adaptations exist within, or relate to, a horror genre that was fostered in a different medium with different industrial structures and economic pressures and is therefore distinct from the literary genre from which King emerged. Crucially, as a result of all these factors, the cinematic and televisual Brand Stephen King emerged as something connected to, but nevertheless different from, the literary brand.

2 / STEPHEN KING FROM VIETNAM TO REAGAN: THE EARLY ADAPTATIONS AND THE ESTABLISHMENT OF BRAND STEPHEN KING ON THE SCREEN

De Palma made the film,
King once commented, and the film made him.

MICHAEL COLLINGS, *THE FILMS OF STEPHEN KING*

AS NOTED IN CHAPTER I, *THE SHINING* BECAME KING'S first hardcover best seller partly on the back of sales of the movie tie-in paperback of *Carrie*, meaning Brian De Palma's adaptation of *Carrie* has some responsibility for King's breakout success as a horror author. That the film drew huge audiences, and then drove many viewers toward the book, sets *Carrie* apart from almost all the other films discussed in this analysis because when the film came out, King was virtually unknown, having published only *Carrie* and *Salem's Lot*, both modest sellers. So the box-office success of De Palma's film had little to do with King's name. King himself said that "with *Carrie* none of us had a reputation. Nobody knew De Palma. Nobody knew me" (Wood 1991c, 30). Instead, that success can be attributed to the quality of the film itself, but also to the fact that *Carrie* the film was a well-made entry in an established type of quality, mainstream horror cinema that had already been attracting large numbers of American moviegoers in the 1970s.

Carrie was a studio-based film financed by United Artists, which packaged it as a horror film in the style of *The Exorcist* and *Rosemary's Baby*. This was picked up by reviewers like Bill Kelley in *Cinefantastique*, who noted that De Palma "knows what films like *Rosemary's Baby* and *The Exorcist* have conditioned the public to expect" (1976, 20). The film *Carrie* was therefore part of the mainstream "acceptable and authorized" horror movement in the 1970s, identified by Gregory Waller, that saw "the major studios [approach] horror principally as a matter of adapting best-selling novels for the screen" (1987a, 5, 10). A number of King's contemporary horror novelists also saw their works adapted by studios in the 1970s. These included Frank De Felitta, whose *Au-*

drey Rose was filmed in 1977, also by United Artists, and Peter Straub, whose novel *Julia* was adapted as *Full Circle* in 1977 in Canada.

These adaptations from King's peers, along with *Carrie*, sought to replicate the formula of *Rosemary's Baby* and *The Exorcist*, both of which drew upon talented young, yet established, directors and actors, some of whom had prior links to the horror genre, to provide a mark of quality. In the late 1960s, Roman Polanski straddled both horror and art cinema through films like *Repulsion* (1965) and *Cul-de-Sac* (1966). While his film prior to *Rosemary's Baby* was the parodic vampire tale *The Fearless Vampire Killers* (1967), *Rosemary's Baby* drew far more upon the stylization of *Repulsion* than that Hammer-inspired romp. Before *The Exorcist*, William Friedkin had won a best director Oscar for *The French Connection* (1971), and star Ellen Burstyn had been nominated for *The Last Picture Show* (1971).

In keeping with this formula, *Audrey Rose* was directed by Robert Wise, who had been responsible not only for *West Side Story* (1961) and *The Sound of Music* (1965), but also for *The Haunting* (1963) and *The Andromeda Strain* (1971). Moreover, he had worked for horror producer Val Lewton at RKO in the 1940s. Wise was therefore, like Polanski, genre savvy, but he was also, like Friedkin, a proven director of mainstream popular cinema. The cast featured non-horror actors, including the then relatively unknown Anthony Hopkins and Marsha Mason, who that year received her second Oscar nomination for *The Goodbye Girl*. *Full Circle* starred Mia Farrow, who had played Rosemary in *Rosemary's Baby*, and was directed by Richard Loncraine, a British director who had worked for the BBC. Before *Carrie*, Brian De Palma had established himself as a director of stylish low-budget horror/thrillers with *Sisters* (1973) and *Phantom of the Paradise* (1974), but he was in need of a hit film after the poorly received Hitchcock homage, *Obsession* (1976). Star Sissy Spacek had received critical acclaim for her performance in Terrence Malick's *Badlands* (1973), and Piper Laurie, who De Palma tempted out of retirement to play Carrie's mother, had been nominated for an Oscar for her role alongside Paul Newman in *The Hustler* (1961).

All these films therefore were part of the mainstream, acceptable, literary horror cinema that Waller identifies as a consistent approach to the genre by the studios in the late 1960s and 1970s. The films were designed to appeal to general audiences through a combination of horror elements via generic ties and non-horror prestige supplied by the quality cinematic pedigrees of the creative personnel. The industrial and cultural moment of the film *Carrie* is therefore significant. The film's success drew attention to King as a writer and launched his rise to literary best-seller status. It also, as argued in chapter 1, tied King to the mainstream through its production history as an incarnation of the cinematic horror genre packaged for a mass-market audience.

The film versions of *Audrey Rose* and *Julia* fared less well than *Carrie* at the box office. As a result, neither De Felitta nor Straub could claim King's impact on the film industry or his profitability in bookshops. Partly, and this arguably forms the other reason why King's success blossomed, this is because, like *The Exorcist*, *Carrie* was a relatively uncompromising horror film. As screenwriter Lawrence D. Cohen put it, "De Palma brought just a wallop of style to [the film]" (Wood 1991c, 35), and right from the start, De Palma directed *Carrie* as a horror film by pushing the boundaries of acceptable representation. The shower sequence that opens the film (after a brief scene of the girls playing volleyball) begins with a slow-motion tracking shot of the girls' locker room that features a large amount of full-frontal female nudity. The room is filled with steam, giving the image a soft focus that adds a dreamlike aura to the scene, and while it is clear from the action that this is a noisy space—the room is full of girls talking and laughing—there is no diegetic sound. The sequence is accompanied only by a melodic and lyrical music score by Pino Donaggio that adds a poetic quality.

The camera then tracks forward to Carrie, enjoying her shower. Accompanied again by a soft music theme expressing beauty, De Palma shows Carrie soaping her breasts, chest, and thighs. At this point, lyricism gives way to realism. Carrie's period has begun, and once she sees blood in her hands, the score is replaced by the diegetic sound of the shower. The steam dissipates, and then, after a series of close-ups of Carrie's reaction, De Palma's roving dolly shots are replaced by a handheld camera when she leaves the shower and enters the locker room. The fetishized nudity of the slow-motion opening is contrasted with Carrie's gaunt naked body, revealed in all its vulnerability under harsh lights, and with the frenzied close-up camerawork as the girls attack her both verbally and physically with towels and tampons. This opening is both sensuous and brutal, soft-core pornography turned to hardcore cruelty.

This sequence is referenced during the climax at the prom in which Carrie uses her telekinetic powers to wreak havoc on her peers. Once Chris Hargensen and her boyfriend, Billy Nolan, upend a bucket of pig's blood on Carrie, the film adopts her traumatized and distorted point of view, combining swirling visuals with a complex soundscape in which key phrases from the story—her mother's warning that "they're all gonna laugh at you" and, from the opening, the chant of "plug it UP, plug it UP"—overlap in Carrie's mind. As the revenge sequence begins, De Palma adopts a split screen. Carrie bursts the lights, bathing the entire gym in a blood-red wash of color, eventually replaced by an icy blue as she uses electricity as a weapon. Covered in blood, Carrie is made monstrous, while the gym, where the prom takes place, becomes a metaphorical and literal hell, a cacophony of screaming voices, vio-

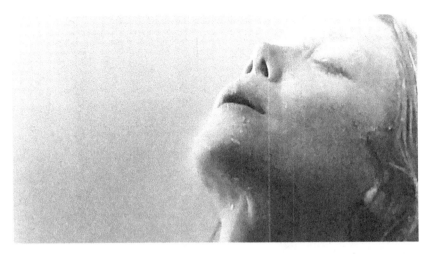

Soft-core pornography turned to hard-core cruelty in Carrie *(1976)*.

lent threat, and panicking students, all bathed in red. As the doors to the gym open, Carrie emerges in slow motion, framed by the doorway before a wall of flames, a demon stepping from hellish depths into our own world.

The violence, the sound, the imagery of hell, the music by Donaggio that echoes the shrieking strings of Hitchcock's *Psycho*, and the visuals all clearly mark this sequence as horror. The style that De Palma brought to *Carrie* therefore follows the example set by *Rosemary's Baby* and, in particular, *The Exorcist*, which, like the more low-budget horrors of Romero and Hooper but in a more mainstream production context, pushed the limits of acceptable representation. Friedkin's film provided a "visceral visual onslaught" (Kermode

1997, 9). This was horror for the masses, but it was horror nevertheless. What the violence in *Carrie* lacks by way of the kind of elegantly staged, effects-driven set pieces—for example, the possessed Regan's spinning head and the green vomit—in *The Exorcist* is matched by De Palma's staging of Carrie's revenge at the prom. With its innocent heroine, religious theme, and scenes of explosive violence, *Carrie* closely echoes the cinematic horror style that made *The Exorcist* such a phenomenon.

However, *Carrie* also marked the apex of this form of boundary-pushing, studio-based mainstream horror, and immediately following its release, the horror genre began to change. Released after *Carrie*, *Audrey Rose* and *Full Circle* focused on character and psychological drama rather than on visceral shocks. The climax of *Audrey Rose* sees the young girl Ivy undergoing regression hypnosis to see if she is indeed the reincarnated spirit of Elliot Hoover's (Anthony Hopkins) daughter, Audrey Rose, who died in a car fire at the moment that Ivy was born. Under hypnosis in controlled clinical surroundings, as onlookers watch through a one-way mirror, Ivy remembers the moment of Audrey Rose's death. While there are glimpses of Audrey Rose trapped in the burning car intercut with the present day, the main focus of the horror is internal as Ivy beats at the one-way glass, screaming as she relives in her head Audrey Rose's terror-filled final moments and finally dies of asphyxiation. Ivy's death is tragic and bleak, but directly afterward, Hoover repeats over and over to Ivy's mother, Janice, "It's all right now. Her soul is set free." The film ends on a somber but positive note about Ivy/Audrey Rose's reincarnation, with Janice writing to Hoover in India, saying that while Ivy's body has died, her soul lives on, that "we are all immortal," and that someday she "will be reborn" to "parents who are generous, understanding, and who will love her as we all loved her."

As mainstream "acceptable and authorized" literary horror turned toward the psychological, the more explicit depiction of violence in *Carrie* and *The Exorcist* found a home in the slasher or splatter film, a new form of horror that eschewed literary adaptation and would dominate the genre until 1984. This same period also saw the emergence of the cinematic Brand Stephen King. By the time that brand was fully formed in 1983–1984, the cinematic horror genre had made a cautious return to literary adaptation, but the position of these mainstream horror adaptations within the cinematic genre was very different.

THE CHANGING FACE OF CINEMATIC HORROR, 1977–1983

The history of the horror film in this period has been covered in numerous works and so is well known. According to Vera Dika, "during the years

1978–1981 [I would argue this should be extended to 1983], the American film market was flooded by the largest number of horror films in recent history [many of which] exhibit an unprecedented level of explicit violence and so have commonly become designated as 'splatter' or 'slasher' films" (1987, 86). The change began shortly after *Carrie*, but the template for the slasher film was largely John Carpenter's *Halloween* (1978), although its origins extend as far back as Alfred Hitchcock's *Psycho* and Michael Powell's *Peeping Tom* (both 1960). However, as Kim Newman has pointed out, "the closest recent cinema had come to *Halloween* was Bob Clark's . . . *Black Christmas* (1974)," which also featured a hidden killer stalking victims during a named holiday season (2011, 200). However, the horror film genre in 1979 saw relatively little by way of slasher films, the main one being *When a Stranger Calls*. Instead, the trend of mainstream, big-budget, literary horror continued to dominate, notably with the adaptation of Jay Anson's 1977 book *The Amityville Horror* (1979) and John Badham's film version of *Dracula* (1979).

In keeping with the movement away from the more overt violence of *The Exorcist*, *The Omen*, and *Carrie*, neither *The Amityville Horror* nor *Dracula* focuses on "visual, visceral" horror. Despite one scene presenting Mina as a zombie-like vampire, *Dracula* takes a gothic romantic approach to its subject, emphasizing Dracula (Frank Langella) as a kind of seductive aristocrat rather than a vampiric monster. Equally, *The Amityville Horror* accentuates the psychological horrors of the story rather than physical effects, as good father George Lutz becomes increasingly sullen and aggressive after he and his family move into the house.

Both films, however, draw upon the established theme of a fractured family under threat, albeit in very different ways. Unlike *The Exorcist*, *The Omen*, and *Carrie*, where the threat comes from a child, *Amityville* focuses on a father who becomes possessed by the house and poses a danger of violence to the family. Badham's *Dracula* reworks Stoker's novel so that Mina is the daughter of Van Helsing and is turned and therefore "possessed" by Dracula. Likewise, Lucy becomes the daughter of Dr. Seward and is depicted as independent and sexually awakened before being courted by Dracula. These two female characters together are presented as different threats to a patriarchal order that is woefully ineffective, Dr. Seward and Van Helsing being notably inept at dealing with the vampire throughout the film. Both films are illustrative of the fact that in 1979, the most high-profile horror movies were still mainstream literary adaptations. Also, they remained interested in the familial middle-class milieu of *The Exorcist* and *Rosemary's Baby* (less so, of course, in the case of *Dracula*, which did not have a contemporary setting), but were becoming less violent than horror films of the early 1970s.

However, in addition to these mainstream horror adaptations, there was also an increase in the use of the kind of visual horror effects pioneered by Dick Smith for *The Exorcist*, which would ultimately become a key element of both the slasher and splatter film. In 1979, the film that arguably most closely mirrored the more explicit mainstream horror films of the early 1970s was a horror/science fiction hybrid, Ridley Scott's *Alien*. Like *Rosemary's Baby*, *The Exorcist*, and *Carrie*, *Alien* was a big-budget studio production, in this case, from 20th Century Fox. The film took a very serious approach to its material, reworking both a traditional monster movie and a haunted house plot with a carefully crafted realist aesthetic and challenging scenes of physical horror, such as its infamous "chest-bursting" scene in which the alien creature is "born" by pushing through the rib cage of the crewman Kane.

Also in 1979, outside of the mainstream in the independent horror film movement, came *Dawn of the Dead*, George Romero's follow-up to *Night of the Living Dead*. Filmed in Monroeville Mall, close to his hometown of Pittsburgh, Romero's film maintained the political concerns of his earlier films. Here the zombies, clearly demarcated by their costumes as people from everyday walks of life, become the ultimate consumers, desperate to enter the mall in order to fulfill their needs. Romero's film was not only a savage satire on consumerism, but also a showcase for the delightfully gory visual effects by Tom Savini, which would shape the horror genre for the next few years.

For example, director Sean S. Cunningham turned to Savini to create the murder sequences in *Friday the 13th* (1980). *Friday* is far more visually explicit than either *Black Christmas* or *Halloween*, and it was the emphasis in Cunningham's film on physical dismemberment and body horror that provided the final piece for the template that would form the slasher genre. Equally, Savini's work on *Dawn of the Dead*, which featured far more depictions of blood than those seen in *Night of the Living Dead*, *The Exorcist*, the set-piece deaths in *The Omen*, and indeed in the final massacre in *Carrie*, would set the stage for the splatter film.

As a result, the horror genre of the early years of the 1980s was dominated by films in which maniacs armed with sharp, stabbing, or chopping implements stalked and murdered mainly teenagers, more often than not around some sort of named celebratory holiday or event. The release of *Friday the 13th* in May 1980 was quickly followed by *Prom Night* in August and *Terror Train* in October, and, in 1981, *Bloody Birthday*, *Happy Birthday to Me*, *My Bloody Valentine*, *Night School*, *Final Exam*, and sequels to both *Friday the 13th* and *Halloween*. Literary adaptations continued, including versions of both Straub's *Ghost Story* and James Herbert's *The Survivor* in 1981. But the lion's share of the cinematic horror audience, and a great deal of the marketing, promotion, and impetus of the horror film, shifted away from literature and the decreasing violence of literary adaptations toward a more explicit form of horror epitomized by both slasher and splatter films. The essence of the splatter film, as John McCarty describes it, is an emphasis upon explicit violence, something also often endemic to the slasher film as victims were dispatched in increasingly gory and imaginative ways (1984). The slasher film was therefore one strand of the splatter film, which also included the kind of cerebral explorations of the body found in David Cronenberg's films, *The Brood* (1979), *Scanners* (1981), and *Videodrome* (1983), as well as in Italian exploitation films such as *Zombie Flesh Eaters* (1979) or *The New York Ripper* (1982), both directed by Lucio Fulci.

Philip Brophy offers perhaps the best assessment of the horror genre in the early 1980s, describing it as using new special effects technology to revel in "the destruction of the body" in a mode of "showing as opposed to telling" (1986, 8). Also significant is the fact that while films like *The Exorcist*, *Rosemary's Baby*, and *Carrie* were widely seen by American and international audiences in their local cinemas, Brophy was researching his article in 1983 in Australia, seeking out the films via "Drive-in Doubles, Dusk til Dawns and hired video-cassettes" (4).

In short, between 1978 and 1983, the cinematic horror genre largely handed back the mainstream audiences it had won in the late 1960s and early 1970s and moved into niche territory, both literally in terms of leaving cinemas for the drive-ins and home-viewing market and figuratively in terms of dropping the kind of serious political or social considerations of 1970s horror in favor of a celebration of bodily dismemberment. This is not to say that slasher and splatter films were unsuccessful, that studios never financed them, or that they never appeared in mainstream movie houses across the United States and elsewhere. Rather, it indicates that in the late 1970s and early 1980s, the driving force behind the horror film moved away from the oppositional strands of low-budget horror, aimed largely at the midnight movie art house and drive-in circuits, and bigger-budget mainstream literary horror for the mass audience of the 1970s and moved toward the slasher/splatter model that predominantly consisted of low- to medium-budget horror films aimed mainly at fans of the genre and burgeoning teenage audiences.

When Brophy coined his term "horrality" to encompass those elements, he was not writing about a particular subgenre of horror, but rather what he calls "the modern horror film" (3), a term also used by Waller to describe the horror films of the early 1970s (1987a, 2). Thus, in the transition between the 1970s and 1980s, the definition of the "modern horror film" shifted from expensive mainstream literary horror to lower-budget splatter and slash. But as the likes of *The Amityville Horror* and *Ghost Story* attest, the types of horror film that Brophy highlights were not the only ones on offer. So what Brophy and Waller refer to in their definition of "the modern horror film" is not an all-encompassing generic tradition, but rather a slasher/splatter model that for a brief period became horror's primary form.

AVOIDING SPLATTER IN DEVELOPMENT HELL: THE CINEMATIC BRAND STEPHEN KING, 1976–1983

Carrie first hit cinema screens in the United States in November 1976. Three years later, Tobe Hooper's version of King's second novel, *Salem's Lot*, aired as a TV miniseries on CBS on November 17 and 24, 1979, with Kubrick's film version of *The Shining* released in cinemas in May 1980. *The Shining* was King's third novel and the third to be adapted, and by the release of Kubrick's film, the author had also published *Night Shift* (1978), *The Stand* (1978), and *The Dead Zone* (1979). The next three years saw a flurry of new books by King (as well as two under his pseudonym, Richard Bachman): *Firestarter* in 1980 followed by *Danse Macabre* and *Cujo* in 1981; *The Dark Tower: The Gunslinger*, *Different Seasons*, *Creepshow*, and *Cycle of the Werewolf* in 1982; and *Pet Sematary* and *Christine* in 1983.

Yet, this period of literary productivity was not mirrored in the adaptations. Although all of King's works were optioned (with the exception of the nonfiction *Danse Macabre* and the atypical and limitedly available *The Gunslinger*), after *The Shining*, no adaptations were released until *Cujo* in August 1983. Thus, between the film versions of *Carrie* in 1976 and *Cujo* in 1983, *The Shining* was the only King adaptation to be released in cinemas (putting aside the two-hour cut of *Salem's Lot* released in Europe). While King was building both his literary brand and his audience of Constant Readers by publishing book after book, the cinema adaptations of his works stalled. The August 1983 release of *Cujo* heralded a glut of five adaptations within a nine-month period: *The Dead Zone* (October 1983), *Christine* (December 1983), *Children of the Corn* (March 1984), and *Firestarter* (May 1984).

Given the box-office achievements of *Carrie*, the lull of King adaptations between it and *Cujo* is worthy of further investigation. Even before *Carrie* came out, Warner Bros. had optioned *Salem's Lot* immediately upon its publication in 1975, with a view to producing a feature film, but numerous writers, including Stirling Silliphant, were unable to reduce King's novel to a 120-minute feature. The property was eventually taken on by Richard Kobritz, executive vice president of production at Warner Bros. Television. He proposed that it be turned into a miniseries and hired Paul Monash, who had produced *Carrie* for United Artists, to write the screenplay (Earnshaw 2013, 16–18). Meanwhile, also at Warner Bros., Kubrick had optioned *The Shining* from Robert Fryer at the Producers' Circle Company.

King's first three novels were in production by the end of 1978, but what followed was a period of so-called development hell in which King-related projects were delayed as they went through numerous changes of production personnel. British-based producer Milton Subotsky acquired the rights to several of the short stories in *Night Shift*. King produced a screenplay with the same title, which was an anthology film based on three stories from the collection, "Strawberry Spring," "Battleground," and "I Know What You Need." The three tales are linked by a framing story in which Harold Davis, an old man living in Weathersfield, Maine, reminisces with his grandson, Rich, who edits the local paper (Stephen King Special Collection, Orono, box no. 2318). Following the success of *Salem's Lot*, a different proposal was put forward: King would rework *Night Shift* for NBC and become a latter-day Rod Serling, introducing weekly adaptations of his stories in the style of *The Twilight Zone* and *Night Gallery*. The proposal was scrapped in 1980 because, according to King, "the standards and practices office felt it was too intense for television" (Gagne 1980b, 34). Meanwhile, King's fourth novel, *The Stand* was sold to George Romero and his producer Richard P. Rubinstein for their company, Laurel Productions. As Romero remembers, "Steve gave us the choice of any book or story of his that wasn't sold . . . we chose *The Stand* (Anon. 1979b, 78). As with *Salem's Lot*, however, the challenge of reducing King's novel to manageable feature length delayed the project.

King's next novel, *The Dead Zone*, was optioned in 1979 by Lorimar Productions to be produced by Sydney Pollack. Carol Baum, who worked for Lorimar at that time, approached Canadian director David Cronenberg, who had just completed *The Brood*. However, Pollack had already lined up veteran director Stanley Donen, who was then completing a sci-fi/horror film, *Saturn 3* (1980) (Collings 2006, 91). Eventually, Lorimar passed on the project, and the rights were acquired by US-based Italian producer Dino De Laurentiis. Meanwhile, *Firestarter* was optioned by Dodi Fayed in 1980, the rights eventually passing to Universal where John Carpenter was scheduled to direct from a screenplay by Bill Phillips. Universal balked at the potential cost, especially after the failure of Carpenter's *The Thing* (1982). So Carpenter and Phillips took on another King novel, *Christine*, their adaptation hitting screens only eight months after the book was released. Finally, one of the *Night Shift* stories, "Children of the Corn," was adapted by King in 1979–1980 and was to be directed by a Maine-based documentary filmmaker, Harry Wisland, but the producer, Joseph Masefield, was unable to secure the funding (Gagne 1980b, 34).

Such development delays are by no means unusual, but this confluence of events meant that projects that were originally planned at different times were all in limbo until, suddenly, they all began moving forward simultaneously.

In 1981 and 1982, De Laurentiis produced the two sequels to *Halloween*, acquiring in the process the services of *Halloween*'s original producer, Debra Hill. According to Cronenberg, Hill suggested he direct *The Dead Zone* for De Laurentiis, seemingly unaware of the director's earlier discussion with Baum at Lorimar (Rodley 1992, 109–110). De Laurentiis, evidently seeing a potential King franchise, also acquired *Firestarter* from Universal once Carpenter and Phillips left the project, handing scriptwriting duties to veteran writer Stanley Mann and hiring Mark L. Lester, director of the violent high-school thriller, *Class of 1984* (1982). *Children of the Corn* landed at Roger Corman's New World Pictures, where producer Donald Borchers offered the project to his friend Fritz Kiersch, a director of commercials who was looking for his first feature (Jones 1984a, 16–17).

These films moved into production simultaneously, along with *Cujo* and *Christine*, both of which had comparatively smooth and speedy transitions to the screen. Therefore, following a long hiatus, cinemagoers were seeing an unprecedented number of King adaptations in a short space of time. While the reasons for this delay appear to be purely practical, it is nevertheless notable that these adaptations of King's stories effectively straddle the rise and fall of the slasher and splatter subgenres. As noted above, within these subgenres, the emphasis upon body horror and transformation effectively took over the horror genre from independent political horror and big-budget literary adaptations. *Carrie* came out at, and benefitted from, the high point of the latter, but by the time *The Shining* appeared, the movement was waning, about to be replaced by the juggernaut that was *Friday the 13th* and its many derivatives.

Yet, by the end of 1983, both the slasher and the splatter movements within horror were played out. As Ian Conrich notes, while the slasher film "dominated the genre . . . by 1984 this subgenre had collapsed" (2010, 173) as the endless repetition of generic tropes sent the slasher film into a spiral of diminishing returns. The emphasis on physical mutilation at the heart of splatter was also waning, due in no small part to the reaction to the inventive brutality of Rob Bottin's work for John Carpenter's *The Thing*. This film marked a watershed moment in horror effects. In his positive review of the film, Phil Edwards in *Starburst* told his readers, "YOU ARE NOT GOING TO BELIEVE YOUR EYES." However, he also noted that "the horror effects represent a new dimension in mainstream cinematic grossness" and that the film "may take some time to realize its potential audience due to its relentlessly grim nature and high physical disgust factor" (1983, 22). This "physical disgust factor," coupled with a bleak ending that had the two surviving characters, one or both of whom might be the Thing, waiting for death, prompted negative reviews. As Anne Billson notes, David Denby in *New York* magazine described the film as "disgusting rather than frightening" (1997, 8), and Gary

Arnold in the *Washington Post* called the film "a wretched excess" (1982). A science-fiction horror crossover backed by Universal and Carpenter's first big-budget effort, *The Thing* was not aimed exclusively at horror fans but had a large summer release in June 1982 on 840 screens. As these reviews attest, it failed in part because it was simply too gory, crossing the boundary of what was acceptable to mainstream audiences.

It has been often said—by Billson, for example—that part of Carpenter's problem was that his nihilistic depiction of an invading alien life form was released two weeks after Steven Spielberg's *E.T. the Extra-Terrestrial* (1982). Just as *Alien* was the polar opposite of Spielberg's *Close Encounters of the Third Kind* (1977) in terms of tone, style, and approach to aliens, *E.T.* stood in stark contrast to *The Thing*. Spielberg had redressed the balance and made alien encounters hopeful again, severely damaging the appeal of Carpenter's vision in the process.

But in many ways more pertinent to this discussion is another Spielberg-related film, *Poltergeist* (1982), also released just before *The Thing*. An evidently unhappy collaboration between Spielberg as writer/producer and Tobe Hooper as director (Spielberg initially approached King to write the screenplay), *Poltergeist* is, as John Brosnan stated in his review for *Starburst*, "a really scary movie," but also "a *cosy* horror movie. It's not going to disturb you on any deep level, like *The Exorcist* did . . . nor will it disgust you with blood and gore effects" (1983, 10). *Poltergeist* draws upon, but reworks, the themes of big-budget horror from the 1970s. Like those films, it displays a largely ineffectual form of patriarchy. Head of the family Steven Freeling is a good-hearted but problematic figure who, unable to protect his home, is finally ejected from it along with his family. Further, as a salesman for a corrupt real estate business that built upon hallowed native burial ground, he is also implicitly responsible for the horrors visited upon them. Despite this, the fractured and perverted family unit of *The Exorcist*, *Rosemary's Baby*, *The Omen*, and *Carrie* is gone, replaced by one that is endearingly chaotic but nevertheless stable. The threat to the family via the child comes not from within but from without. Carol Ann, the youngest daughter of the Freeling family, is taken, not possessed. So unlike Regan in *The Exorcist* or Robert Thorn's lost child in *The Omen*, she is never replaced by an Other. Also, aside from one single moment where parapsychologist Marty has a vision of tearing off his own face, body horror is largely replaced by the ethereal light-based visual effects created by George Lucas's Industrial Light and Magic. At the end, though the family home is destroyed and the Freelings forced to flee, they are nevertheless safe, the final lingering image of the television set pushed onto the walkway outside their hotel room being tinged with humor. As Brosnan argued, the film shows "just how canny Spielberg has been with *Poltergeist*. In a real sense he has made a *family* horror movie, designed to offend as few people as possible and appeal to the majority" (1983, 10). Unlike *The Thing*, which took the "visceral visual" excesses of *The Exorcist* to extremes, *Poltergeist* offered a relatively "safe" form of horror, tempering the excesses of horror effects that had become endemic to the genre and signaling a shift in mainstream horror away from the visceral visuals of *The Exorcist* toward something cozier.

The success of *Poltergeist* and the corresponding failure of *The Thing* in summer 1982 therefore marked a pivot point in the horror genre that saw the impetus move away from slasher films and body horror, although the genre would return to these tropes a few years later. In their place, the horror film returned to literature for its inspiration. However, in keeping with the shift away from the violence evident in adaptations from the late 1970s, these new films did not contain the more explicit elements of those of the early 1970s. For example, summer 1983, when *Cujo* came out and the flood of King adaptations began, saw the release of *Psycho II*, Richard Franklin's eloquent sequel to Hitchcock's masterpiece. Considering that Hitchcock's original in 1960 marked a turning point, along with *Peeping Tom*, a proto-slasher narrative with equivalent levels of violence, and also considering that slasher films had dominated the horror genre since 1980, Franklin's film largely, albeit not entirely, avoids gore, and, as star Anthony Perkins pointed out at the time, is "very restrained" and "tastefully discreet" (Jones 1983, 15). While there were some late entries, such as *The House on Sorority Row*, into the slasher cycle in 1983, and body horror did continue through, for example, *Spasms* (1983), which featured spectacularly gloopy effects by Dick Smith, the movement in 1983 in studio-based horror cinema generally echoed MGM's *Poltergeist* and Universal's *Psycho II* in a move toward restraint and a cozier form of horror.

Other literary adaptations in 1983 included a version of Frank De Felitta's novel, *The Entity*, released by 20th Century Fox (released in the United Kingdom in 1982), and Michael Mann's interpretation of F. Paul Wilson's *The Keep* for Paramount. Again, both films, while using some physical makeup, place more emphasis on the kind of ethereal visual effects pioneered in *Poltergeist*. In April 1983, Disney released its first foray into the horror/science-fiction/fantasy genre with an adaptation of Ray Bradbury's *Something Wicked This Way Comes*. These films evidence both a revival of horror literary adaptations in 1983 and a shift within the mass-market end of the horror genre toward a less gory form, harking back to the trend that started in the late 1970s with the likes of *The Amityville Horror* and rose again to prominence after the mainstream moviegoing public emphatically rejected the visual excesses of the horror genre of the early 1980s as epitomized by *The Thing*. Thus, during the hiatus between *The Shining* in 1980 and *Cujo* in 1983, the horror genre adopted stalk and slash as its principal form, but returned to literature in a different, "safer" form from that of the early to mid-1970s. It was from this new iteration of the horror genre that the Stephen King films emerged.

First was *Cujo*, which was in keeping with the general trend away from the violence visible in studio-based literary horror films since 1977 and which represented a first step in establishing the cinematic Brand Stephen King. The director of *Cujo*, Lewis Teague, was not familiar with King's work and was not keen to do another horror film after his tongue-in-cheek monster movie *Alligator* (1980). Upon reading the book, however, Teague saw it primarily as a psychological drama and "got very excited because of the dynamics that existed in the family . . . . Donna's fears of wasting her life in the country . . . the husband's fear of financial insecurity . . . . To me, Cujo's materialization is a manifestation of their internal fears" (Horsting 1983, 43).

In a decision that would become a familiar refrain for King adaptations, stars Dee Wallace and Christopher Stone said at the time, "We're not interested in doing it if it's a horror film . . . . We really took great pains to make it psychological, a suspense thriller. . . . See, in America a horror film is . . . what's the word . . . exploitative and graphic. And I thought they treated that side of it very well in *Cujo*. There's nothing that makes you go eeoough" (Crawley 1983, 27). The first film that began to cement the identity of the cinematic Brand Stephen King, *Cujo* took pains not to be defined as a horror film in the style of stalk and slash. The makers of *Cujo* looked around at the horror genre in 1983 and declared their film to be different.

BRAND STEPHEN KING ON THE BIG SCREEN, 1983–1985

The literary Stephen King brand evolved during the period between the films of *The Shining* and *Cujo*. This led to the development of the cinematic Brand Stephen King, but because of the gap between *The Shining* and *Cujo*, that cinematic product only really coalesced between 1983 and 1985 and did not really exist before *Cujo*. De Palma's *Carrie* makes no mention of King in its advertising beyond acknowledging that the film is "based on the novel by Stephen King" in the credits. By the time Kubrick's film was released, King's literary brand was established, but *The Shining* also does not overtly foreground King's name. While the original trailer contains the caption "Based on the Bestselling Novel by Stephen King," the poster, like that of *Carrie*, included King's name only in the credits at the bottom. This lack of emphasis was likely due to Kubrick, who maintained control over all aspects of the production, including the marketing. Designer Tom Beauvais, who produced one version of a poster for *The Shining* using a photographic still from the film said that "it was Stanley's idea and we executed a design he had carefully detailed" (Shannon 2013). Not one of the posters for Kubrick's films foreground the author of the original work, even *Lolita*, the screenplay for which was written by Vladimir Nabokov himself. In the case of *The Shining*, King had written a script that was jettisoned by Kubrick, who proceeded to write his own with Diane Johnson.

The impending arrival of *The Shining* certainly attracted considerable interest in the fantasy press. In its first issue, *Fangoria* noted that "most of the breathless anticipation in Hollywood horror circles is being reserved for . . . *The Shining*." Describing King as "the author of such well-received books as *Carrie*, *Salem's Lot* and *Night Shift*," the piece focuses on Kubrick, who is "universally regarded as one of the greatest filmmakers in cinema today" (Anon. 1979a, 65). By the time the film came out, *Fangoria* was clearly excited, noting that after "a long wait . . . horror fans and film aficionados alike are ready to reap the rewards for their patience," going on to describe *The Shining* as "the terror film of the century" (Wynorski 1980, 21). In that year, King had gone from being the "author of some well-received books" to "the best-selling author of horror tales in the world" (Winter 1980, 26). Nevertheless, in the publicity aimed at cinema-going audiences, *The Shining*, like *Carrie*, was not a branded Stephen King cinematic product but rather a Stanley Kubrick film.

The first film to prominently feature King's name in its advertising was *Creepshow* (1982). The script was his original screenplay, with two of the segments, "The Lonesome Death of Jordy Verrill" and "The Crate," based on previously published stories. The first screenplay King had written to be filmed, *Creepshow* was the result of a partnership between King and George Romero that emerged from the development process of *The Stand* and from a shared love of E.C. horror comics from the 1950s. While King and Romero were, by 1980, lauded in fanzines like *Fangoria* and *Cinefantastique*, neither had proved themselves with the kind of budgets that *The Stand* might require, so *Creepshow* became a kind of test project. For Romero, it was about working with a large $8 million budget and handling big-name stars for the first time; for King, it tested whether he could actually write a successful horror movie, given that he had had no involvement in *Carrie*, *The Shining*, or *Salem's Lot*. *Cinefantastique* voiced concerns, suggesting that "while the King/Romero collaboration sounds like dynamite, many genre fans may be a little skeptical after such promising, but inevitably disappointing combinations as King and Tobe Hooper and more specifically King and Stanley Kubrick." King confirmed that this was about taking responsibility for his own work, noting that, until then, "none of them [the films] have been King! In a way I've been safe all through this. But if *Creepshow* is a bad movie and people don't like it, then I can't very well duck it, can I? I'm tied to this in a hundred ways" (Gagne 1982a, 21).

King's greater involvement, as both screenwriter and actor, and the mutual respect between King and Romero led to *Creepshow* being sold on his name alongside that of Romero. The trailer features King's name first, alone on a black screen with a voice-over announcing, "From the author of *Carrie, The Shining*, and *Cujo*," followed by a similar credit to Romero, as "The Creator of *Night of the Living Dead* and *Dawn of the Dead*." The US poster announced at the top that the film was from "The Masters of Terror and the Macabre" followed by Romero's name on the left and King's on the right, with King billed as "the author of *Carrie, The Shining, The Stand, Firestarter*, and *Cujo*." The UK poster similarly attributed the film to "Masters of Terror and the Macabre," but rather than listing their credits, it billed the film as "Stephen King's *Creepshow*. Directed by George A. Romero."

Creepshow premiered in 1982 at the Cannes Film Festival where it was sold to numerous international territories and to Warner Bros. in the United States, in addition to receiving a glowing review in *Variety* (Gagne 1982b, 24). Solid, but not outstanding, box-office returns followed, meaning that King and Romero's experiment had worked. This did not ultimately lead to their production of *The Stand*, but it did mark the first time that King's name was marketed as a selling point of a film. As a result, *Cujo* became the first adaptation of a King novel (as opposed to *Creepshow*, which was an original screenplay) to highlight his name in the advertising, the US poster for the film announcing:

First *Carrie*
Then *The Shining*
Now Stephen King unleashes the most terrifying fear of all . . .

The trailer also emphasized that the film is "from the novel by Stephen King, creator of *Carrie* and *The Shining*." What is noticeable here is that the poster and trailer both equate the idea of "Stephen King" solely with the prior film adaptations of his work, avoiding references to TV through the absence of *Salem's Lot*, to his original screenplay for *Creepshow*, and indeed to any of the as yet unadapted books he had written. The *Cujo* poster and trailer also do not refer to King as a writer. The trailer specifically refers to him as a "creator," while the poster makes no mention of his specific role, which is only as the author of the original work, King having written a screenplay that was rejected by Lewis Teague. By 1983, King was the most successful author in the United States, and *Cujo* was the first cinematic adaptation of his work to foreground his contribution, and it does so in a very different way from *Creepshow*, highlighting King as "the creator" and thus implying some form of input while being deliberately unspecific as to what it was.

Two months later, *The Dead Zone* went one step further, the poster imply-ing creative oversight on his part by referring to "Stephen King's *The Dead Zone*." Here, King is allocated the stamp of authorship of the film, despite the fact that it was directed by David Cronenberg and adapted by Jeffrey Boam. Cronenberg had rejected King's script, which he described as "terrible. It was not only bad as a script . . . it was basically a really ugly unpleasant slasher script. The Castle Rock killer . . . becomes the lead and it was 'let's show lots of his victims'" (Rodley 1992, 113).

It is worth noting here that Cronenberg's assessment of King's screenplay is unfair. King's revised first draft and second draft are held in the Stephen King Collection at the University of Maine, Orono, and both follow the book quite closely. The revised first draft opens with Greg Stillson, a young Bi-ble salesman, poisoning a dog, and it subsequently follows the book by focus-ing upon Johnny Smith and Sarah Bracknell at the county fair wheel of for-tune, Johnny's accident, and his eventual awakening and rehabilitation. Both drafts do show more of the Castle Rock murders, the first including a scene that takes place just after Johnny's crash in which Frank Dodd kills Alma Fre-schette with a hatchet on which the word "Destroyer" is written (27) and a later scene in which two young boys find the feet of a woman sticking out of the snow (35). Johnny's vision at the bandstand when he identifies the killer as Frank Dodd is also more graphic, especially in the second draft where Johnny sees:

A MIDDLE AGED WOMAN: The hatchet comes down into her head. Blood sprays. AN OLD WOMAN: Crumpling. Bleeding. The hatchet comes down and hits her again. More blood. A TEENAGE GIRL IN A CHEERLEADER'S SKIRT. She's splattered with blood. She crumples to the ground. A shadow falls over her . . . Dodd grins . . . and blood pours out of his mouth as his lips form the word "Destroyer" over and over. (75)

Despite this explicit description, this is not, as Cronenberg suggested, a slasher script. As with *Cujo*, the film was sold on King's authorship and vi-sion, notwithstanding the fact that he did not write it. This decision also highlights the nature of the audience to which the producers were appealing. Thanks to his low-budget films such as *Shivers* (1975), *Rabid* (1977), and *Scan-ners*, Cronenberg was, like Lewis Teague after *Alligator*, an established name among horror film fans, but he was not yet a familiar name to general audi-ences, making King's name more high profile.

Released in December 1983, *Christine* was a different case. In contrast to *The Dead Zone*, the poster and trailer for this film refer to "John Carpen-ter's *Christine*," a stamp of authorship that has been a standard feature of all of Carpenter's films since *Halloween*. The trailer makes no mention of King by name, referring only to "the mind that gave us *Salem's Lot*," an interesting choice in that it mentions no other cinematic adaptations, referencing instead the novel, or possibly the miniseries. The posters for *Children of the Corn* return to the approach of both *Cujo* and *The Dead Zone*, naming previous adaptations by announcing that the 1984 film is "From the author of *Carrie*, *The Shining*, *The Dead Zone* and *Christine*"—curiously not *Cujo*—and billing it as "Stephen King's *Children of the Corn*." That same year, *Firestarter* incorporates King's name in the tagline that includes the title, "Charlie McGee is Stephen King's *Firestarter*."

Aside from the anomaly that is *Christine*, the nine-month period between *Cujo* and *Firestarter* saw the emergence of the cinema Brand Stephen King, stemming partly from the fact that his was the most famous name associated with the projects. The concept behind this brand is King as creator, his "mind" being the source of the "imagination" that lies behind the stories that the films tell, those stories being almost exclusively previous film adaptations. None of the promotion mentions *The Stand* or *Night Shift*, both un-adapted at that point, and only *Christine*, the odd one out, references *Salem's Lot*. The publicity for these films seeks therefore to establish King not necessarily as the author of a series of books (which he was), nor indeed as the writer of a group of movies (which he wasn't), but rather as the creative mind behind the series of films.

This process was cemented in April 1985 with the release of *Cat's Eye*, another De Laurentiis production. This time, King wrote the screenplay, adapting three of his short stories with one original tale, loosely linked by the journey of a cat. Here the trailer—mostly using scenes from the opening of the film—makes specific references to previous movies, including an appearance by Drew Barrymore, who played Charlie in *Firestarter*; the dog from *Cujo*; the '58 Plymouth Fury from *Christine*; and even a sequence from *The Dead Zone* on a TV set. These intertextual references are described in the trailer as "all the elements of his [King's] creative imagination," again blurring the lines between the idea and its cinematic depiction. While in 1982 the marketing for *Creepshow* highlighted King as the author of a number of best-selling books, by the 1985 release of *Cat's Eye*, the marketing fell in line with the brand established by *Cujo*, *The Dead Zone*, *Firestarter*, and *Children of the Corn*. The promotion of *Cat's Eye*, although only the second film from his own screenplay, emphasized King not as a novelist but as the imagination behind a series of films.

These films therefore established Stephen King as a form of specifically *cinematic* horror branding, alluding only to other film adaptations rather than to the books or indeed to TV's *Salem's Lot*, but at the same time borrowing, for marketing purposes, his phenomenal literary success and household name. The question remains, however, as to the validity of this brand, given King's negligible involvement in the cinematic projects outlined, and more importantly, what that brand actually meant within a changing horror landscape.

BRAND STEPHEN KING FROM LITERATURE TO FILM

Chapter 1 argues that the essence of King's literary brand is hybridity and the notion of "horror in disguise." Novels like *Firestarter*, *The Dead Zone*, and *The Stand* explicitly blend horror with other generic forms, such as the political paranoid thriller and the epic fantasy. On a textual level, however, King's focus is on the everyday elements of American life, from brand names to familiar places to identifiable, largely blue-collar characters who speak a recognizable, often profane, American language. The result is that King writes stories that reflect the concerns of contemporary America, both literally and figuratively. He presents real-world situations, such as the bullying that Arnie and Carrie endure, alongside the supernatural elements of a haunted car and telekinesis in order to highlight, for example, the perils of consumerism and religious fundamentalism. Similarly, King uses the ghosts of the Overlook Hotel to comment upon issues of child, spousal, and substance abuse, or Charlie McGee and John Smith's supernatural powers to expose governmental misuse of power. This focus on realism and the supernatural, on the blue-collar worker and the trappings of Americana, infused with a highly moralistic standpoint, is evidence of a clear literary brand based on an authorial vision that encompasses both narrative preoccupations and writing style.

The cinematic Brand Stephen King that emerged in 1983–1984 shares fewer of these characteristics. As noted above, there was a lack of regularity in terms of the output—with the films coming in rapid succession after a substantial gap—and also a lack of authorial control, with only *Creepshow* and *Cat's Eye* using screenplays by King. In reality, King's name and his marketed status as the "creator" are the only things that link the films. Therefore, the film versions represent a disparate, rather than a single, creative vision and furthermore offer a different set of preoccupations and themes.

This disparity between the books and films is due in part to the interests of the screenwriters and directors (and, indeed, in the case of De Laurentiis, the producer), but also to the fact that in this early period of King adaptations, significant sociopolitical changes had taken place in the United States between the writing of the books and the making of the films. For example, both *The Dead Zone* and *Firestarter*, two of King's most political novels, were written in 1978 and 1979, and both books reflect the political paranoia of that post-Watergate period. In particular, *Firestarter* uses The Shop—the fictional agency that reappears in other King stories, including "The Mist," *The Stand*, and the original TV miniseries *Stephen King's Golden Years* (1991)—to place Charlie and Andy McGee within a conspiracy story reminiscent of paranoid thriller films of the 1970s, such as *The Parallax View* (1974) and *Three Days of the Condor* (1975), and books such as Woodward and Bernstein's *All the President's Men* (1974), Richard Condon's *Winter Kills* (1974), and the works of Don DeLillo and Thomas Pynchon.

Within the novel, the sole supernatural element is the pyrokinetic ability of Charlie to set fires using the power of her mind. Her capacity to manipulate elements, often destructively, echoes that of Carrie White, although different in terms of the detail. Further, as in *Carrie*, the narrative builds to a literally explosive finale as the young female protagonist finally allows her supernatural ability free rein as a result of trauma—in the case of Carrie, humiliation at the prom, and in the case of Charlie, the death of her father. But in *Firestarter*, the supernatural element is not the focus of the story. In *Carrie*, the inserts such as the retrospective newspaper reports hint at the destruction to come and therefore place the supernatural events of the climax at the center of the narrative in absentia. In contrast, apart from a brief early flashback, *Firestarter* has a more straightforward chronological narrative. Obviously influenced by Watergate, the bulk of the story deals with the ongoing oppressive actions of a secretive branch of government. As Whitley Strieber describes it, *Firestarter* is "a book of rage against the cancerous spread of secrecy in our government" (1986, 40), while King himself describes it as "a political novel" (Fletcher 1988, ix).

The Shop pursues the McGees because of their psychic capabilities. Charlie has developed the power of pyrokinesis through tests in which her father and mother were given doses of an experimental drug, Lot Six, by The Shop in the late 1960s. Andy has the ability to "push" people and influence their actions, a power that is slowly killing him via pinprick brain hemorrhages every time he uses it. In contrast, Charlie's destructive power is potentially limitless. As a result, The Shop pursues Charlie in order to test the reaches of her power and decide whether she should be harnessed or destroyed. As Tony Magistrale points out, "The Shop is a visible manifestation of the post-Vietnam/Watergate skepticism" with the result that the book "focuses on the estrangement of individuals caught in the machinery of social institutions no longer adequate to human needs" (2003, 34–35). The Shop is King's own vision of a secretive government out of control, and Charlie and Andy, who are typical of King's ordinary protagonists thrust into extraordinary situations, find themselves at the mercy of forces that wish to take away their freedom and control and confine them.

Of all the film adaptations of King's works in this period, *Firestarter* is the most faithful to the book. As Bill Warren points out, the film is "entirely an effort to put the book on the screen . . . . Writer Stanley Mann regards the novel as a sacred text and follows it slavishly" (1988, 127–128). Yet, for all this, the result, Warren argues, is that the film "is hollow, unbelievable. It is as close an adaptation as any feature based on King, but miles from the book: it's a paint by numbers kit of the Mona Lisa" (129). King agrees, stating that "there's no Stephen King in *Firestarter*. And it's very faithful to the book, but it's just that—I'm not in that movie at all, whatever it was that was in the book that people liked" (Collings 2006, 30). As such, *Firestarter* represents a key text in that it is, as Warren and King assert, one of the adaptations closest to King's prose and story, but also one of the least successful in terms of "capturing" the novel. King criticizes the film for not being "King" in the same way that he criticized *The Shining*, but while he was outspoken about his dislike of the changes that Kubrick made, here he is equally critical of a film that follows his work meticulously. The case of *Firestarter* seems to suggest that elements that make the literary Stephen King brand can be transferred to the screen, but nevertheless leave something nebulous but fundamental behind.

In *Firestarter*, the story, the characters, and the dialogue are transferred to the screen almost verbatim, but what gets lost in the process is King's subtext. James Egan describes the novel as a place where "the dark fantastic joins with the espionage thriller," yet the timing of the film version stripped the espionage element of much of its commentary (1987, 95). King's novel was written in the late 1970s and released in September 1980, four months before Ronald Reagan took office as the fortieth president of the United States and reinvigorated America's self-belief and confidence. By the time the film *Firestarter* was released on May 11, 1984, Reagan was only months away from winning a landslide second term, and his policies were overturning the uncertainties and paranoia that had spawned King's novel in the 1970s, replacing fear of the government with fear of the external threat of the Soviet Union. As a result, for all the script retained the political overtones of the 1980 book, by 1984, these lacked relevance. While the film ostensibly maintains the original's hybridity of supernatural tale and conspiracy thriller, it lacks the hybridity of *meaning* of King's original work; the shadiness of The Shop and the abuse by the government of its own citizens stands in stark contrast to the image of the US government of the 1980s protecting its citizens from the threat of communism through mutually assured nuclear destruction. *Firestarter* was a paranoid thriller film released in the middle of a decade in which this type of film was no longer current. This lack of politically allegorical meaning partially explains how King can be absent from the film despite its closeness to his text.

The timing of the film undercut the meanings that King had placed behind the story, leaving only a series of narrative events.

Equally complex in terms of presence and absence is the film's relationship to what Egan describes as the other half of this generic hybrid, the "dark fantastic." As noted above, King himself refers to *Firestarter* as "a political novel," (Fletcher 1988, ix) rather than horror, but the label that King had acquired through his first three novels overwhelmed the categorization of *Firestarter* as anything other than a horror book. Thus, the dust jacket for the UK first edition, published by Macdonald, calls *Firestarter* "the latest magnificent horror novel from Stephen King" and "a masterpiece of sophisticated terror [from] the world's foremost living horror writer." Despite the jacket referring to Charlie as a "full genetic horror," there is relatively little by way of traditional horror tropes in the novel, certainly compared to the vampires of *Salem's Lot* and the ghosts of the Overlook Hotel.

Although she has powers like Carrie and the story draws upon the theme of the child as Other, King's Charlie is a sad and innocent little girl with a strong moral compass who uses her pyrokinesis sparingly throughout the novel. The first time she uses that power, she sets the boots of a soldier on fire. She overhears his conversation with his girlfriend on the phone and she has "a feeling that he was trying to trick the girl he was talking to" (1980, 25). Charlie is in the Albany airport using her gift to steal quarters from the pay phones. She knows using her power is bad, and that stealing is bad, but her father is hurt and needs help. This inner conflict leads her to allow her power to "get away from" her toward, as her father says, "someone you don't like" (26). Later, she uses pyrokinesis to protect her father when The Shop comes to get her at Irv Manders's farm, but she only unleashes its full force after her father's death when she destroys The Shop's plantation headquarters. Unlike Regan from *The Exorcist* and Damien from *The Omen*, who threaten their own loved ones and disrupt the family unit, Charlie and her pyrokinesis are not the main horror element in the story. In *Firestarter*, as with *Poltergeist*, the threat comes largely from without. The locus of horror in *Firestarter* is the idea of government persecution, the loss of control of one's own life, and the specter of child abuse through The Shop's experimentation with Charlie and through John Rainbird's obsession with killing her in order to absorb her power at the moment of death. Despite its labeling as a horror novel, and Egan's assertion of the film's links to "the dark fantastic," the horror within the story is, at its core, political, just as the horror at the heart of *Carrie* is both social and religious.

When it came to the film, producer Frank Capra Jr. made a concerted effort, as had those involved with *Cujo*, to inform audiences that *Firestarter* was "not a horror picture, in the sense that we're not looking for scares to carry it. It has excitement and thrills" (Collings 2006, 122). As Collings argues, the emphasis of the script was therefore on "stunts and special effects . . . [and] pyrotechnics," resulting in the decision to hire as director Mark L. Lester, who had a background not in horror but in the choreography of action (123). In this respect, the film paralleled the book by not concentrating on traditional horror tropes, but it shifted the emphasis in a different direction, not toward highlighting political paranoia but instead toward introducing a new hybrid element of action. This suggests the essential problem that the film *Firestarter* faced. The filmmakers attempted to faithfully replicate the book to the extent that producer Capra said, "I think King's readers will find every memorable and important scene included" (Collings 2006, 125) and also to make it clear to audiences that this would not be a horror film. Yet, the way in which they chose to make it "not horror" was very different from the way that King chose, which ultimately is another reason why he was absent from the finished film. The emphasis on ordinary people thrust into extraordinary situations, the blue-collar milieu, the identifiable American dialect, the political persecution, and Charlie's unusual talent are all retained in the script, but ultimately what the film is about, where its purpose lies, is in action set pieces, something that King never intended.

For example, in the film, the final showdown between Rainbird and Charlie in The Shop's barn involves a stalemate posed by the presence of three weapons: Rainbird's gun, Charlie's pyrokinesis, and Andy's ability to "push." Charlie enters the barn with a Shop agent and then forces him to leave by burning his hand and threatening to set him on fire. Once the agent leaves, Rainbird, hiding in the loft, calls to her and they have a friendly exchange before Andy and The Shop's leader, Cap Hollister, arrive and Andy tells Charlie that Rainbird has lied to her. As the sequence plays out, Charlie first has to force herself not to burn Rainbird so as not to harm the horses in the barn, then she agrees to go to him because he threatens to shoot her father if she doesn't. Following this Andy "pushes" Cap to kill Rainbird, but Rainbird shoots Cap, and then Andy "pushes" Rainbird to jump. He does, but then shoots Andy. The sequence therefore builds suspense through a series of potential threats before shifting to action-oriented gunplay as each threat is played out, ending with Charlie setting fire to Rainbird.

In the novel, the scene plays differently. When Rainbird and Charlie meet, she is already aware of his duplicity. Instead of willingly going to him, Charlie confronts him, calling him a liar. Rather than hide, Rainbird sits on the edge of the loft, feet dangling, and says, "Lied to you? No, I mixed up the truth, Charlie, that's all I ever did. And I did it to keep you alive." Charlie responds by calling him a dirty liar, but is "dismayed to find she wanted to believe him . . . wanted to believe he had liked her." Gradually, Rainbird persuades her with inexorable logic, saying how he, like her, is different from those around them and explaining just how dangerous she is. She begins to see Rainbird as a kind of release, "ending the doubt, the misery, the fear . . . in his own twisted way he was talking about being her friend in a way no-one else could be" (1980, 382–383). The book emphasizes the paranoia created by lies and mind control, the conversation about duplicity taking place between Rainbird and Charlie alone, with Rainbird out in the open, speaking softly and twisting her thoughts and understandings until she believes that he is her friend and that his solution is the best. In the film, the same conversation takes place with Andy present and Rainbird hidden, running behind bales of hay and brandishing a gun, shifting the emphasis toward action.

Although this changing of the focus of the story and the lack of political relevance go some way in explaining how the film is "not King," his name nevertheless was an essential selling point in the marketing of the movie. However, by selling the film as a branded Stephen King product, as Collings argues, "*Firestarter* was inextricably associated with King's name and reputation, in spite of the clear statements by its producer and director that it was not a horror film" with the result that "the film was nonetheless part of the King mystique, and that implied an expectation of horror that simply did not materialize" (2006, 121, 122). *Firestarter* therefore suffered because the association with the established screen Brand Stephen King carried with it an expectation of the film being a horror film, even though neither it nor the book purported to be one.

More importantly, King's own label as "the master of horror" carries with it an expectation that the film would be a strong example of the genre, which *Firestarter* was not. Further, it was never intended to be because, stylistically, the film has more in common with action cinema than with horror. This aesthetic choice is evident when comparing the climatic destruction scene of *Firestarter* with that of *Carrie* since both revolve around young girls unleashing their powers. As discussed above, in the final prom sequence of *Carrie*, De Palma used color, sound, music, and visuals to create a vision of hell. Carrie's thin, blood-drenched face, flat hair, and wild, staring eyes convey her fall into madness. The audience is introduced to this transition through a sudden shift to Carrie's subjective perspective, showing a swirling image of everyone laughing, though actually many are not. This immediately encourages a difficult and ambivalent attitude toward her. Previously sympathetic to Carrie, the audience is forced to accept that her violent killing spree is not entirely justified. Although she is most definitely wronged, many of the people she kills are innocent. Through the visuals and this morally ambiguous perspective, De Palma forces the viewer to see the horror in what Carrie does.

The high school gym as hell in Carrie *(1976).*

The ending of *Firestarter*, by contrast, is constructed as an action sequence with the emphasis upon the spectacle, rather than the horror, of destruction. At the end of *Firestarter*, Charlie is far from being a wide-eyed, blood-stained monster. She is instead a focused young girl, her blonde hair blowing around her head in an invisible breeze. Like Carrie, Charlie emerges from a burning building, but this is not presented as a vision of hell in the same way. De Palma frames the gym in long shot and shoots in slow motion, so Carrie is a small figure emerging from a huge doorway, the building engulfed in flames looming behind her.

The soundtrack emphasizes the crackle of the flames, the screams of the dying, and the whoosh of a strong wind. Visually and aurally, the shot foregrounds the high school gym as hell. In *Firestarter*, Charlie is framed in a medium long-shot that becomes a medium-shot as she walks toward the camera. There are flames behind her, but the entire building is not engulfed as it is in *Carrie*, so not only is the focus on her face, which shows her new-found resolve to, as her father says, "burn it all down," but also the image is clearly that of a girl emerging from an empty barn that is on fire, rather than from a scene of hellish death and destruction.

Furthermore, the people she kills are not innocents but gun-toting Shop stooges who come to kill her, and so there is little by way of moral ambiguity in the destruction she wreaks. Her actions, unlike Carrie's, are justifiable. This is further confirmed by the fact that she is no longer conflicted about her power, having been given permission to use it by her father. By the time she firebombs The Shop's headquarters, most of the support staff have left and so by implication have survived. In *Firestarter*, the innocent escape because what matters is the demise of the institution of The Shop, as represented not by office workers, but by armed agents and by the plantation house itself, which is consumed by flames. Charlie destroys a thing, while Carrie destroys people. *Carrie* then is a horror film in both its affiliation and its execution, while *Firestarter* is conceived and directed as an action film.

Firestarter therefore embodies the fractured identity of a branded Stephen King film as it emerged in 1983–1984. The film is King in that it is faithful to the original source text in terms of story, structure, character, and dialogue and also not-King in that, despite this faithfulness, "King" is absent. It is not horror, as it was conceived as an action film, and yet is horror-by-association, as it was sold with an emphasis on King's brand name. The film draws upon King's mass appeal and, indeed, the non-gore approach of literary horror in the mid-1980s, but it runs into the problem that both these things are linked to horror, thus importing the *requirement* of horror to a film that is not attempting to be so and is operating in a medium that has very different generic tropes. The ultimate failure of *Firestarter* is an inability to negotiate these different elements.

In comparing *Firestarter* with David Cronenberg's version of *The Dead Zone*, released seven months earlier, the first thing to note is that *The Dead Zone*, unlike *Firestarter*, maintained its political relevance in its transition to the screen. In King's novel, while the implication is that Johnny sees that political candidate Greg Stillson will instigate some form of apocalyptic event, Johnny's actual vision is just a series of images of "the screams of the dying; the smell of the dead. And a single tiger padding through miles of twisted metal, fused glass and scorched earth" (1979, 339). King's screenplay for the film is equally interpretive. What he describes in both the revised first and second drafts is as follows:

> Exactly how this is to be shot rests entirely with the director. All I can say is that it's the equivalent of that big, almost psychedelic rush in Kubrick's 2001—we get flashes of:
> 1. Jet fighters streaking across the sky
> 2. The wheel of fortune, spinning
> 3. Titan-II missiles vomiting out of their silos
> 4. An Iowa farm kid looking up at a sky full of B-52 Bombers
> 5. A Ukrainian farm kid looking up at a sky full of Ilyut bombers
> 6. (p. 114) The wheel of fortune, slowing . . .
> 7. An alarm clock, at less than a minute to midnight
> 8. Stillson at a big desk, railing at Sonny Elliman . . . whose long hair is sheared in a buzz-cut a la H. R. Haldeman . . . screaming "Eyeball to Eyeball and We're not gonna Flinch!"

9. (p. 115) The alarm clock with its hands now at straight-up midnight
10. The wheel of fortune . . . clicks into the green Double Zero slot
11. Cars slamming together in a fiery crash
12. The alarm clock stops ticking: ALARM SOUND: BRRRINNNG!
13. Mushroom clouds, maybe? Bombers? The director will know
14. Frank Dodd lurching across the White House Oval Office . . . He attacks Sonny Elliman with the DESTROYER hatchet
15. The alarm clock with its springs sprung
16. The wheel of fortune at dead stop (p. 117)

(Stephen King Special Collection, Orono, box no. 2317)

In the film, however, the vision is more straightforward, showing Stillson in his pajamas at what appears to be Camp David, setting off the nuclear warheads and whispering, "the missiles are flying. Hallelujah. Hallelujah." At the time of the film's release in 1983, tensions between the United States and the Soviet Union were around their highest level since the Cuban missile crisis of 1962, and the possibility of nuclear Armageddon had therefore increased. Thus, *The Dead Zone* replaces King's conceptual montage with the much more concrete and, in 1983, recognizable depiction of a US president literally pushing the red button, giving *The Dead Zone* far greater political relevance than the paranoid conspiracies of *Firestarter*.

The Dead Zone was Cronenberg's first horror film as a director for hire and was a departure for him, as had been the drag-racing film, *Fast Company* (1979). Before then, he had established himself as a horror auteur, a writer/ director whose thematic obsessions focused on sexuality, repression, and, through special effects, the physical manifestation of psycho-sexual states. Cronenberg's approach was, as Stacey Abbott points out, "intensely cerebral," leading to the films having a "coldly clinical aesthetic characterized by a modernist mise en scene" (2010a, 57). Drawing upon the clinical representation of medicinal practices, alongside the explicit representation of the body in distress, Cronenberg's early films are highly scientific and therefore merge the tropes of science fiction with those of horror.

In this respect, *The Dead Zone*, with its initial emphasis on Johnny's recovery after his accident, also focuses on science and medicine, but not in same cold and futuristic way as Cronenberg's previous films. Sam Weizak's clinic is a homely New England mansion that is neither overtly medical nor threatening. Johnny's room is just a re-purposed living room or bedroom, with slightly peeling green wallpaper and a fireplace. When Weizak and Johnny discuss his psychic abilities, they are seated at a large oak table, surrounded by lamps and plants, in a comfortable wood-paneled drawing room. Cronenberg presents only one brief scene of what must be a slow and painful reha-

The president launches nuclear war in The Dead Zone *(1983)*.

bilitative process for Johnny, showing him learning to use his crutches on the driveway. Here, to match Johnny's isolation, it is the outside world that is cold, represented by the snowy landscape of a New England winter as he recovers under Weizak's guidance.

Alongside the less clinical aesthetic, Cronenberg's thematic concern with body horror is still embedded in the film through the character of Johnny, but in a more muted form than in the director's previous work. In King's novel, the "dead zone" of the title is an area of the future that Johnny cannot see with his gift and is caused by a brain tumor that would eventually have killed him if he hadn't been shot attempting to assassinate Stillson. In the film, the dead zone is virtually absent, Cronenberg instead drawing upon his own interest in the physical manifestation of psychic states—evident in the venereal parasites that manifest extreme sexual desire in *Shivers*—by having the visions have a bodily effect on Johnny. Early in the film, when Johnny sees Weizak's past during World War II, the vision ends with Johnny collapsed on the floor, breathing heavily and visibly in shock. Later, when he witnesses members of his student Chris Stuart's hockey team drown, his eyes widen, and he reacts as if the vision has slapped him across the face. A similar effect occurs when Johnny grasps Stillson's hand at a rally, the moment that precipitates the final section of the story. Again, the emphasis is on the physical, Johnny jolting as if the vision goes through him like an electric current. This is very different from King's description of "a familiar compact coldness . . . the trance feeling" (1979, 324), showing Cronenberg's decision to represent the visions as physical attacks. This is in keeping with his interest in body horror, but in a manner far less explicit, both physically and sexually, than, for example, the armpit penis in *Rabid*, the exploding head in *Scanners*, and the vaginal open-ing that appears in Max Renn's stomach in *Videodrome*.

In his review of the film in *Starburst*, Phil Edwards bemoaned this fact, say-ing that *The Dead Zone* was "short on shock value" and that there was only "one gruesome scene" with the result that the film had little of Cronenberg in it and "could have been directed by anyone" (1984, 41). In the one scene of violence, the Castle Rock killer, Frank Dodd, commits suicide by impal-ing himself on a pair of scissors, again a change from King's screenplay in which Dodd slits his own throat. The impalement, however, takes place off-screen and all we see are Dodd's preparations and his dead body after the fact. Cronenberg's abandonment of his trademark body horror, sexual themes, and clinical mise-en-scéne led many to consider that *The Dead Zone* "looked sus-piciously like a director's move towards the mainstream" (Rodley 1992, 110). Cronenberg denies this, stating that it "wasn't a calculated attempt to get a bigger audience" (110), but, in many ways, the point is moot. *The Dead Zone* was a move to the mainstream for Cronenberg, certainly in comparison to his previous films.

By contrast, John Carpenter had already made the leap from low-budget to big-budget studio-based filmmaking, which had resulted in the disastrous *The Thing*. Carpenter was, as noted, lambasted by the critics for the visual ex-cesses of the Thing's various manifestations, and *Christine* represented an at-tempt to repair his reputation. As such, it avoids any moments of gore, and, in Collings's view, "wisely pulls back on the more gruesome visual effects" (2006, 110). In the main sequence where Christine dispatches the teenagers who vandalize her, all the deaths are more implicit than explicit. Detective Junkins reports to Arnie that Moochie Welch was "cut in half . . . they had to scrape up his legs with a shovel," but in the depiction of this moment, Car-penter focuses on Moochie's face while the screen fades to black. In the book, however, Moochie is hit by Christine from the rear, breaking his back and knocking him out of his boots. The attack then continues: "The car roared forward and over him. . . . Moochie was pulled first one way and then the other as Christine reversed into the street again. . . . She screamed forward. And back. And forward. . . . The thing in the street no longer looked like a human being; it looked like a scattered bundle of rags" (1983a, 251).

In the film, Don Vandenberg and Richie Trelawney die when Christine rams into the gas station in which they are sitting, causing an explosion that is shot from a distance, emphasizing the spectacle of the gas station blowing up rather than the deaths of its occupants. Buddy Repperton escapes and runs off—conveniently right down the middle of the road—and is run over by Christine, now on fire. The film again shies away from the depiction of the impact, instead cutting to a long shot of Repperton's flaming body lying in

The "rape" of Christine.

the road. In contrast, in the book, Trelawney and Repperton die together as Christine rams Buddy's Camaro. Trelawney is crushed by the engine while Buddy suffers a number of injuries, including losing his ear, which is "clipped off with surgical neatness," and breaking his leg and several ribs. As he rolls away from Christine's attack, Buddy feels "the splintered ends of his broken leg ground together," while "blood from his mouth now mixed with the snot running freely from his nose; one of his broken ribs had nicked a lung." Finally, Buddy's broken ribs puncture his heart and he dies, cold, bleeding, and terrified (300–306).

There is very little by way of similar violence in the film, with two main exceptions. Arguably, the most jolting moment comes at the beginning when Christine's hood slams down on the fingers of a factory supervisor on the production line in Detroit. This is not seen in close-up; rather, the film shows the raised hood dropping down out of shot with a slam before cutting to the shocked and screaming face of the worker. The most extended and explicit scene is when Buddy and his friends vandalize Christine. Buddy climbs on Christine's roof before smashing her windshield and hood with a sledgehammer. The others punch holes in her bodywork, rip open her seats, and use a hammer to destroy the radio, which Carpenter has established as Christine's "voice" through the playing of scene-appropriate songs.

This sequence ties into the key thematic change that Carpenter and Bill Phillips brought to the script, which was to make Christine inherently evil rather than, as in the book, a car possessed by the spirit of its former owner, Roland D. LeBay. In King's novel, LeBay appears in the car at various points as a corpse, "rotting and stinking of the grave, half skeleton and half rotting, spongy flesh . . . . Maggots squirmed their sluggish way up from his collar" (434). Carpenter's monster, however, has no such visceral impact. Indeed, unlike LeBay, who is more terrifying as he decomposes, Christine is at her most threatening when she is at her most pristine. She rips off her doors when squeezing into the alleyway to get at Moochie, but we never see the result of this damage, and it is only after she runs over Buddy that we see Christine return to the garage as a burned-out wreck. Carpenter's film therefore does contain sequences of violence and body horror, but these are targeted at an inanimate yet personified object, Christine. This is reinforced in the final sequence of the film when Christine is systematically destroyed by Dennis, who drives a Caterpillar tractor into and over her time and again. As the tractor rips into her, the car begins to wheeze and limp like a wounded animal.

In this respect, *Christine* is similar to *The Thing* in that the extreme physical manifestations in the latter always represent not the human—or animal—body being ripped apart and dismembered, but rather the plasticized and artificial alien entity metamorphosing for its own protection. In *The Thing*'s infamous *Alien*-inspired chest-bursting scene, Doc Copper attempts to defibrillate Norris, one of the men stationed in the remote Antarctic research station. Norris's stomach opens, produces teeth, and releases some form of monstrous Norris-like shape from his chest cavity. Meanwhile, his head comes off, grows legs, and scuttles across the floor. Yet, while this is one of the sequences that prompted commentary about the level of gore in the film, it is, in fact, only Copper who is actually hurt, his arms being bitten off at the elbows. Norris is not only long dead, he is not even there. What we see is the Thing itself, a shape-shifting entity that is merely doing what it must in order to survive. It looks like a human body being torn to pieces, whereas Christine, of course, does not.

In terms of violence, the unprovoked attack by Buddy and his goons on Christine, described as "rape" in Bill Phillips's screenplay (59), is depicted first through Christine's vulnerable and isolated position in Darnell's darkened garage and then coupled with the whooping and hollering of the assailants and the penetrative violence of the attack. This ought to be far more disturbing than the sight of an alien creature simply shrinking from a threat as best it can, but the fact that Christine is metal, chrome, and glass, rather than flesh and blood, greatly reduces the impact and denies any form of abjection. The only rotting corpse on display is Christine herself.

Like *The Dead Zone* and Cronenberg, *Christine* is thematically consistent with Carpenter's earlier work. As Peter Nicholls points out, Carpenter's films have a Manichean tendency—that is, "he seems to believe in evil as existing outside humanity as an absolute force . . . there is usually a Shape or a Thing—a Malevolence out there, waiting to get us" (1984, 79). Christine, like the Thing and Michael Myers in *Halloween*, represents a kind of objective evil presence, the motivations of which derive somewhat loosely from narrative threads but equally from the simple existence of supernatural evil within the world. In addition, it is worth noting that *The Thing* represents Carpenter's sole foray into the landscape of body horror, *Halloween* being known for its restraint and lack of blood and gore. While *The Dead Zone* therefore sees Cronenberg reworking his thematic and visual preoccupations for a wider, more general audience, *Christine* sees Carpenter returning to the kind of restraint that characterized his low-budget work, combined with the bigger-budget studio support that he had for *The Thing*.

There is, however, one way in which *Christine* does push the envelope of excess and that is in its use of language. As Bill Phillips points out in the documentary on the DVD special edition, the *New York Times* called *Christine* the "most foul language film in the history of English speaking cinema," even though it opened close to Brian De Palma's *Scarface*, which instantly eclipsed *Christine* in terms of swearing, violence, and, indeed, box-office returns. In particular, Phillips's script does not shy away from Buddy's referral to Arnie as "Cuntface" or "Cuntingham" at a time when this particular word was relatively rare in mainstream cinema. As mentioned in chapter 1, the language used in the film is very similar to that in King's book. In a scene in the book, the auto shop teacher Mr. Casey asks Buddy to turn out his pockets in order to find out if he has a switchblade. Buddy replies, "Yeah, try it, try it . . . I'll knock you through that wall, you little bald fuck," which is also the line in Phillips's screenplay (1983a, 15). In the final film, however, the response is exaggerated, with Buddy saying, "Yeah, try it, you little bald fuck, and I'll knock you through the wall. Fuck!" According to Bill Phillips, he and Carpenter put more swearing into the film to ensure that it got "a hard R" rating from the MPAA; otherwise, the visuals were sufficient to merit a PG-13, which they considered too moderate for a horror film. Therefore, while King's book has a broad mainstream appeal, Carpenter and Phillips adopted more swearing in order to make *Christine* an R-rated picture and thus appear more in keeping with the kind of rating expected for a horror film, having deliberately downplayed the violence and horror. Carpenter's film therefore is, like *Firestarter*, very faithful to King's book at least in its replication of King's language. Unlike *Firestarter*, it jettisons much of the story, but, as *Firestarter* did, it abandons King's thematic preoccupations—in this case, around consumerism and the death of the dream of 1950s America—in favor of Carpenter's own Manichean view of the world.

The Dead Zone treads something of a middle path between the two. Both the novels of *The Dead Zone* and *Firestarter* contain less swearing than *Christine*. Even so, Greg Stillson's language in the book is further toned down for the film, along with some of his more appalling acts such as killing the dog, which, as noted earlier, was in King's screenplay but rejected by Cronenberg.

Yet, by and large, the key events of King's episodic text are replicated in the film in the same order: Johnny's crash, his recovery, his discovery of his powers, his involvement in the Castle Rock killer case, his work as a private tutor, and his collision course with Stillson. By concentrating on Johnny and limiting the parallel story of Stillson's rise to power, the film loses much of King's emphasis on political corruption, or rather the corruption at the heart of the political soul, in favor of a more simplified, and timely, Reaganite vision of an out-of-control, gung-ho president with the nuclear launch codes. Cronenberg, then, was left to pursue his personal themes of the physical manifestations of psychological states.

Unlike Lewis Teague and Mark L. Lester, both Cronenberg and Carpenter are recognized horror auteurs, so there is no suggestion that *Christine* and *The Dead Zone* are anything but horror films. But they are mainstream horror films from the perspective of Cronenberg and Carpenter, tying both into the emerging cinematic Brand Stephen King. In an interview on the DVD of *Christine*, Carpenter refers to the film as "a haunted car story, but with really interesting characters," and so in keeping with *Cujo*, *Firestarter*, and *The Dead Zone*, the emphasis of Carpenter's film is on character rather than horror.

The same however cannot be said for *Children of the Corn*, the other film in this period released alongside those of Teague, Lester, Cronenberg, and Carpenter. As noted above, unlike *Cujo*, *Christine*, *Firestarter*, and *The Dead Zone*, *Corn* was gestated outside of Hollywood—first in Maine and then at Roger Corman's New World Pictures—and it was director Fritz Kiersch's first feature. The budget for the film was set somewhere between $800,000 and $3 million, which, compared to the $10 million- to $15-million budgets for *Firestarter*, *Christine*, and *The Dead Zone*, clearly marks the film as low budget. Even *Cujo*, itself relatively cheap, cost around $5 million, but while that film had a shooting schedule of eight weeks for principal photography and two additional weeks for second unit (Horsting 1983, 42), Kiersch was given only eighteen weeks to prepare, shoot, and edit the entire film, with principal photography allotted only twenty-five days. The result, Kiersch suggests, is a film that "looks like an homage to all those '50s B-movies that ran out of money" (Jones 1984a, 17).

This reference to B-movies, the small budget, the quick shooting schedule, and the involvement of Corman's New World Pictures, rather than a big studio, all signal *Children of the Corn* as a film apart from the other Brand Stephen King films discussed so far in this chapter. In addition, the film had a much smaller release, opening first on a limited basis on 350 screens in the United States before moving the following week to a wider release on 653 screens. Each of the earlier films opened on more than 1,000 US screens. Yet, the approach to the subject matter taken by Kiersch is similar to that of his contem-

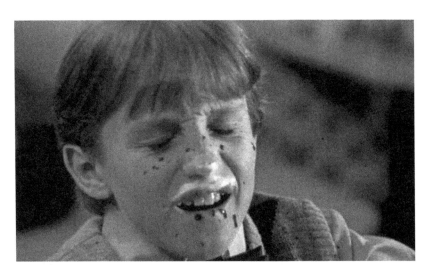

Muted gore in Children of the Corn *(1984).*

poraries. As Alan Jones reports, Kiersch did not like "the gore approach to horror movies," saying, "I hate the pain conjured up by all the recent splatter-squirting offerings. Our picture was much more suggestive." He admits this suggestiveness was partly driven by the budget, noting that "we did have very poor special effects support. The effects at the ending really do suck" (Jones 1984a, 18). About this he is undoubtedly right, and King agrees, referring to the final appearance of the supernatural monster, He Who Walks Behind the Rows, as looking like "a gopher from hell" (Collings 2006, 119).

The suggestive approach Kiersch took is, however, very effective in the early sequence where the children butcher the adults in a coffee shop. Here, the owner is held by three children who force his hand into a meat slicer. A close-up of the hand, seemingly millimeters away from the blade, cuts immediately to a shot of the face of Job, one of the key young children in the film, being splattered with a few drops of blood. His father is then killed with a meat cleaver, but the camera lingers on the cleaver itself, which, similar to the opening murder scene in *Halloween*, moves in and out of the shot as it is repeatedly brought down. The final shot of the dead father again shows minimal blood, as indeed does an earlier shot of another adult victim with his throat cut. There is no arterial spray here, merely a shot of his blood-stained neck. For all its lack of gore, the sequence is very effective, a largely bloodless massacre seen from a child's point of view.

Tonally, *Children of the Corn* therefore has the same safer approach to its subject matter as its more expensive counterparts. It is also worth noting here that King's original story, and indeed his own screenplay, end with the death of the central couple, Burt and Vicky, who stumble upon the town of Gatlin, Nebraska, where all the adults have been murdered by the children. In Kiersch's version, they not only survive but also defeat He Who Walks Behind the Rows. Written in 1973, King's story captures the nihilistic and unresolved endings of independent horror films such as *The Texas Chainsaw Massacre*, but in the film the ending has been softened.

Each of the films discussed here therefore represents in different ways the particularly cozy form of horror film that John Brosnan identified in *Poltergeist*. *Firestarter* and *Cujo* were not conceived as horror films, but rather as an action film and psychological drama, respectively, and so are horror films principally through their association with King. *The Dead Zone* and *Christine* have stronger ties to horror cinema through their directors, but while both films remain thematically consistent with their respective directors' works, they nevertheless present these thematic elements in less confrontational ways, both representationally and stylistically. *Children of the Corn*, in contrast, had no such pedigree and so was sold primarily as a horror film. However, in keeping with the general movement in the horror genre by 1983 away from the visual excesses of stalk and slash, that film, like the others, deliberately avoids gore in favor of a more suggestive approach and offers a happy and resolved ending.

These films together formulated the cinematic Brand Stephen King. This means that, with the exception of *Children of the Corn*, these were studio-funded, modestly budgeted films, featuring strong casts and high production values. But in all cases, regardless of cast or budget, it also meant a release aimed at general audiences rather than specifically targeting horror fans. The broad appeal was achieved either through denying a relationship to horror or downplaying the kind of visuals with which the horror film had become associated. In keeping with the 1983–1984 general trend in horror cinema, the branded Stephen King film was a largely middlebrow and safe form of horror, prompting Alan Jones to describe it as "the Stephen King blandwagon" (1984b, 8). Jones's description of this cycle of films is erroneous inasmuch as "bland" denotes tastelessness when, arguably, the problem with the films was that, in seeking a mainstream audience, they were trying to be too tasteful.

This idea surfaces in Jones's review of *Cat's Eye*, the final film in this first cycle of King adaptations. Here he suggests that the film uncomfortably mixes humor and scares, so that they cancel each other out, meaning the film is neither frightening nor funny. As a result, *Cat's Eye* is, in his words, "limp" because it spends too much time "painfully avoiding trying not to make the audience have kittens" (1985, 15). Despite Jones's confusing sentence structure, his implication is that the film, the first King adaptation to get a PG-13 certificate in the United States and a 15 certificate in the United Kingdom, is trying not to be too scary. It is thus part of the mainstream cinematic Brand Stephen King in keeping with *Christine, Firestarter*, and *The Dead Zone*. It employs a cast of respected character actors, including Kenneth McMillan and James Woods, and, like the other films, *Cat's Eye* downplays the horror. This time, however, it does so by exploiting the humor in King's work, which, with the exception of *Creepshow*, was largely absent from the adaptations in this period.

In the opening segment of this anthology story, Dick Morrison (James Woods), in an attempt to give up smoking, acquires the services of Quitters Inc. Their methodology is simple: they watch you, and if you smoke, they put one of your loved ones in a wired room and electrocute them. Alan King, playing the part of Dr. Vinny Donatti, the head of Quitters Inc., like a mafioso from a B-picture, demonstrates this to Morrison by putting the unfortunate cat in the electrocution room. The scene is, as Jones asserts, an unsuccessful mixture of comedy and horror, the latter visible through Morrison's shocked reaction. The comedy is a result of the way the scene was shot, framed in such a way that the cat is seen jumping into shot from the bottom, as if on a trampoline, accompanied by a jaunty cover version of "Twist and Shout." The tone is set in King's original script (in which a rabbit, not a cat, is electrocuted) as he describes the scene as "horrible, surreal—but it's also rather funny, in an admittedly sadistic way: the rabbit looks like it is dancing to 'Twist and Shout'" (53). From there, the film mixes scenes of paranoia as Morrison is convinced that someone is hiding in his closet in the middle of the night, watching him trying to sneak a cigarette, with scenes of broad humor, such as the party where Morrison's cravings manifest themselves in a series of nightmarish visions of giant cigarette packets, people with smoke coming out of their ears, and, finally, Donatti, dressed as Elvis, miming along to the Police's "Every Breath You Take."

When Morrison's wife goes into the electrocution room, the sequence is again played largely for comedy. Donatti assures Morrison and the audience that she won't be hurt. Then, her hair standing up due to static electricity, she dances around to "96 Tears" by Question Mark and the Mysterians, as both Donatti and Junk, his henchman, laugh and assure Morrison that his wife will be fine. In the short story, this sequence has a far more serious tone, Morrison comparing it to being a witness at the gas chamber: "Junk pressed the button with one hand and kept the pistol jammed firmly into Morrison's back with the other. It was the longest thirty seconds of his life" (1978, 230).

Cat's Eye is one of only two films in this chapter written by King, the other being *Creepshow*. What is immediately noticeable about both is that they are the only two films that contain this strong streak of humor. They are serious films in the sense that they are not genre parodies, but they are unique among the titles discussed here in that they are also silly in places and therefore very distinct from the gravitas of *The Shining*, *Cujo*, *Firestarter*, *The Dead Zone*, and *Christine*. *Creepshow* and *Cat's Eye* capture that spirit of "*fun*, dammit, *fun*" that King highlights in his own assessment of what a good horror film can be. In *Danse Macabre*, as mentioned in the introduction, King divides his analysis of the American horror film into two chapters. In the first, he considers what he determines to be horror films of "value—of art, of social merit" (1981b, 132), and in the second, he looks at what he calls horror films "as junk food," bad movies that are nevertheless endearingly enjoyable. While the above quote about "*fun*, dammit, *fun*" is from a review of *The Boogens*, which he doesn't discuss in *Danse Macabre*, that film is clearly an example of the latter, what King calls "a nugget, the horror film fan's reward" (204).

Although King's categories—films of social merit and films as junk food— don't quite fit the analysis I offer here, the distinction he draws in *Danse Macabre* between "good" horror films and trashy but enjoyable ones illustrates one final key point in the establishment of the cinematic Brand Stephen King. As this chapter argues, the films discussed here established this brand as one of mainstream literary adaptations that either downplay or deny their links to horror. With the exception of *Christine*, they highlight King as the primary creative force in an attempt to appeal to his fans and also attract a mass audience for whom his name is, by and large, the most familiar and therefore marketable involved with the project. As studio-based pictures (for the most part) that are aimed at the mainstream, they carry with them Abbott's and Waller's connotations of prestige and legitimacy through their serious treatment of the subject matter and through their drawing upon either non-horror directors and talent or established horror directors. In doing so, these King-brand products tie into trends within the cinematic horror genre for a softer, cozier form of mass-market horror. Yet, when King is directly involved, these elements still remain, but they are underpinned by a subversive humor that reminds the audience that horror films are not necessarily supposed to be great and serious works that are horror. Rather, they can simply be entertaining genre pieces. This is particularly noticeable in *Creepshow* in which, alongside genre-related quality actors like Hal Holbrook, Adrienne Barbeau, E. G. Marshall, and Leslie Nielsen, King himself appears, hamming it up outrageously as Jordy Verrill, a kind of uber-hick figure who is turned into a giant plant by what he describes as "meteor-shit."

Therefore, in this period, the cinematic Brand Stephen King emerges, and within it can be found a split between a more reverential form of "serious" yet cozy horror for the mainstream and a more cheerful irreverence that comes from King himself. This split would become more evident after this slew of films between 1983 and 1984 firmly established the cinematic Brand Stephen King. It can be seen, for example, in 1986 with the almost simultaneous release of *Maximum Overdrive* and *Stand by Me*. As noted previously, the latter was lauded as great cinema and confirmed the idea that King's work, by bringing in quality directors and talent and downplaying the horror to the point of nonexistence, could produce outstanding cinematic results. In contrast, the former was derided as a cheap and silly exploitation film of little redeeming merit. Between them, these films represented two of the four strands that would come to define the form of King adaptations for the next twenty years.

3 / THE MAINSTREAM ADAPTATIONS, 1986–2007

The best Stephen King movies of the last few years have been those
that deal with "reality"-based psychological horror, concentrating
on character development and interaction above scary monsters.

STEWART EDWARDS, "*APT PUPIL:*
A LESSON IN TERROR FROM STEPHEN KING"

CHAPTER 2 ARGUES THAT THE CINEMATIC BRAND STEPHEN
King was developed through a group of adaptations in 1983–1985. These were
representative of a movement within the cinematic horror genre back toward
literary adaptations aimed at mainstream audiences in the 1970s, but shorn of
their more violent and stylistic excesses. In contrast to the slasher and splatter films of the early 1980s, these King adaptations were a particular type of
horror film for general audiences, one that was cozier, safer, and less likely to
incur the disdain of the non-horror or the casual horror fan tired of endless
on-screen teenage murders. For genre directors like Carpenter and Cronenberg, King-related projects signaled a move toward mainstream respectability. Movies such as *Firestarter, Cujo,* and *Children of the Corn* denied ties to the
horror genre to reassure audiences that they did not contain the kind of violence associated with splatter and slash. *The Thing* proved conclusively in
1982 that gore was a turn-off for mainstream audiences, meaning that mainstream horror could be downbeat but not nihilistic, scary but not gory, and, as
Cat's Eye indicated, it could also be funny.

However, as Alan Jones's reference to the King "blandwagon" attests,
these films may have been representative of a movement in mainstream horror, but both the reviews and the box office were mixed. By the time that *Cat's
Eye* came out in 1985, it was clear that the popularity of branded Stephen King
horror films was declining. Compared to the $21 million each earned by *Cujo*
and *Christine* at the US box office, *Cat's Eye* made only $13 million. This, how-

ever, was better than *Silver Bullet*, a 1985 adaptation of King's novella *Cycle of the Werewolf* released six months after *Cat's Eye*, which took in only $12 million. These films were followed in 1986 by the disastrous *Maximum Overdrive*, adapted by King from his short story "Trucks" and also directed by him. This opened on 1,200 screens across the United States and took in only $3 million in its opening weekend, earning $7 million before disappearing after only a couple of weeks.

Stand by Me was released within a month of *Maximum Overdrive*. A sleeper hit that opened on only sixteen screens across the United States, but expanded to almost 750 screens by its third week, *Stand By Me* was number one at the US box office by the fourth week after its release. As the cinematic horror Brand Stephen King faltered, its demise indicated by *Maximum Overdrive*, which, thanks to King's writing, directing, and appearing in the trailer, was the most emphatically King-branded product of this cycle, *Stand by Me* became a hit by avoiding both the King name and any ties to the horror genre. In doing so, it captured and transferred elements of King's hybrid success to the screen in a very different form and marked the way for a new strand of King projects on the big screen.

Screenwriters Ray Gideon and Bruce Evans purchased the rights to King's novella, *The Body*, early in 1984. According to Gideon, "at this point in his career King was kind of dead in Hollywood and at the same time he had soured on Hollywood. He had hated *Christine*. He had hated *The Shining*. 'The Body' wasn't a particularly personal story for him. He just didn't want Hollywood screwing it up" (Matthews 2005, 70). They secured the rights after King's agent, Kirby McCauley, helped persuade him to sell them after Gideon and Evans brought director Adrian Lyne on board, as well as two producers, Martin Shafer and Andrew Scheinman. These producers are among the founders of Castle Rock Entertainment, which was named after King's fictional town and would have a long and largely fruitful relationship with King's works. Shafer and Scheinman took the project to Embassy Pictures, headed by Norman Lear. According to Evans, the original script played up the horror, including having lead character Gordie Lachance's dead brother appearing to him as an increasingly rotting corpse (71). When Lyne was forced to withdraw, Lear turned to Rob Reiner, who was finishing up his second feature, *The Sure Thing* (1985), at Embassy. Reiner, says Evans, "rejected all the horror elements we had added to the script. He said the movie just had to be about the four boys" (71). Reiner would later say that it was this decision to "play down the horror element" that meant the film "succeeded where other King adaptations failed" (Wood 1991a, 21).

This is not to say that there are no horror elements in *Stand by Me*, which is essentially about loss and trauma. The story involves four friends traveling to see the dead body of another boy, Ray Brower, who has been hit by a train. So behind their very quest is the loss of a life. Furthermore, Gordie has lost his brother while both his friends Teddy Duchamp and Chris Chambers have "lost" their fathers, Chris through his dad's abusive behavior and Teddy through mental illness. Other corresponding themes of the story include the loss of innocence as the four boys' journey pushes them from boyhood to manhood and the loss of friendship as the boys drift apart as they grow older. Fear is present in the form of bully Ace Merrill, who terrorizes the boys. While horrors are very much present, *Stand by Me*, like *The Body*, tips the balance of King's hybrid writing and focuses on horrors drawn from the real world rather than from the supernatural and weaves them through a nostalgic depiction of childhood in a bygone America. Reiner emphasized this, saying that "King spins a good yarn. So you've got *that*. You don't have to push *that* into the foreground. You can spend time concentrating on the characters" (21).

Reiner and Lear—who, after he sold Embassy to Columbia, financed the film on his own—decided to change the title and avoid any references to King in the marketing. Said Reiner, "We actually played down King's name because we didn't want people to have the idea that this was a bloody, gory horror movie. . . . That's why we changed the title to *Stand by Me. The Body*, with Stephen King, *sounds* like a horror movie" (21). By downplaying King's name and removing the requirement to *be* horror that came with the cinematic Brand Stephen King, *Stand by Me* could instead concentrate on the characters, the world, and the dialogue, letting the horror come from them.

Despite the changes to King's story, the film sought to capture his nostalgic depiction of the late 1950s/early 1960s and how the four preteen boys, Gordie, Chris, Vern Tessio, and Teddy, come of age. The film charts their journey into adolescence/manhood as they face up to their problems and who they are. Chris, for instance, is finally able to overcome his and everybody else's belief that "he would turn out bad" and "never . . . get out of this town" (King 1982b, 316, 439). Like the book, the film is structured around how the relationships among the boys develop over a series of adventures, such as getting covered by leeches while swimming, running from a train over a rickety bridge, and evading Chopper, the dog that guards the town dump in Castle Rock. The dialogue follows the book closely in these key scenes, although King's use of profanity, especially by the boys, is played down. In the confrontation with Milo, Chopper's owner, much of the script is lifted verbatim from the book, albeit in a slightly different order, but gone is Teddy shouting at Milo that "your mother blows dead rats . . . and if you call my dad a loony again I'll fucking kill you, you cocksucker" (358), replaced with the quiet threat that "if you call my dad a loony again, I'll kill you." The hard

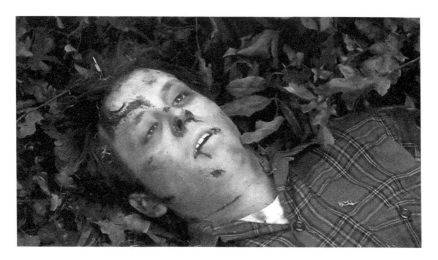

The body in Stand by Me *(1986)*.

edges of the boys' dialogue have been softened, although the essence of their banter remains.

Also softened is the dead and decaying body behind King's story. King adds detail to his description of Brower's condition: "there were ants and bugs all over his face and neck . . . his eyes were . . . terrifyingly out of sync—one was rolled back so far that we could see only a tiny arc of iris; the other stared straight up" (422). In contrast, Reiner shows Brower only as a lifeless boy. There is a small smear of blood on his forehead and around his nose, and his eyes are open and staring, but there are no ants, flies, or bugs. This again was a conscious decision by Reiner. As Bruce Evans says, "In all honesty, we argued strongly for the more disturbing aspects of the dead body. But when Rob cut it all together, it didn't go with the rest of the movie. In the end, the story isn't about finding the body" (Matthews 2005, 72).

Thus, while maintaining the real-world horror elements of the story, Reiner's film subtly shifts the focus. As the very title *The Body* suggests, King's novella is about a quest to actually confront death and about the understanding of mortality that comes with that confrontation. In the film, the boys do find Brower's body, but that moment represents not a confrontation with the physical characteristics of violent death and decay, but rather a sense of facing the pain of loss, as Brower's body allows Gordie to come to terms with his brother's death. The horror of King's original is reduced in favor of the emotional journey of the boys.

The softening of the horror in the adaptation is echoed by the film's concealment of its relationship to King. This is significant because it highlights the fact that these adaptations are mainstream films for general audiences, rather than primarily aimed at King fans. King's name wasn't absent entirely from the promotional material for *Stand by Me*. Contractually, his name and the name of the original story were in the credits on the poster, meaning anyone who was a fan of King or who looked closely enough would know it was an adaption of a King story. But the film was not sold as *Stephen King's Stand by Me*, so his connection was not foregrounded as it had been in the first group of adaptations. The publicity was not therefore so much an attempt to hide King's name as it was an attempt to disassociate the film from the cinematic Brand Stephen King as it was understood by mainstream audiences.

Nevertheless, the success of *Stand by Me* is significant to the cinematic Brand Stephen King in that it introduced to cinema the idea of King not just as the creator of cinematic horror tales but also as a chronicler of America, which is a significant element of his literary success. As King said:

> It's tough to break the gap between the warmth in the novel that makes the characters seem worth loving and caring about, set off against the horror. When they make the movie they concentrate on the moment when the monster comes out and starts waving his claws. I don't think that's what the people are interested in. (Wood 1991d, 51)

Reiner not only didn't focus on the monster waving its claws, he also went so far as to reduce the already slight traces of a clawed monster in King's original story. The result was that *Stand by Me* was a box-office hit. However, as noted in chapter 1, its success became a stick with which to beat King's reputation, the suggestion being that the film succeeded in spite of King, rather than because of him.

Stand by Me would lead to a new strand of King adaptations, but its effect would only be felt some years later. The immediate result of the dual releases of *Stand by Me* and *Maximum Overdrive* was a decrease in the number of adaptations of King's work, owing to the fact that that lack of an overt connection to King and the horror genre meant that, in the short term, the failure of *Maximum Overdrive* had far more impact on the cinematic Brand Stephen King than the achievement of *Stand by Me*. Nine King films appeared between August 1983 and August 1986, but the next four years saw the release of only three. In 1987, Tristar released an adaptation of King's 1982 Richard Bachman novel, *The Running Man*, and Laurel Productions produced *Creepshow 2*, followed two years later by Paramount's film version of *Pet Sematary*.

Together with *Stand by Me*, these films became prototypes for the four different strands of adaptations that would define the cinematic Brand Stephen

King until the new millennium. *Creepshow 2* would herald a number of low-budget films aimed predominantly at horror fans outside the mainstream, and these are discussed in more detail in chapter 4. The other three strands, discussed in this chapter, existed within mainstream cinema. *The Running Man* began a short sequence of films that drew on King's material but reworked it beyond recognition in order to fit into other pre-existing cinematic genres, while *Stand by Me* would inspire a series of prestige projects outside horror. *Pet Sematary*, followed by *Misery* (1990), would continue the trend started in 1983–1984 of horror films aimed at a wide audience; these films claimed their mainstream status through distancing themselves from the then-current tropes of the horror genre. What was different is that *Pet Sematary* and *Misery* would mark a shift in mainstream horror King adaptations toward the thriller, something also reflected more generally in mainstream horror cinema. The strand of King adaptations initiated by *Pet Sematary* and *Misery* in this period would hybridize horror and thriller elements, emphasizing one over the other. For example, *Pet Sematary* would be more of a horror film with thriller elements, while *Misery* would tip the balance the other way.

This movement toward the thriller genre was reflected in King's own writings. While he still produced supernatural horror novels such as *IT* (1986), King was moving away from Straub's "immediately classifiable horror fiction," with *Misery* (1987), *The Dark Half* (1989), and *Needful Things* (1991), leaning toward psychological drama with a supernatural twist. At the same time, he also began to explore science fiction and fantasy with *The Tommyknockers* (1987) and *The Eyes of the Dragon* (1987), and the second book in the *Dark Tower* series, *The Drawing of the Three* (1987). In cinemas, *The Running Man* and later *The Lawnmower Man* would also draw heavily on science fiction.

Now wealthy, King could comfortably write in any genre he wished, regardless of his literary brand. However, cinematically, each King adaptation was an investment of money requiring a suitable return. The larger the project, the more money was required and the bigger the risk. The failure of *Maximum Overdrive*, combined with the success of the non-horror, non-King-branded *Stand by Me*, made using King's name and marketing his work as horror seem more of a hindrance than a help. By the end of 1986, it seemed clear that, as critic Glenn Lovell pointed out, "King's stock in Hollywood is down. His name no longer assures box office success" (Herron 1988, 224). In 1983, *Cujo* could be sold to audiences on the basis that it was a horror film from the mind of the great horror creator, Stephen King. In contrast, *The Running Man*, for example, avoided all references to King, all references to horror, and was sold on an entirely different basis.

Based on the 1982 book published under the pseudonym of Richard Bachman, *The Running Man*, like *Stand by Me*, made no mention of King in its promotional material. Neither the trailer nor the film bears his name, the latter crediting the source novel to Bachman, even though the fact that King is Bachman was public knowledge in 1984, before the film went into production. George Linder, CEO of Quadra Medical Corporation, a company that made wheelchairs, purchased the rights to the book shortly after publication. Linder was interested in dabbling in film and liked the book. Apparently, he was puzzled when informed that the rights cost $20,000, a large amount for a book by an unknown author, but he bought them anyway. Upon finding out in 1984 what he had purchased, he said, "I felt like I'd found a Rembrandt at K-Mart" (Wood 1991d, 51). The fact that the film's promotion made no reference to King may well have been contractual or at King's insistence. Either way, by the time it reached the screen, the selling point of *The Running Man* was such that any association with King was neither necessary nor desirable.

The premise had been entirely reworked in order to fit a pre-existing genre, the mid-1980s blockbuster action movie, and a pre-existing genre star, Arnold Schwarzenegger. *The Running Man* was released in December 1987, six months after Schwarzenegger had secured the biggest box-office hit of his career with *Predator*. In every sense, *The Running Man* was an Arnold Schwarzenegger film, not a Stephen King film, something King himself acknowledged in 1991, saying, "I didn't have anything to do with making it. They obviously saw it as a book that could be adapted to fit an existing Rambo-Terminator kind of genre" (51).

Written in the mid-1970s, *The Running Man* has strong thematic ties to King's later post-Watergate paranoia tale, *Firestarter*, about a father and daughter on the run, alone and vulnerable, while all around them a powerful government machine works to find them. The same premise forms the basis of *The Running Man*. To make money to support his wife and son, Ben Richards, an unemployed man living in a dystopian, totalitarian America in 2025, signs up to be a contestant on *The Running Man*, the most popular show on TV. The rules are simple. Each contestant can go anywhere they want in the world and for each hour on the run, they win $100, provided that they evade capture from the Hunters, who are network-employed assassins. If not caught after thirty days, the runner wins $1 billion. The longest a runner has evaded capture is eight days.

Like *Firestarter*, this story has echoes of 1970s conspiracy thrillers like

Three Days of the Condor. But in the Reaganite 1980s, as discussed in chapter 2, conspiracy narratives were unfashionable, and the film of *The Running Man* was reworked as a vehicle for Schwarzenegger, then the image of the 1980s Republican hero. Along with Sylvester Stallone, Schwarzenegger embodied, literally, the "hard man" concept fostered by Reagan. As Susan Jeffords has argued, in contrast to the previous president, Jimmy Carter, who sometimes wore cardigans in the Oval Office, Reagan was often pictured dressed in cowboy gear, doing overtly "masculine" things, like chopping wood or riding horses, in order to present himself and his administration as "distinctively masculine, not merely as men but as decisive, tough, aggressive, strong and domineering men" (1994, 11). In the novel, Richards is untrained, desperate, and out of his depth. Schwarzenegger's Richards, however, is a cop, which partially explains his fighting skills and pneumatic physique. He is falsely accused of murdering unarmed civilians during a food riot. In fact, his superiors order him to fire on the crowd, but he refuses. So, from the outset, Richards occupies the moral high ground as a courageous, lone, principled hero, fighting a corrupt system. That system survives through a collaboration between the government and the media, which feeds the people mindless game shows like *The Running Man* and *Climbing for Dollars*, in which men climb a rope festooned with money, while below them, hungry Dobermans snap at their heels.

The image of the show *The Running Man* changed significantly from book to film. In the novel, there is one brief sequence on the show before Richards starts to run, in which he is asked to make a few brief comments to the audience while they bray at him. He offers, "You bastards . . . if you want to see someone die so bad, why don't you kill each other?" (1982c, 50). After that, all that is shown of the series is what Richards sees on TV, and it is not depicted as a game show:

> [The host] Bobby Thompson stared deadpan at the camera from the middle of a brilliant post in a sea of darkness. "Watch," he said. "This is one of the wolves that walk among you." A huge blowup of Richards's face appeared on the screen. . . . Dissolve back to Thompson, looking grave. "I speak particularly to the people of Boston tonight. . . . Who is he tonight? *Where* is he tonight?" (93)

This is presented like a press conference during a manhunt, which ties into the fact that Richards is a fugitive in the real world and that ordinary citizens are asked to inform on him. *The Running Man* of the book is more of a news program than a game show. In contrast, in the film, the rendering of *The Running*

Man draws upon the hyperbole of 1970s and 1980s game shows, such as *The Price Is Right* and *Family Feud*, the latter hosted from 1976 to 1985 by Richard Dawson, cast in the film to play the host of *The Running Man*.

Whereas the book is seen from Richards's perspective, increasing the sense of paranoia because the reader only knows what the character knows, the film returns frequently to the studio to present the audience's reactions to the events taking place. The garish yellow surroundings of the studio contrast with the dark low-key lighting and derelict spaces of the game grid (in the film, Richards is not running in the ordinary world but in a specially constructed location), as do the ludicrous costumes of the Stalkers (as the Hunters are renamed in the film) such as Dynamo, an opera-singing, fat, bald man in an electric suit driving a beach buggy. The excessive depiction of the Stalkers heightens the unreality of the game show, making death seem like a game. So too does the casting of Schwarzenegger, who dispatches each of the Stalkers with a trademark pun. After bisecting the chainsaw-wielding Buzzsaw with his own weapon, Schwarzenegger quips, "He had to split."

The film version of *The Running Man* is not about paranoia. Instead, it is, like the show it features, about death as entertainment, the on-screen audience seemingly mirroring the cinema audience in their desire to see murder and carnage. This is summed up in the title chosen for the *Fangoria* interview with director Paul Michael Glaser, "See Arnie Run! See Arnie Kill!" (Brod 1987, 48). Schwarzenegger's mid-1980s persona overwhelms any critique of the media that the film might be attempting. It is, finally, about seeing the same lone, heroic fighting machine represented by John Matrix in *Commando* embodying Reaganite principles by fighting bad guys for what's right. King's dystopian conspiracy story is reworked on film for the sci-fi action-adventure genre. The fact that King's name is not used—while possibly a contractual matter, given the rights were purchased before King was revealed as Bachman—suggests the state of his reputation in Hollywood in 1987. The filmmakers' re-conception of the story as a Schwarzenegger vehicle implies that, by 1987, the cinematic King brand was effectively dormant.

Yet, the early 1990s saw a change in the fortunes of the cinematic Brand Stephen King, as evidenced by another big-budget, severely altered sci-fi action blockbuster. In 1992, King's seven-page short story, "The Lawnmower Man," was turned into a feature film by UK-based Allied Vision and distributed in the United States by New Line Cinema. According to Gary Wood, the rights to the story were part of the *Night Shift* package sold to British producer Milton Subotsky in 1978 with the idea of producing an anthology project. Some of the stories formed the basis of King's unproduced screenplay *Night Shift*, described in chapter 2. King's tale involves Harold Parkette, an ordinary man who hires a company to mow his lawn. Harold sees a huge red mower in the garden moving by itself and being followed by the Lawnmower Man, who is naked and eating the cut grass. He tells Harold that his boss is, in fact, the god Pan, and if Harold keeps quiet, all will be well. But Harold phones the police at which point the mower bursts into his house, chases, and kills him.

Subotsky sold the rights to De Laurentiis, who then sold them to Ed Simmons at Allied Vision (Wood 1992b, 6). Simmons brought in director Brett Leonard, who hit on the idea of merging King's tale with a project he was developing, called *Cyber God*, about the then relatively new area of science, virtual reality (Wood 1992a, 7). Leonard built a new narrative around King's story. Pierce Brosnan plays scientist Dr. Lawrence Angelo, who is experimenting with virtual reality on chimps. After his work is interfered with by his funders—again, The Shop—Angelo begins to experiment on Jobe, a simple-minded gardener, using virtual reality to make him smarter. Jobe gains super intelligence, kills several people, and inserts himself into the worldwide computer mainframe. One of his victims is Angelo's neighbor, Harold Parkette, an abusive father and husband whom Jobe kills by sending his mower crashing through Parkette's house.

Leonard approached the project as a King fan and tried to create a film around the story that "would fit into his style of work. We set it against a small New England background and had a lot of King-isms. . . . Those coming to see the short story will see it, but the entire context of it has been changed" (7). The inclusion of Parkette, the New England backdrop, and the presence of The Shop link the film to the short story and to King more generally. So too, thematically, does the narrative, which involves both an interfering, militaristic government agency seeking to harness Angelo's research and Jobe's power for military gain, as The Shop does to Charlie in *Firestarter*, and a fear of technology, present in, for example, "Trucks" and *Christine*. Like *The Running Man*, Leonard's film turns King's source material into a sci-fi action blockbuster. In the Schwarzenegger film, Republican heroism and 1980s surface gloss replace 1970s paranoia and dystopian grunge. *The Lawnmower Man* builds an entire narrative around King's single incident, albeit drawing upon King's own thematic concerns to do so.

The Running Man avoided references to King, but *The Lawnmower Man* played up King's involvement. According to the script, the film was "suggested by a short story by Stephen King," and the posters, in keeping with the cinema Brand Stephen King image formed in the early 1980s, described it as "Stephen King's *The Lawnmower Man*." The reasons for this were economic, Leonard saying that "obviously Stephen King is a credible and marketable name" (Wood 1992b, 7), which is notably different from the attitude of the makers of both *Stand by Me* and *The Running Man*. It was this use of his name as a marketing tool to which King objected. At the end of May 1992, about two months after the film's release, King filed a lawsuit in New York against Allied Vision and New Line over the use of his name on publicity for and prints of the film, claiming the work bore "no meaningful resemblance" to his story and that they were using his name and brand for profit. In July, the judge found in King's favor, ruling that the producers had attempted to mislead the public (Syson 1992, 1).

The film had taken in more than $30 million at the US box office by the time of the suit, so the addition of King's name was considered important enough for New Line to defy the ruling and release *Stephen King's The Lawnmower Man* on VHS, prompting two more lawsuits from King before the studio finally relented (Farrow and Avingola 1992, 4). Given that in 1986 and 1987 King's name on a film carried negative connotations, the stance of Allied and New Line, plus the fact that the film made money, demonstrates that by 1992, the cinematic Brand Stephen King had re-acquired both cultural capital and box-office potential. The reason for this resurgence, both in the King brand and in his own interest in it, was two projects that came out in the intervening period and achieved both critical and financial success: *Pet Sematary*, with which King was closely involved, and *Misery*, which reunited King's work with Rob Reiner.

THE EARLY 1990S AND THE RE-EMERGENCE OF THE KING BRAND

According to Douglas Winter, King wrote *Pet Sematary* in 1979 while he was living next to a major road in Orrington, Maine. After a car hit his daughter's cat, he began to wonder about what would happen if the cat came back to life. From there, he developed the story of Louis Creed, a doctor who, after his daughter's cat is run over, is told of an ancient Indian burial ground where what is buried comes back to life. He inters the cat, which does return, albeit considerably more aggressive, and later, when his son, Gage, is killed by a truck, Louis buries him there, too. Gage also returns, in a monstrous form.

In an interview with Winter, King said that when the book was finished, he considered it "nasty" and put it away in a drawer, never to be published. It was only due to a contractual dispute with Doubleday that it came out: he owed them a book, and *Pet Sematary* was the one he had. The darkness of the subject matter troubled him deeply. In 1984, he told Winter, "It hurts me to talk about it; it hurts me to think about it. *Pet Sematary* is the one book that I haven't reread. I never want to go back there again" (Winter 1989, 152–156). Yet, for all King's reluctance, *Pet Sematary* went on to become his biggest seller to that date. The producer of the film, Richard Rubinstein noted that the book "sold 750 thousand copies on hardback publication—more than double the sales of his previous book *Christine*" (Hughes 1990, 12).

Rubinstein acquired the rights for Laurel Productions around the time that he was working with King and Romero on *Creepshow*. By 1983, *Pet Sematary* was on Laurel's production slate, with George Romero set to direct, but another six years would go by before the film came out (Szebin 1989b, 4). This was possibly due to the fact that King had put provisos into the deal. He insisted that the film be shot in Maine, that he have director approval, and that his script be used as written. If *Pet Sematary* was scheduled to go into production in 1983, and the book was delivered to Doubleday in 1982, the sale of the rights must have taken place in 1982, before the King adaptations of the early 1980s. If, as seems the case, these provisos were in the original contract, they were likely added as a result of King's disappointment over Kubrick's version of *The Shining* and after the rejection of his scripts for *Cujo* and *The Dead Zone*, as well as his own personal thoughts about the story itself. If the requirements were added later, it is probable that they were the result of King's general dissatisfaction with the adaptations of his works in 1983–1985. Either way, during the production delay, *Silver Bullet*, *Cat's Eye*, and *Maximum Overdrive* were released, all scripted by King and all box-office and critical failures. In the wake of these projects, it is not surprising that the prospect of granting King a level of creative control was not appealing to the studios.

Paramount finally agreed to make *Pet Sematary* on a small $9 million budget, in King's words, "as quick and dirty exploitation," but, he continued, "that wasn't what they got" (Wood 1991c, 39). The film version replicated the success of the novel. Released in April 1989, *Pet Sematary* grossed $12 million in its opening weekend (Hughes 1990, 11), ultimately making upward of $50 million at the US box office in the summer of 1989. According to Rubinstein, part of the success of the film came from the fact that it attracted a large female audience, which he considered unusual for a horror film in the late 1980s. He said, "I was particularly surprised and impressed by the age range of the audience, and by the above-average number of women going to see the picture" (12)

Although it attracted an audience not typically associated with the horror film, *Pet Sematary* was seen by Rubinstein as very specifically a horror film. He said, "I had a very short pitch. I said, 'Do you remember *The Exorcist*?' I felt *Pet Sematary* was just as disturbing" (Wood 1991c, 39). Despite his low-budget origins working with Romero on the likes of *Dawn of the Dead*, Rubinstein considered *Pet Sematary* to be a mainstream genre film in *The Exorcist* vein. This was partly due to thematic similarities—for example, the inclusion of a monstrous child—but it was also due to the dark nature of the material, in which a child dies and then is revived by his father only to find a demon in its place. Rubinstein wanted the grimness to remain in the story, as did King who had placed it in the script. "I don't think anybody wants to go to a movie, an adaptation of a horror novel that really scared them" said King, "and see a *Reader's Digest Condensed Books* version that's been sanitized and cleaned up" (39).

In approach, therefore, *Pet Sematary* closely echoes *Carrie*, and the ties to *The Exorcist* are more than tonal and thematic. By linking *Pet Sematary* to that earlier success, Rubinstein was trying not only to position the film as horror, but also, more importantly, to distance it from the horror genre as it stood in 1989. In a manner similar to the way in which the directors of *Cujo* and *Children of the Corn* had sought to reassure audiences that they were not slasher films, Rubinstein said of *Pet Sematary*: "the story's most horrific and disturbing elements may be its greatest strengths [meaning it] stands apart from the more standard horror fare being offered through sequels and rehashes" (quoted in Szebin 1989b, 6). Director Mary Lambert, brought in when Romero was unavailable, said the same thing: "*Pet Sematary* is not a slasher movie . . . . When I originally was approached about directing this movie they told me they wanted someone who could bring a little more to it than just babysitters getting killed" (Szebin 1989a, 122). Furthermore, there was a deliberate attempt to downplay gore, which, up until then, had been something of a trademark for Laurel. David Hughes noted that "*Pet Sematary* is a departure from the splatter-schlock movies Rubinstein has produced in the past" (Hughes 1990, 12), while Lambert, as noted by Frederick Szebin, "refrained from blood and gore shots until the very end" (Szebin 1989a, 122).

Rubinstein's and Lambert's summations of the horror genre in 1989 as being made up of sequels, rehashes, slasher films, and gore goes some way in explaining the success of *Pet Sematary*, as it was markedly different from much of the generic output that year. This was the year that saw the release of, among others, *The Fly II*; *Friday the 13th, Part VIII: Jason Takes Manhattan*; *Halloween V: The Revenge of Michael Myers*; *A Nightmare on Elm Street 5: The Dream Child*; and *Sleepaway Camp III: Teenage Wasteland*. By 1989, the slasher film, which, as noted in chapter 2, had effectively played itself out as the main horror subgenre by 1983, had transformed into a commercial franchise. This started in 1984 when Wes Craven's *A Nightmare on Elm Street* (1984) reinvigorated the genre by bringing in an element of the supernatural. *Nightmare*'s Freddy Krueger was not just a crazed killer, he was also a crazed killer who was already dead and could attack teenagers in their dreams. The popularity of the film led to a sequel the following year, which also saw a very belated follow-up to Craven's 1977 film, *The Hills Have Eyes*, and a fifth installment in the *Friday the 13th* series.

As scholars, including Waller (1987a, 2) and Mathijs and Sexton (2011, 197), have pointed out, the mid-1980s was an era in which sequels and franchises dominated the horror genre. Andrew Tudor agrees, noting that in what he calls late [twentieth-] century horror "the concept of a 'sequel'—or, if you like, the process of 'sequelling'—has itself become a major convention" (2002, 167). For instance, the mid-1980s saw the release of *The Texas Chainsaw Massacre 2*; *Poltergeist II: The Other Side*; *The Howling II*; *Demons 2*; *Psycho III*; *Silent Night, Deadly Night 2*; and, of course, *Friday the 13th Part VI: Jason Lives*. Both Jason and Freddy appeared in more and more sequels as the decade wore on, and by 1989, Freddy was not only the star of five films, but also the host of a TV anthology series, *Freddy's Nightmares* (1988–1990). He could be found on the shelves of Toys"R"Us in a range of children's toys, including the Freddy knife glove.

By the end of the 1980s, thanks to Jason and Freddy, franchise properties were stretching credibility and turning toward campiness. Whereas the unresolved endings of *The Texas Chainsaw Massacre* or *Halloween* once broke the conventions of closure endemic to Classical Hollywood narrative and left the audience feeling uncertain and unsettled, by 1989, a lack of resolution pointed toward the likelihood of yet another film in the franchise. Even when there appeared to be a definitive ending, owing to the supernatural element, the writers of the next installment could simply change the rules by coming up with inventive ways to bring the killer back. The one-time villain had become the star, and open endings and franchise security implied the inevitable return of Jason or Freddy, who no longer represented a serious threat to be eliminated, but a jolly ongoing danger to be enjoyed, temporarily defeated, and enjoyed again.

Against this backdrop, *Pet Sematary* reinstated the serious themes, ambiguous characters, and the downbeat ending that had categorized horror films in the 1970s, and it did so in a hybridized form that embraced the mid-1980s movement toward a cozier form of horror—for example, by showing only muted gore and saving it to the very end. The film does not shy away from presenting the demonic creature that Gage becomes after his rebirth in the burial ground, but, considering that he was hit head-on by a fast-moving 18-wheeler, the Gage-creature does not look like a demon inhabiting a body that must have been barely recognizable as human after the accident. Like Ray Brower in *Stand by Me*, Gage is knocked out of his Keds, but like *Stand by Me*, *Pet Sematary* doesn't show the full horror of what that means. The film also doesn't show, in the final showdown in Jud's house, what Gage does to his mother, Rachel, with Louis's scalpel, instead showing her drop from the ceiling with a noose around her neck, her face hidden in shadow. The audience does, however, see her resurrected corpse at the end, one eye and half her face

The Gage-creature in Pet Sematary *(1989).*

missing. The image of a re-animated mutilated human corpse is something to which the audience has been already exposed through the figure of Victor Pascow, the ghostly cadaver of a runner who dies earlier in the film, having been, like Gage, hit by a truck. Pascow appears to Louis and to Rachel, his eyes pale and milky and his head matted with blood, but he is not a threatening presence. He is instead a warning spirit who tries to help them.

The horror that the film presents is that of loved ones transformed beyond the grave, revenants displaying either the damage inflicted at their death or the crazed bloodthirsty behavior of a being devoid of humanity. What the film doesn't show are the unthinkable images that prefigure these revenants; a child dragged under the wheels of a truck and a mother having her face mutilated by her two-year-old son.

Pet Sematary therefore stood out from the pack of horror movies in 1989 as a mainstream but serious horror film that had thematic reach beyond the standard horror audience, in part because of its focus on the idea of losing a child. As Mary Lambert put it, "The important thing to remember is that *Pet Sematary* is not a film about children being killed. . . . It's a film about the fear your child will die" (Szebin 1989a, 122). *Pet Sematary* achieved mainstream success by following the pattern set in the adaptations of the early 1980s and downplaying gore. But in foregrounding the dark nature of the subject matter and presenting a scenario with which many ordinary people could identify, it also harks back to *Carrie* and the more challenging horror films of the 1970s. Thematically, there is nothing cozy about *Pet Sematary*.

Pet Sematary became the most profitable King adaptation to that point, and, in the words of Rubinstein, gave Hollywood "a great deal more confidence in the horror film" (Hughes 1990, 13). Despite this influence, and despite Rubinstein's comparisons of his film to *The Exorcist*, what followed *Pet Sematary* was a trend in mainstream horror films toward psychological, rather than supernatural, horrors. *Pet Sematary* encompassed both, exposing the real terror of loss before the paranormal fear of resurrection. The following year, 1990, saw the release of a number of high-profile horror films that shifted the balance more toward psychology. This was accompanied by a reduction in franchise properties, with no *Friday the 13th*, *Nightmare on Elm Street*, or *Halloween* sequels appearing that year. Morgan Creek Productions and 20th Century Fox teamed up to produce *The Exorcist III*, William Peter Blatty's own sequel to his original story, based on his novel *Legion*, published in 1983. The film bore little of the makeup effects of the original, instead centering on a serial killer narrative and a series of philosophical discussions between Detective Kinderman (played by George C. Scott, who was cast after the death of Lee J. Cobb, the original Kinderman, in 1976) and an unidentified patient in a mental hospital, who is both the serial killer Gemini and Father Karras from the original film. Also in 1990, Tristar released the equally psychological horror film *Jacob's Ladder* in which Tim Robbins's traumatized Vietnam veteran experiences ever more terrifying hallucinations. That same year, Columbia released *Flatliners* about a group of medical students who also experience visions as they investigate what awaits after death.

These were bigger-budget horror films than *Pet Sematary*, but they also used the genre to offer psychological horrors, focusing on themes such as fear of death, post-traumatic stress in the case of *Jacob's Ladder* and *Flatliners*, notions of sin and responsibility, and, in the case of *Exorcist III*, the serial killer. The movement toward the mainstream horror film as psychological thriller in 1990 therefore saw a blending of elements of the supernatural with natural horrors in much the same way that *Pet Sematary* did. Just as *Stand by Me* would influence a strand of King adaptations in the 1990s that focused upon non-horror, character-based tales and *The Running Man* and *The Lawnmower Man* would use King as the basis for science fiction-inflected action blockbusters, so too would *Pet Sematary* introduce a strand of King films that used horror elements under this guise of the psychological thriller.

The idea of placing horrors within the real world was a key theme in King's writing from the beginning, and one of the elements that contributed to his literary success. Cinematically, *Stand by Me* had been able to capture King's character-driven depiction of the real world, and while *Pet Sematary* was not as restrained as *Stand by Me*, its focus was still more on the real fear of loss than on the supernatural revenants. The next big-screen King adaptation, *Misery*, also released in 1990, eliminated the supernatural entirely. Director Rob Reiner was drawn to the project because "it really is reality oriented . . . it's something that could actually happen" (Wood 1991b, 16). While Rubinstein evoked *The Exorcist* in an attempt to distance *Pet Sematary* from contemporary conventions of the horror genre by saying it was a darker, more serious film, Reiner and Castle Rock, which produced *Misery*, sought to distance themselves from the genre altogether. Said Reiner, "I think that people are going to see *Misery* is the same [as *Stand by Me*] . . . in that if you're a hardcore blood-and-guts fan, you're not going to like *Misery*. We really didn't focus in on that. It's certainly there in the story, but it's played down. I've allowed the characters to drive the story and that's hopefully what the audience will find interesting" (19). Martin Shafer, head of Castle Rock, also confirmed that Reiner "made it very much a suspense/thriller" (20), while Reiner claimed, "It'll probably get an R but it's not one of *those*, you know, slasher, *Nightmare on Elm Street* kind of things" (20).

In contrast to *Stand by Me*, there was no attempt to change the title and to avoid references to King. "We're going to use Stephen's name prominently," said Reiner. "It's still a Stephen King project and I think his fans will like it. What I hope is that we don't fall into the cracks between people who are going to be hardcore Stephen King fans—horror fans who are going to be disappointed there isn't enough blood and guts" (20). The decision to foreground King's name this time most likely derived first from the fact that *Misery* was a best seller, and second, from the fact that, thanks to *Pet Sematary*, the cinematic Brand Stephen King had regained cultural capital. King's direct association with *Pet Sematary* made him, in Gary Wood's words, "a hot property in Hollywood again" (1991d, 39). The third reason is that *Misery* was not a horror novel, but rather an exercise in psychological suspense in which King critiqued his pigeonholing as a horror writer. While *Pet Sematary* was conceived and sold as a serious *Exorcist*-style horror film, *Misery* could be marketed as the psychological thriller that it was.

In this respect, Reiner's approach to the subject matter harks back to late 1970s adaptations of the works of King's literary peers such as Frank De Felitta and Peter Straub. As discussed in chapter 2, the reason why De Felitta's *Audrey Rose* and Straub's *Julia* fared less well than *Carrie* was because those films were out of step with the genre at that time. In contrast, early 1990s films such as *Exorcist III*, *Jacob's Ladder*, and *Flatliners* evidenced a movement *toward* the horror film as psychological thriller, and *Misery* tapped into a growing generic trend away from outright horror, gore, and supernatural monsters toward suspense.

Misery was a box-office hit, but in addition, it marked an important step in seeing the literary mainstream horror film as psychological thriller achieve breakthrough popular success. It also added to the mix the conventions of the police procedural as it follows the attempts of Buster, the local sheriff, to find Paul Sheldon, who is trapped in Annie Wilkes's house. Furthermore, Rebecca Frost argues that, while never described as such, Annie Wilkes can be read as a serial killer because she "fits the description of the classic angel of death" (2015, 121). This combination of serial killer story, police procedural, and psychological suspense thriller was replicated the following year by *The Silence of the Lambs*, which contains a similar mix of themes. Like *Misery*, *Jacob's Ladder* (Adrian Lyne), and *Flatliners* (Joel Schumacher), *The Silence of the Lambs* was helmed by a non-horror director, Jonathan Demme, and featured a cast of serious actors led by Anthony Hopkins and Jodie Foster. It, like *Misery*, became a full-fledged horror blockbuster, and an Oscar winner.

As Stacey Abbott points out, *Lambs* was "a prestige picture . . . marketing itself as a psychological horror film/detective drama, specifically targeting adult rather than teen audiences." Furthermore, she argues that the success of the film "specifically renewed Hollywood's interest in the horror genre in the 1990s" (2010b, 29). Abbott suggests that this new interest took the form of a resurgence of literary horror "with the main studios returning to classic horror tales taken from literature, comics, folklore and film history" (29). As discussed in chapter 1, these tales, as Abbott notes, were reinvented and repackaged as "prestige" blockbuster projects such as *Bram Stoker's Dracula* (1992). This prestige came partly from the foregrounding of their classic literary heritage, but also through using respectable acting talent and marshaling generic hybridity, selling the films not so much as "not horror" but as something "more than horror." As Mark Jancovich states, the publicity for *Silence of the Lambs* tried "simultaneously to present the film as offering the pleasures associated with the horror movie—that it will be gripping, terrifying, shocking etc.—while also legitimizing the film through its distinction from the genre" (2002, 156). It did this by avoiding the supernatural and emphasizing the psychological and procedural aspects of the story.

This approach to mainstream horror differs from that of *Pet Sematary*, which was clearly a horror film, but one that sought to distinguish itself from the genre as it stood at that time. Yet, it also displayed a tendency toward thriller/horror hybridity. In a similar manner to *Bram Stoker's Dracula*, the film was called *Stephen King's Pet Sematary*. Although Rubinstein pitched the film as being like *The Exorcist*, the poster refers to the film being based on "the best-selling thriller," while at the same time presenting horror imagery with an extreme close-up of Victor Pascow's corpse looming over a gothic image of the pet cemetery with ghostly trees in the background and a stalking cat staring directly out of the image in the foreground. The poster implies that the film offers, like Jancovich argues *Silence of the Lambs* does, the pleasures of both horror *and* thriller, but here horror genre tropes play a more significant role. This differs from the manner in which Rob Reiner and the producers sold *Misery* to audiences, emphasizing King's name, but stressing that the film prioritized psychological thrills and suspense over gore and was therefore a thriller.

However, the era of the mainstream hybrid horror blockbuster was to be short-lived. *Bram Stoker's Dracula* was a hit in 1992, but in 1994, neither *Mary Shelley's Frankenstein* nor the Columbia Pictures reworking of the wolf man legend *Wolf*, directed by Mike Nichols and starring Jack Nicholson, achieved similar success. Instead, 1993 brought the return of the horror franchises, with *Jason Goes to Hell: The Final Friday, Maniac Cop III, Amityville: A New Generation, Puppet Master 4*, and even, almost ten years on from the original, *Children of the Corn II: The Final Sacrifice*. That year also saw Steven Spielberg marshaling the tropes of the horror genre in his adaptation of Michael Crichton's novel *Jurassic Park*, a film about genetically engineered dinosaurs running amok at a theme park. *Jurassic Park* draws on jungle adventures like *King Solomon's Mines* (1950) and Spielberg's own *Raiders of the Lost Ark*, hybridizing them with horror elements including the Frankensteinian cautionary tale about scientific discovery overreach, the monster movie (including *Jaws*, 1975), and the conventions of the slasher film. As the velociraptors chase the two children, Tim and Lex, around the kitchens of the Jurassic Park visitor center, they are, to all intents and purposes, stalking their victims in the vein of Michael Myers or Jason Voorhees. This horror element is also evoked when Laura Dern's Dr. Ellie Sattler finds herself suddenly jumped by a hidden raptor that has been lurking in the shadows by the corpse of its last victim.

After a brief period of breakthrough success with the likes of *Pet Sematary, Misery, Silence of the Lambs*, and *Bram Stoker's Dracula*, the mainstream literary serious horror film for adults, offering horror hybridized with the gothic love story, the psychological thriller, or the police procedural, receded in 1993, and the genre returned to the franchises of the late 1980s. Into this situation came two more King adaptations, *The Dark Half* and *Needful Things*, although he was involved in neither of these films. Both drew their inspiration from *Pet Sematary* by presenting themselves primarily as horror films that also drew upon elements of the psychological thriller. *Needful Things* also added an element of humor.

George Romero was adapting *The Dark Half* for Orion Pictures at the same time that Orion was preparing *The Silence of the Lambs* for its February 1991 release. Like *Misery*, *The Dark Half* was a self-reflexive novel: in this case, a supernatural take on King's Richard Bachman pseudonym and a continuation of *Misery*'s exploration of King's relationship to his generic labeling. In the novel and film, Thad Beaumont is a writer of "serious" literature who invents a pseudonymous persona, George Stark, to pump out violent pulp crime novels featuring vicious killer Alexis Machine. When he is about to be exposed, Beaumont goes public and kills off Stark, who then comes to life and begins to murder the people around him, implicating Thad in the crimes.

In the trailer for *The Dark Half*, a voice-over intones that "Thad Beaumont has a secret, a piece of himself that he keeps hidden" before cutting to the scene where Thad sees a psychiatrist who tells him, "these behaviors could be interpreted as schizophrenia." The voice-over continues, saying "sometimes secrets take on a life of their own." The implication is that the story revolves around a serial killer with a literal split personality. Thad's wife says that when Thad writes as Stark, "it's like watching Jekyll turn into Hyde." Her quote is followed by shots of the police investigation and Sheriff Pangborn, a character in both *The Dark Half* and *Needful Things*, saying that Thad is being investigated and that "the evidence says you did it." The trailer brings in horror elements at the end, calling *The Dark Half* "George A Romero's masterful vision of a nightmare come true," thus selling the film as a serious thriller and police procedural with a horror component.

The film was aimed at adult audiences but again avoided gore. Romero diluted the violence in the novel, toning down, for example, the death of Fredrick Clawson, who threatens to expose Thad as George Stark. In the book, Clawson is found dead, his penis cut off and stuffed down his throat, his tongue pinned to the wall (King 1989, 76). In the film, Clawson's body is shown only from behind, in shadow, and Pangborn later describes his injuries.

Orion saw *The Dark Half* as another *Silence of the Lambs* and *Misery* and "put the project together with lightning speed specifically for Romero" (Leyman 1993a, 16). It should have been a hit. King's novel was a best seller and Orion conceived it as being, like *Silence of the Lambs*, part horror, part psychological thriller, and part police procedural drama. Yet, upon its release, it garnered fewer than $3.5 million in its opening weekend. John Kenneth Muir describes the film as "out-of-step with the times [in which] it was created" (2011, 275), which is odd given its similarities to *Silence of the Lambs*. Unfortunately, the film fell afoul of Orion's financial troubles when in December 1991, ten months after *Lambs* swept the board at the Oscars, Orion filed for bankruptcy, resulting in *The Dark Half* being shelved and not released until April 1993. Because of this delay, the film may not have been out of step with the time it was created, but it was out of step with the time it was released. In April 1993, mainstream adult literary horror was in hiatus, so both it and the other adaptation that year, *Needful Things*, failed to attract audiences.

Both it and *Lambs*, which came out on Valentine's Day, were holiday releases. *The Dark Half* appeared at Easter, and *Needful Things* was released for Labor Day. Both highlighted their links to King in the advertising: *The Dark Half* poster declared the film to be "Based on the Book by Stephen King" and the *Needful Things* poster similarly stated, "Based on the Best Selling Book by Stephen King." The two films were marketed differently, however. *Needful Things* is a novel that is as much a satire of consumerism as it is a horror story, and the film connected to the idea of the hybrid horror film and police procedural. In contrast to the seriousness of *The Dark Half*, however, the trailer for *Needful Things* is humorous. It opens with a voice-over saying, "Castle Rock Entertainment and Stephen King invite you to visit Castle Rock, Maine, a quiet little town whose population has just increased. By one." The soundtrack uses Edvard Grieg's "In the Hall of the Mountain King" from *Peer Gynt*, which can also be heard in the film in the set-piece comic sequence where Nettie Cobb plasters corrupt town selectman Danforth "Buster" Keeton's house with citations for offenses like "Cornholing your mother," "Horse fucking," and "Being King Shit." The trailer adopts a wry tone as Sheriff Pangborn asks Catholic priest Father Meehan, "Do you believe in the devil?" to which Meehan replies with irony, "I guess I have to. You can't have one without the other." Matching Pangborn's question, "What does he look like?" to a shot of Leland Gaunt establishes Gaunt as Satan. This is then followed by a moment in which Baptist preacher Willy Rose asks Gaunt, "May I take this opportunity to welcome you to Castle Rock on the Good Lord's behalf?" After a pause, Gaunt responds, "Why not?"

From there, the trailer focuses on a mixture of humor, action, and, like *The Dark Half*, police procedural. The comedy centers around Gaunt. Pangborn tells the people of Castle Rock "He came here to destroy us," to which Gaunt replies, "Oh, you wussy." A shot of Keeton is followed by Gaunt saying, "You are disgusting. I like that in a person." Meanwhile, Pangborn says, "There's been two murders and an attempted suicide in this quiet little town and Mr. Leland Gaunt is at the bottom of it." Finally, as the tempo of Grieg's piece increases, the trailer includes explosions, fights, and car crashes, before ending with Gaunt asking, "Are we having fun now?" Keeton then asks Gaunt, "I killed my wife. Was that wrong?" to which Gaunt replies, "Hey, these things happen."

Tonally, the trailer suits the film, which is also a mixture of action, drama, investigation, and comedy. Ed Harris and Bonnie Bedelia, as Pangborn and his love interest, Polly, play their roles straight, while at the other extreme,

J. T. Walsh offers an exaggerated caricature of Keeton. He is first seen arguing with Deputy Norris Ridgewick over a parking ticket in a scene played for comic effect, with Ridgewick calling him a "bloated cigar-sucking used car salesman" to which Keeton replies with gusto, "BOATS, shithead! I sell quality used yachts, you miserable fucking scuzz-bucket!" Walking a path between Harris and Walsh is Max von Sydow as Gaunt. At times, his performance is humorous, sometimes broadly so, as when, for example, he emerges from the burning ruins of his shop, Needful Things, unscathed and says, "Sometimes, I really hate this job." At other times, Gaunt has a more subtle twinkle, telling one character, "The carpenter from Nazareth. I knew him well. A promising young man. He died badly." Meanwhile, in the sequence where he sells Polly an amulet to cure her arthritis, he is entirely seductive and even, in Polly's vision of having sex with Gaunt, monstrous.

Needful Things, like *Stand by Me*, captures King's hybrid approach to his material, placing the emphasis upon location and character, the latter driving the narrative forward as each person's desire for a particular thing in the shop allows Gaunt to persuade him or her to undertake a prank that sets the townspeople against each other. The film suffers because, arguably more than any other King adaptation, *Needful Things* displays problems from being reduced to a two-hour running time. Evidently, more footage was shot as the director, Fraser C. Heston, produced a three-hour version that was broadcast as a miniseries on TBS. Given the emphasis on character in the story, and the fact that character traits drive the narrative forward in both book and film, the absence of many of the townsfolk in favor of a few key pairings—Pangborn/Polly, Keeton/Ridgewick, Nettie/Wilma, Meehan/Rose—robs the film of the world in which these characters live. For all that the trailer invites the audience to visit Castle Rock, the film shows little of both the town and its people.

With its elements of comedy and horror, the film captured the hybridity of King's writing, but it also marked a turning point in both the literary and cinematic Brand Stephen King. The book sold well, around 1.5 million copies, but it was the first King book in years not to hit number one on the *New York Times* best-seller list in either hardcover or paperback (Hendrix 2013). *Needful Things* performed better than *The Dark Half* at the US box office, but it too was gone within a few weeks, demonstrating conclusively that the cinematic Brand Stephen King was struggling once more.

Furthermore, the novel *Needful Things* was not only King's farewell to Castle Rock—hence the apocalyptic narrative for the town—but it also represented a good-bye to a series of familiar conventions that had emerged in his work in the 1980s. It includes cameos from previous stories: Ace Merrill, the bully who torments the boys in *Stand by Me* turns up, and in the final confrontation with Gaunt, Pangborn uses his hands to make two sets of shadow puppets that come to life, the first being a sparrow—a reference to *The Dark Half*—and the second being a St. Bernard dog. Castle Rock is destroyed by fire, as was the Overlook Hotel in *The Shining* and Salem's Lot, the destruction of which was also orchestrated from the interior of a new store. *Needful Things* therefore represents a point of closure for more than just Castle Rock and signaled a new direction for King as a writer. Three of his next four novels, *Gerald's Game* (1992), *Dolores Claiborne* (1993), and *Rose Madder* (1995), were much smaller in scope and developed the psychological thriller territory of *Misery* even further, but in a far more intimate manner, revolving mostly around the internal life of a single central character. Only the intervening *Insomnia* (1994)—King's fourth-longest novel behind *The Stand*, *IT*, and *Under the Dome*—would return to the idea of a town, Derry, being torn apart by outside influences.

King's writing in this period therefore moved away from horror as the main element, as in *Pet Sematary*, toward psychological thrillers, like *Misery*. At the same time, cinematically, the mainstream Brand Stephen King would achieve success by focusing on the psychological and avoiding horror, and indeed avoiding ties to King. As the next section will consider, the thriller *Dolores Claiborne* (1995) would draw upon the example of *Misery*, while *Apt Pupil* (1998) would be more heavily influenced by *Pet Sematary*. Alongside these, all influenced by *Stand by Me*, would come a second strand of highly popular, entirely non-horror, and non-King-branded prestige projects.

THE KING BRAND IN THE MID-1990S

By the mid-1990s, the American cinematic horror genre was struggling. Writing in 2010, Steffen Hantke offered a bleak retrospective of the genre from the mid-1990s to the end of the first decade of the twenty-first century. The essence of his critique is embedded in the title of his essay, "They Don't Make 'Em Like They Used To." He asserts that there is a general sense among horror fans that, during this period, the genre "has fallen into a slump" (vii), in which "one subgeneric cycle followed another" (viii). In a loose chronology, Hantke highlights a number of these subgenres. The first is the postmodern slasher film that was launched with Wes Craven's *Scream* (1996) and followed by a slew of what David Church calls "slick, teen-oriented horror films (many featuring young TV stars) with far less imagination [than *Scream*] and self-reflexive awareness" (2006).

This was followed, according to Hantke, by a series of remakes of 1950s and 1960s B-horrors that emerged from the Dark Castle company and included *The House on Haunted Hill* (1999), *13 Ghosts* (2001), and *House of Wax* (2005). Alongside this came a slew of US remakes of Asian horror films, including Gore Verbinski's *The Ring*, a 2002 reworking of Hideo Nakata's *Ringu* (1998), and Brazilian director Walter Salles's 2005 remake of *Dark Water* (2002), another Nakata original. A third group remade independent horror films of the 1970s, such as *The Texas Chainsaw Massacre* (2003), *Dawn of the Dead* (2004), *Halloween* (2007), and *The Last House on the Left* (2009). For Hantke, the low-budget, angry political films of the 1970s, the B-pictures of the 1950s, and the unsettling horrors of Japan were, in the 1990s and 2000s, being appropriated as mid-budget fare for a younger market of undiscerning viewers in a process that he describes as "the mainstreaming of recent American horror" (2010, xxiii). Hantke argues that this mainstreaming process "expand[s] the audience demographics for the horror film genre to include large audiences without a pronounced genre preference" (xxi), and the result is that in the 1990s, the American horror genre aimed itself primarily at moviegoers with only a tangential interest in the genre, leaving genre fans to "retreat from the commercial mainstream" (xxiii). They in turn had to seek out "more exotic and extreme forms of horror film" (xxii), such as those coming from Asia. The implication is clear. Hard-core horror fans watched Hideo Nakata's *Dark Water*, while more undiscerning viewers were satisfied with the Walter Salles remake.

In the same period, King's novels moved further away from the "immediately classifiable horror fiction" noted by Peter Straub (2000). As mentioned above, between 1991 and 1995, with the exception of *Insomnia*, King turned to a series of more intimate novels exploring the psychology of a particular female character—Jessie in *Gerald's Game*, Dolores in *Dolores Claiborne*, and Rose in *Rose Madder*—partly as a reaction to criticism of the treatment of women in his work (see Simpson 2011, 47–48). Each woman is a victim of domestic abuse, and each book blends the notion of her recovery with supernatural elements. For instance, while she is handcuffed to the bed, Jessie receives visits from the "Space Cowboy," who may be supernatural, a hallucination, or a man. Nevertheless, each book falls into the territory of the psychological thriller, the real horrors being not so much the supernatural as the specter of an abusive male relation.

In many of King's novels, like *Needful Things*, *Salem's Lot*, or *Desperation*, the horror element appears from the outside as devil or vampire and preys upon human weaknesses. The supernatural threads in *Gerald's Game* and *Rose Madder* are presented ambiguously as potential hallucinations in a troubled mind. In this respect, the balance of fantasy and reality that categorized his early works—bringing the supernatural into a clearly recognizable and identifiable American world—becomes in these 1990s novels more subjective, based around one character's perception of reality as his or her trauma unfolds. King's next novel, *Desperation* (1996), was more of a return to horror. A group of travelers are terrorized in the town of Desperation by the sheriff, Collie Entragian, who is possessed by an ancient being called "Tak." King then followed this with a series of novels, *The Green Mile* (1996), *Bag of Bones* (1998), and *The Girl Who Loved Tom Gordon* (1999), in which horror is a smaller part of the hybrid mix.

The same period saw the mainstream film adaptations increasingly occupying non-horror territory that negotiated this relationship between fantasy and reality—and indeed, between the cinematic Brand Stephen King and the projects themselves. It is an indication of the shift in fortunes for the Brand that, despite the presence in the title role of Kathy Bates, who had won an Oscar for *Misery*, a film that acknowledged its ties to King, *Dolores Claiborne*, the film that followed *Pet Sematary*, *Misery*, *The Dark Half*, and *Needful Things* in this particular stand of hybrid horror/thrillers, did not acknowledge those ties. As noted above, the novel was, like *Gerald's Game* (with which it is narratively linked), a psychological character study via a first-person testimonial monologue delivered by the title character at a police station. Questioned about the death of her employer, Vera Donovan, Dolores reveals what happened to her husband, who disappeared years earlier. In opening up the story from this internal monologue, screenwriter Tony Gilroy increases the role of Dolores's daughter, Selena, who, after fifteen years away, returns to see her mother because she's been accused of Vera's murder. Remaining a character study of Dolores, the film is also a police procedural, emphasizing Dolores's relationships with the estranged Selena and also with Christopher Plummer's Detective Mackey investigating Vera's murder. The emphasis on the police investigation connects the film to *The Dark Half*, *Needful Things*, and *Misery*, which in turn links it to *Silence of the Lambs*. *Dolores Claiborne*, however, has few connections to horror, to the extent that when director Taylor Hackford read the script he "didn't even know it was King. I don't read him because I'm not into horror and fantasy" (Blair 1995, 70)

In contrast, Bryan Singer, director of *Apt Pupil*, was well aware of the source material and of King, having wanted to make a movie of the story ever since reading it in *Different Seasons* when he was nineteen. The rights were acquired by Richard Rubinstein, who produced an unfinished film version in 1988, directed by Alan Bridges and starring Nicol Williamson and Ricky Schroder. The rights eventually reverted back to King, who was impressed with Singer's *The Usual Suspects* (1995), and so granted them to the director for one dollar, provided he could get the film financed within six months (Scapperotti 1998, 20).

Singer embraced both King's name and the horror genre. The top of the poster announces that the film is from "the author of *Misery* and *The Shining*." Like Richard Rubinstein with *Pet Sematary* in 1989, Singer saw his film as a horror movie, albeit, as many had emphasized before him, one that was different from the genre as it stood in 1998. As Anthony Ferrante noted in *Fangoria*, "Singer cautions that the terrors of this movie are of the very real kind, a far cry from the franchised boogeymen flicks that have become the genre norm" (1998, 67). To avoid the tropes of the "boogeyman" franchises, Singer and writer Brandon Boyce jettisoned the section of King's novella in which both Tod Bowden, the young boy who becomes obsessed when he finds that his elderly European neighbor is a former death camp commandant, and that neighbor Kurt Dussander start murdering homeless men. Singer argued that to include many murders would make *Apt Pupil* "look and feel like an exploitation film" and so he included one death to make the point rather than going for "graphic repetition" (Scapperotti 1998, 21). Singer declared, "There haven't been a lot of real horror movies in a long time. There have been a lot of fun horror movies like *A Nightmare on Elm Street*, *Scream* and *I Know What You Did Last Summer*. But I miss movies like *The Shining*, *The Exorcist* and *The Innocents* . . . so this is a movie sort of in the spirit of a real horror movie. I like the idea of doing a Stephen King horror film but I like the idea of less supernatural and more character driven terror" (20). Boyce agreed, saying, "These days being called a horror film seems to carry some sort of slight. Back when *The Exorcist* was released, horror meant upscale scary drama of a first-class nature. I wish we could get the modern perception of horror movies changed to what it really should be about: a great story full of character and characters that find themselves in frightening situations" (Jones 1999, 31).

The evocation of *The Shining*, *The Exorcist*, and *Misery* resonates across the cinematic Brand Stephen King, linking *Apt Pupil* with the quality literary mainstream horror of the 1970s, the reclamation of Kubrick's film in the 1980s as a horror classic, and the new incarnation of the King brand in the 1990s as part horror and part psychological thriller. Indeed, *Fangoria* would describe the film as a "superior psychological chiller" (Ferrante 1998, 67). Singer argued that "the movie is about evil that endures through the ages . . . . In this case it emerges in not only the man who committed these horrible crimes in Nazi Germany, but in the young, impressionable boy who is exposed to them" (67), and this was picked up in the reviews. Matthew Saunders wrote in *Cinefantastique* that, "what the audience is left with is a meditation not only on the corrupting influence of power, but the genesis of everyday evil. While we can easily dismiss such popularized horror icons as Freddy Krueger and Jason as simple boogeymen, we often find it too disturbing to fully address the lingering existential questions surrounding the true nature of evil" (1998, 117).

Arguably, however, the subject matter was too disturbing. Roger Ebert considered that the treatment of the Holocaust was "trivialized with standard horror clichés" and that "the material deserves a more respectful treatment" (1998). Despite overall positive reviews and a Halloween release, the film performed badly, taking in only a little more than $3 million in its opening weekend and barely making the top ten movies that week. Less than a month earlier, the slasher movie *Urban Legend* took in more than $10 million in its first weekend, a figure almost matched by *John Carpenter's Vampires* the week after *Apt Pupil* came out. *Apt Pupil* was billed as a horror film, and in 1998, the horror genre, mired in the remakes, sequels, and franchises noted by Hantke, was seemingly not serious enough to sustain a character-based drama about the Holocaust and the enduring nature of evil. The result was that *Apt Pupil*, a horror film and a visibly branded King product, disappeared from cinemas very quickly, as had *The Dark Half* and *Needful Things*, taking in less than a third of the $24 million that *Dolores Claiborne* had made, a film that was neither King branded nor horror.

By the mid-1990s, after *Pet Sematary* and *Misery* led a resurgence in the cinematic Brand Stephen King, connections to King and to horror were once again as problematic as they had been after *Maximum Overdrive*. At the same time, as also in 1986, a group of films that were the direct descendants of *Stand by Me* in that they existed entirely outside of the King/horror brand and genre, would demonstrate the ongoing appeal of King's stories and provide his biggest critical and box-office hits.

THE PRESTIGE ADAPTATIONS, 1994–2001

The first of this group of films outside the King/horror brand was *The Shawshank Redemption* (1994), which was followed by *The Green Mile* (1999) and *Hearts in Atlantis* (2001). Like *Stand by Me*, *Shawshank* was based upon a novella, *Rita Hayworth and Shawshank Redemption*, from *Different Seasons*. Also like *Stand by Me*, the film version of *The Shawshank Redemption* made no references to King in its marketing, beyond his name in the credits at the bottom of the poster and at the end of the trailer. Finally, again like *Stand by Me*, the film shows a real world that could exist, but imbues that world not with supernatural horror, but with real-world horrors that are, in this case, overcome through magic realism. Prison life in Shawshank is brutal. The inmates place bets as to which of the new arrivals, or "fresh fish," as they call them, will break, and when one does, prison guard Captain Hadley beats him to death. Andy Dufresne is locked up for more than thirty years for a crime he didn't commit; he is repeatedly raped by a group of male cons; he helps Warden Norton embezzle money, joking that "I had to go to prison to become a crook"; and the same warden denies him his chance for freedom when evidence emerges that someone else committed the crime.

This has all the hallmarks of a harrowing prison drama, but tonally, the film avoids this due to the messianic serenity with which Andy does his time. Mark Kermode discusses the various ways in which Andy can be read as a Christ-like figure (2003, 29–34). For example, in the scene where Andy and fellow inmates are tarring a roof, and Andy offers to help Hadley keep an inheritance at the cost of a beer apiece for his co-workers, Kermode counts thirteen cons, including Andy. He describes this scene as a parallel to the Last Supper, something equally suggested by the fact that Andy doesn't have a beer, which, for Kermode, echoes "Jesus blessing, giving, but crucially not partaking of the wine" (32). Kermode also argues that Andy, like Jesus, is a character seen purely through the eyes of others. In Jesus's case, the story is told through the Gospels; in *Shawshank* (both film and novella), the story is told through the eyes of Red (Morgan Freeman).

The same is true of John Coffey in *The Green Mile*. Beyond the obvious parallels that mark *The Shawshank Redemption* and *The Green Mile*—for example, the films share a director (Frank Darabont) and are both set in prisons—both are also stories of people who enter the lives of the narrators and touch them with their goodness and serenity. Coffey, whose initials are J. C., is, like Jesus, a gentle healer who changes the worldview of those around him before prejudice leads to his execution. A similar case can be made for the character of Ted Brautigan in *Hearts in Atlantis*, also produced, like *The Green Mile* and *Shawshank*, by Castle Rock. In the 1950s, Brautigan, an enigmatic older man, moves into the apartment above the one shared by a young boy, Bobby Garfield, and his mother. Like Andy and John Coffey, Brautigan has magic within him—in his case, a form of telepathy. He is pursued by the FBI, which wants to use his powers in the search for communists. His telepathy allows him to help Bobby, who is traumatized by an absent father and a mother too busy working to pay him any attention. The boy is bullied, but learns from Ted not to be afraid of bullies, or of life. As the adult Bobby narrates, after Ted is captured by the FBI, "my mom got a job in Boston. I was upset, but not afraid. Ted taught me that."

Hearts in Atlantis is a parallel piece to *Stand by Me*. It is set in the 1950s, narrated by the lead character's older self, deals with his reflections on his now-dead childhood friends, and focuses upon a specific and life-changing summer event. But in this case, the catalyst is not a dead body, but an elderly man with a gift. It is, like *Shawshank* and *The Green Mile*, a story of faith and hope. Whereas, as argued in chapter 1, King traditionally sets up a real world that is disrupted by supernatural horrors, *Shawshank*, *Hearts*, and *The Green Mile* disrupt a harsh and unpleasant world with the introduction of a force for

Goodness in a bad world: John Coffey in The Green Mile *(1999).*

good. In *Shawshank*, Andy's patient tranquility offers hope, not of rebellion or escape, but that humanity can prevail in such a terrible place. Coffey offers the possibility of goodness in a world filled with men who will rape and murder little girls, while Ted offers the chance for a frightened young boy to, in the older Bobby's own words, "open my eyes, and let the future in." In both the stories and their adaptations, the focus shifts from the idea that there is evil in the world and that good men have to fight it toward the idea that there is good in the world that can fight against the evil of men.

Like *Shawshank* and *Stand by Me*, the filmmakers of *The Green Mile* and *Hearts in Atlantis* avoided using King's name in the marketing, and also, like many King adaptations, distanced themselves from the horror genre. *The Green Mile* was billed as a film "from the director of *The Shawshank Redemption*" and the only other name in both poster and trailer is that of the star, Tom Hanks. In a short documentary accompanying the DVD release of *The Green Mile*, director Frank Darabont notes that "it's not the kind of story that people immediately think of when you hear Stephen King mentioned. It didn't have the fur and the fangs and the haunted car." Star Tom Hanks adds that "usually you throw around the name 'Stephen King' and you think that you are going to be getting this very particular brand of a horror story and this is really not." Similarly, the *Empire* magazine review of *Shawshank* begins, "This movie is based on a novella by Stephen King, but don't let that put you off. It's not a horror film, rather a thumpingly good ode to friendship, hope, wit, wiles and wisdom" (Anon. 1994). Yet, as has been established, what works in *Shawshank* and *The Green Mile* are elements that had always been present in King's work. Darabont says that, in his view, the story of *The Green Mile* "had this really rich world that it presented. It felt like that Stephen King that I really, really love. That humanistic writer that he is." Hanks adds, "This is what Stephen King does so well. He is able to really create these characters that are flawed but good."

Many of the adaptations discussed so far sold themselves either not as horror or as distinct from the general trends in horror at the time of release, and they often run afoul of the perceived requirement to be both effective and popular horror films through the foregrounding of the King name and the resulting associations. In contrast, *Shawshank*, *The Green Mile*, and *Stand by Me*, partly through their avoiding the use of the King brand and partly through adapting material atypical of the literary King brand, capture more completely the essence of King's hybrid mainstream success: character, language, reality, and morality. These are not horror films; they are melodramas, and like almost all the King adaptations discussed so far, as a strand they appeared, flourished briefly, then declined. In 1994, *Shawshank* was a box-office failure, but the film found its audience on VHS, becoming the most rented tape of 1995. Five years later, *The Green Mile* became the most successful Stephen King adaptation, yet three years after that, *Hearts in Atlantis* barely broke even and signaled the end of this particular strand. The next decade would see the fewest number of mainstream King adaptations since the 1970s, as the brand continued to decline and the horror genre struggled to find its identity.

KING ADAPTATIONS IN THE NEW MILLENNIUM

In 2001, King published *Dreamcatcher*, the first book he wrote after an accident in 1999 when he was hit and almost killed by a van while taking his daily walk. The book draws upon a number of elements from King's previous works. The broader canvas of the story links to the alien invasion narrative of *The Tommyknockers*, as well as the paranoia themes of *The Dead Zone* and *Firestarter* through the depiction of the American military placing ordinary citizens into camps with a view to executing them. At the heart of the book is the relationship among four men, who go on an annual hunting trip in the woods, staying in the same cabin. These men, Jonesy, Pete, Beaver, and Henry, share a special bond and a psychic gift, thanks to their saving Duddits Cavell, a young boy with Down Syndrome, when they were kids. A group of four boys sharing a significant incident echoes the premise of *The Body*, while the idea of children bonded by events who face a challenge as adults connects to *IT*. The book was optioned by Castle Rock and William Goldman, who scripted *Misery* and *Hearts in Atlantis*, wrote the screenplay. Shortly afterward, director Lawrence Kasdan came on board.

Just as the novel was a departure for King from his recent works, so too the film was very different from the King adaptations in the 1990s. Kasdan saw the film as "a real horror movie and a creature feature," adding that "it's not a psychological horror film: it's the real deal" (Longwell 2003, 21). In the same article, Kasdan cited his genre influences: "*Alien* is my favorite horror film. It's really scary to me. And *The Exorcist*" (21). *Dreamcatcher* was therefore, in Kasdan's eyes, a return to the serious adult horror of *Pet Sematary*, downplaying the humorous, procedural, and psychological thriller aspects of the mid-1990s adaptations. But, in following the legacy of *Alien* and *The Exorcist*, it was also a film that, unlike *Pet Sematary*, aimed to reinstate some of the "visceral visual" shocks of horror cinema in the 1970s. The origins of this can be found in King's novel, the working title of which was *Cancer*. Famously, part of the idea for the story came from King thinking about how what goes on behind the toilet door is one of the last great taboos of society and also about the fact that the toilet is where many people first get a sense that something might be wrong with their health when, for example, they find blood in the bowl. In the novel, this thematic strand is manifested, *Alien* style, through the life cycle of parasitic alien hosts called "shit weasels," which grow inside the intestinal tract and burst forth through the anus.

In the film, as in the book, a stranger, Rick, suffering from outrageous flatulence comes to the four men's cabin. Jonesy and Beaver later find him in the bathroom with the door closed, a trail of blood leading from the bedroom. When they ask if he's okay, Rick says he feels sick and "just needs to make a little room." They break the door down to find the bathroom covered in blood, Rick sitting on the toilet. Beaver asks if he is still alive, to which the response is a plopping sound. But Rick is dead, and whatever is in the bowl is alive. The monster, a snake-like creature with many teeth, escapes and kills Beaver. The scene indeed breaks taboos, from bursting through a closed bathroom door with a stranger inside to the sound of someone, in Beaver's phrase, "dropping a clinker," to Beaver wrestling with the monster on a blood-covered, tiled toilet floor. Whereas *Apt Pupil* pushed boundaries through its appropriation of the Holocaust, this sequence draws on the horror of finding something in the toilet that no one wants to see and presents it in visceral terms of abjection. The result, at least in this sequence, is that *Dreamcatcher* is gorier than virtually all the previous mainstream King adaptations.

However, in keeping with the general trend in King films in the last half of the 1990s (excluding the prestige adaptations), gore and horror give way to the psychological, as Jonesy undertakes a mental battle in his "memory palace" with an alien who has possessed him. The film also shifts toward paranoia and conspiracy as the army moves in. *Dreamcatcher*, which came two years after the novel, was, like *Firestarter*, released into a world different from the one in which it was written. The 1990s had been the decade of the alien conspiracy story. On television, *The X-Files* (1993–2002) had made alien invasion and government cover-ups a national obsession, leading the big-screen horror genre to embrace similar narratives through films such as *Body Snatchers* (1993) and *The Puppet Masters* (1994). After the attacks of September 11, 2001, however, the concept of alien invasion seemed far less terrifying than that of global terrorism, while the fear of secretive conspiracies was replaced by confidence in the government as national defenders. According to Chris Carter, creator of *The X-Files*, this was in part responsible for the demise of the show. He notes that "the mood of the country had changed . . . where there was suspicion of government before that there was complete faith that the government could protect us" (Brown 2013, 8).

Opening to poor reviews—Roger Ebert, for example, described it as "a monster movie of stunning awfulness" (2003)—*Dreamcatcher* did reasonably well at the box office, taking in more than $33 million, albeit against a budget of $68 million, the largest ever for a King film. Like *Hearts in Atlantis* and *The Green Mile*, *Dreamcatcher* was produced by Castle Rock and distributed by Warner Bros., and it was to be the last Castle Rock-produced Stephen King adaptation to date. *Shawshank* and *The Green Mile* had demonstrated that, by avoiding the horror-associated King brand, his stories and characters could reach wide audiences, but these were particular types of stories and characters. Audiences stayed away from *Hearts in Atlantis*, despite the fact that the film was tonally similar to the other two, and Kasdan's reintroduction both of branding *Dreamcatcher* as a Stephen King film and of the horror element proved unpopular.

As will be discussed in the conclusion, the years 2013–2014 saw the beginnings of what would become a new resurgence in cinematic King adaptations. In the intervening period after *Dreamcatcher*, however, the mainstream King brand on the big screen consisted of only three films: *Secret Window* (2004), *The Mist* (2007), and *1408* (2007). *Secret Window* was produced by Sony, the other two by Bob and Harvey Weinstein for MGM. They each offer some insights into the relationship of the King brand to mainstream horror in the twenty-first century. *The Mist* was written and directed by Frank Darabont and shot on a relatively low budget of $17 million. The film starred Thomas Jane, who had appeared as Henry in *Dreamcatcher*, but it mainly drew on an ensemble cast. This was in contrast to *Secret Window* and *1408*, the former of which starred Johnny Depp and the latter, John Cusack and Samuel L. Jackson.

A summer release, *1408* was marketed as both a Stephen King and a horror project, with the poster announcing the film was "from the terrifying story by Stephen King." However, in keeping with the pattern of Brand Stephen King films in the late 1990s, publicity emphasized that *1408* was a psychological thriller as much as a horror film, principally to distinguish it from the cinematic horror genre at the time of its release. Significantly, *1408* hit cinemas two weeks after *Hostel II*, the sequel to Eli Roth's notorious film from 2005, and was perceived very much as an antidote to such material. As *Starburst* pointed out, "horror fans who over the last couple of years are growing tired of being served up the same derivative Asian ghost stories over and over or what some have dubbed 'torture porn' . . . could well find *1408* a refreshing return to traditional horror in a modern day setting" (Anon. 2007, 100). Producer Lorenzo di Bonaventura agreed, stating that "I think what this movie does versus what Eli has done in those movies are two totally different experiences . . . this movie is trying to go beyond a call to the extreme, to elicit a reaction. It's going towards the subtle or the nuanced or the emotional" (100). For di Bonaventura, the aim was to make a film that played to audiences who did not want their horror to look like *Hostel* or *Saw*, and to use the film to see "how wide and how broad the genre is" (100).

Original writer Matt Greenberg, according to David Michael Wharton, approached King's short story "with the lofty goal of creating an anomaly in this age of jump scares and torture porn" and significantly used as his touchstone the key texts, both literary and cinematic, to which so many previous adapters of King have referred. He described his vision for *1408* as being "a slow burn, thoughtful horror thriller in the vein of 70s classics such as *The Exorcist* and *Rosemary's Baby*" (Wharton 2007, 26). On meeting producer Bob Weinstein, Scott Alexander and Larry Karaszewski, the writers brought in after Greenberg, found themselves in the same territory, saying, "The points of reference weren't modern horror films. We were discussing *Repulsion* and *Rosemary's Baby* . . . and movies about psychological deterioration . . . we wound up writing it very realistically" (Kaye 2007, 69).

The film proved to be a success. Against a budget of around $25 million, *1408* earned close to $72 million at the US box office, nearly $55 million more than *Hostel II* and $45 million more than *The Mist*. It was the highest-grossing horror film in the United States that year.

The Mist should perhaps have been the bigger hit. It was another collaboration with Darabont, and while King remained hands-off on *1408*, he made himself available for publicity interviews with Darabont for *The Mist*. But unlike *The Green Mile* and *Shawshank*, *The Mist* was both a horror film and a branded Stephen King project, described on the poster as being "Stephen King's Legendary Tale of Terror." Furthermore, in contrast to the story, it had a downbeat ending. The hero David Drayton kills his family to save them from the monsters in the mist, just before the US army comes to the rescue. Said Darabont, "From my viewing experience, the best horror movies have the most horrifying endings—the ones that don't pull their punches and leave you truly disturbed and discomforted" (Goldsmith 2007, 28). The downbeat ending of *1408*, in which Mike Enslin dies, was changed after test audiences rejected it. In the theatrical version, he survives the terrors of room 1408, is rescued by the fire department, and returns home, where he hears a tape recording of his dead daughter. Still subdued, the theatrical ending provides some closure to the narrative while allowing the lead character to live.

The change to a (slightly) more positive ending shows the other crucial differences between the two films. While *The Mist* had an R rating in the United States and came out in November, *1408* was PG-13 and a summer horror film. This has echoes of the year 1999, which Stacey Abbott refers to as "the summer of horror," when an abundance of CGI spectacle horror films were released (2010b, 34). Discussing the dominance of horror films like *The Mummy* and *The Haunting*, Abbott notes that these films, like *1408*, had family-friendly ratings that "de-emphasize the horror" (37) in order to accommodate the fact that "the target audiences for summer releases are consistently young people" (35). Dispensing with the physical destruction of torture porn, *1408* instead favors psychological torture. Trapped in the wrecked room, Mike is visited by his dead daughter, who dies again in his arms, crumbling to ash to the strains of the Carpenters' "We've Only Just Begun." Prior to that, he is released from the room and allowed to live a happy life before he realizes that, in fact, he never left. This is followed by Mike seeing a vision of a noose, then of him hanging himself, and finally, his grave. The film is a dark portrait of a traumatized man confronting his past sins in a hotel room. Presented as a special effects spectacular without gore, it tapped into an increasing desire for mainstream horror films that offered nonviolent scares for younger audiences, such as the *Paranormal Activity* (2007–) and *Insidious* (2010–) franchises.

The film is also less of a King-branded product than *The Mist*. The script is less faithful to the original than is Darabont's for *The Mist*, and whereas *1408* claims it is based on "the terrifying story by Stephen King," *The Mist*, with its added pedigree of being another Darabont/King collaboration, describes the King story as "legendary." Despite Darabont changing the ending, there is a reverence to *The Mist* that is missing from *1408*. Much of King's story can be found within *1408*, including the crooked pictures, Mike Enslin's habit of keeping a cigarette behind his ear even though he does not smoke, and the lengthy conversation with hotel manager Gerald Olin that opens the tale. But once in the room, the film embellishes King's sparse description and adds depth to the character of Enslin. In the book, he is arrogant and fairly successful, while in the film, he is, like Thad Beaumont, a writer of serious literature, slumming it for money. He's also more of a failure, the film open-ing with him doing a poorly attended signing. The film also expands the role of his estranged wife and introduces his deceased daughter. In King's novel, the horror Enslin faces is small scale: the paintings move, a menu changes languages, a strange voice on the phone babbles incoherent numbers, and fi-nally the room begins to shift and melt. The film adds the digital radio alarm clock that counts down one hour and keeps playing the Carpenters, the scald-ing water from the faucet, the specters leaping from the window, the bleeding walls, the flooding, and the room reduced to a frozen wasteland, then a black-ened shell. Nothing is explained beyond Samuel L. Jackson's helpful descrip-tion that it's "an evil fucking room." The film expands King's story to make an effective summer horror movie for mainstream audiences.

After 1986, the cinematic Brand Stephen King suffered inconsistent for-tunes. Moneymakers or critically acclaimed films like *The Running Man*, *The Lawnmower Man*, *The Green Mile*, *Dolores Claiborne*, and *1408* either avoided using the King brand or used King mainly as a starting point to create some-thing new, while overtly branded cinematic King projects such *The Dark Half*, *Needful Things*, *Apt Pupil*, and *The Mist* faltered. These latter films also sold themselves as mainstream, serious horror films for adults and distin-guished themselves from the general run of cinematic horrors at the time of their release. The more successful films, in contrast, broke away from the hor-ror genre almost entirely, becoming magical realist texts, thrillers, or youth-oriented summer blockbusters, with only *1408*, still conceived as a PG-13 summer movie, linking to horror.

Behind the brand are the stories and those hybrid elements that made King such a mainstream literary phenomenon. Putting aside *The Running Man* and *The Lawnmower Man*, in which little of King survives, *The Green Mile*, *Dolores Claiborne*, *Shawshank*, and even *1408* focus mainly on characters, using them to draw the audience into the story world. The same holds true for *Misery* and *Pet Sematary*, two films that bucked the trend by being King-branded (*Mis-ery*) and both King-branded and horror (*Pet Sematary*). Both focus on charac-ters about whom the audience can care before, in King's words, "the monster comes out and starts waving his claws."

Ultimately, these mainstream adaptations evidence this tension between a focus on character and upon the monster, the former proving far more popu-lar than the latter, be it a supernatural monster (*Needful Things*) or a human one (*Apt Pupil*). In many ways, in this scenario, it is the cinematic King brand itself that has become the clawed monster, the filmmakers having to decide whether to sell their work as a King project, given that the ebb and flow of the King brand capital in this period offered potential for a breakout hit (*Pet Sem-atary*) or a box-office flop (*Dreamcatcher*). The monstrous elements are the expectations that come with the King brand: that it must be a horror tale and that the film will not be particularly good, either as an adaptation of the book or as a horror film in its own right. In 1989, *Pet Sematary* demonstrated that a King-branded horror project could achieve breakthrough success by offering a kind of horror film that was different from the then-current genre tropes, as indeed did *1408* in 2007. But other projects, like *The Dark Half*, *Needful Things*, and *Apt Pupil*, suffered from being out of step with the genre and, evidently, with audience expectations. Above all, these mainstream films had to negotiate, as did those in the early 1980s, their relationship to the genre and the expectation of mainstream success that came with the King brand, often bringing in other elements such as humor, psychological drama, police procedural, or teen-oriented special effects action to bolster a broader appeal. The mainstream adaptations are fundamentally hybrid works, either not-horror or "more than horror," and in this respect, they tie into the formula of King's mainstream literary success.

But not all King adaptations in this period were mainstream, just as not all horror films were aimed at multiplex audiences. As Hantke pointed out, the trends within the mainstream horror genre sent horror fans out of the multiplexes in search of different, arguably "purer" horror experiences.

4 / STEPHEN KING AS LOW-BUDGET
AND STRAIGHT-TO-DVD HORROR

*Videotapes enabled horror fans to get hold of films that were too narrow
in their appeal to market to a theatrical audience.*

GLYN DAVIS, "A TASTE FOR *LEECHES!* DVDS,
AUDIENCE CONFIGURATIONS, AND GENERIC HYBRIDITY"

AS DISCUSSED IN CHAPTER 3, *THE SHAWSHANK REDEMP-
tion* failed on its initial cinema release in 1994, but went on to find its audience
on home video, becoming the most rented videotape of 1995. Given the status
of the film as a beloved classic of Hollywood cinema, the fact that it found its
audience on the VHS home-viewing platform is noteworthy, but *Shawshank* is
by no means unique among the Stephen King canon in terms of finding an audience outside of cinemas.

The first wave of King films from 1983 to 1985 coincided with the rise of
home video, and many of the films that formed part of that wave would continue to circulate and find new audiences on VHS. In some cases, this was a
natural follow-up to the theatrical release, while in others, home video release played a more significant role. As the market developed, it became clear
that there was a voracious appetite among consumers to watch films on video,
and more product was needed. The result was that in the mid-1980s, companies began to emerge that had an eye primarily on the revenues from VHS,
rather than those from theatrical releases. Chief among these was Cannon
Films, established in 1967 and purchased in 1979 by cousins Menahem Golan and Yoram Globus. In the 1980s, Cannon specialized in producing low-
budget action films and sequels. The expanding VHS market was their target, and quantity, not quality, was their guiding principle. As Golan said at a
press conference in 1986, "theatrical is not the only mouth to feed. If Hollywood produced five times as many films as it does now, it would still not meet
demand. There is space for the mediocre" (Wasser 2001, 123). Companies like

Cannon and, in the case of Stephen King, producers like Dino De Laurentiis funded their films by pre-selling not only foreign distribution rights but also home video rights, the latter proving more lucrative by 1986 when a prospectus for De Laurentiis confirmed that "domestic home video contributed about 10 percent more than foreign pre-sales—50 to 60 percent of negative costs versus 40 to 50 percent from foreign distribution rights" (125).

The year of De Laurentiis's prospectus saw the release of *Maximum Overdrive*, the third in a trilogy of De Laurentiis adaptations of King's work that began with *Cat's Eye* and *Silver Bullet* in 1985. De Laurentiis had also produced *Firestarter* in 1984, but the crucial differences between it and the other three were that the later films were all scripted by King and budgeted much lower than *Firestarter*'s $15 million. According to King, De Laurentiis pursued both him and the rights to his material, seeing King as "the Great White Whale, and he was going to have me. No matter what" (Wood 1991d, 40). De Laurentiis captured King first by buying rights to his work from other people, such as Milton Subotsky, who sold his option on various *Night Shift* stories after the collapse of the TV project, and then by approaching King with the promise of a greater degree of involvement in the process. The trade-off was lower budgets because De Laurentiis's objective was the home video market. As part of the cost savings, relatively inexperienced directors were hired. Lewis Teague, who had made *Cujo*, directed *Cat's Eye*, but both *Silver Bullet* and *Maximum Overdrive* were directed by newcomers—Daniel Attias and Stephen King, respectively.

King has been openly critical of *Maximum Overdrive*, telling Tony Magistrale that "I was coked out of my mind all through production, and I really didn't know what I was doing" (Magistrale 2003, 20) and describing it as "a stinker" in his book, *On Writing* (2000b, 173). But closer to its release, he described the film as "the kind of picture I'd go see . . . . It's just the sort of picture where you go see it and you say, yeah, that was good. That was fun" (Fletcher 1988, x). Later, in 1991, he told Gary Wood, "I wanted to make a chicken-circuit picture. That's what I like" (Wood 1991d, 49). As discussed in the introduction, King has a stated affinity for horror films that are fun and do not try to "rise above the genre" (Collings 2006, 18), and this embracing of the conventions of low-budget horror, epitomized in King's mind by *The Boogens*, certainly informs *Maximum Overdrive*.

The film features scenes of violence presented in an arguably throwaway fashion. An early sequence, for example, shows a young boy being crushed under a grass roller, albeit without graphic detail, and the unfolding narrative is punctuated at regular intervals by shots of people being run over by big rigs. Yet, alongside this is an irreverent humorous streak. The film opens with King himself playing a man who walks up to an ATM to find it calling him an asshole. Above the ATM, an electronic banner outside the bank informs the customers that it is 79 degrees outside before adding, "Fuck you." At times, the violence and comedy are presented uneasily together—for instance, when a little league baseball team is attacked by high-velocity soda cans shot out of a vending machine. Indeed, in the original unpublished script, the homicidal Coke machine was on the set of a western being shot at De Laurentiis's studio in North Carolina, the sequence ending with Dino himself being flattened by a truck. A handwritten note on the first page of the first draft outlines King's approach to the film, saying "Basic philosophy. It's about trucks going bazonka, not people and their problems" (Stephen King Special Collection, Orono, box no. 2318a).

The *Toronto Star* described the film as "the year's silliest, most amateurish horror picture, a kind of crude, camp classic of badness," a review that, while entirely negative, nevertheless seems in line with King's aim to make "a chicken-circuit picture" or, as he described it on the promotional tour for the film, "a moron movie [where] you check your brains at the box office" (Von Doviak 2014, 101). Despite the fact that the underlying thematic fear of machines running amok echoes *Christine*, *Maximum Overdrive*, unlike Carpenter's film, does not take its material seriously. King's script abandons the ending of the short story in which a bleak future for mankind seems the only way forward. The script resolves the situation with the survivors of the Dixie Boy Truck Stop boarding a boat and taking to the water. This is followed by a written coda implying that the earth moves out of the tail of the comet that started the phenomena, and everything goes back to normal. The final sound heard in the film is not a revving engine, but a seasick survivor vomiting over the side of the boat.

Four years earlier, *Creepshow* had included humor, but the comedy of Jordy Verrill's battle with "meteor-shit" was offset by the seriousness of Romero's visual approach to the horror. For instance Fluffy, the ancient monstrous killer residing in "The Crate," is presented as genuinely terrifying and violent, a werewolf-like beast with huge teeth that kills one of its victims by tearing his throat and slashing his face with its razor sharp claws. In *Maximum Overdrive*, King offers the same uneasy mix of horror and comedy evident in *Cat's Eye*, and this also appears in the next King-scripted film, *Sleepwalkers* (1992). Unlike the De Laurentiis films, *Sleepwalkers* was produced by Columbia Pictures, but like *Maximum Overdrive*, the film had a wide release across the United States and was sold exclusively on King's name, the poster calling the film *Stephen King's Sleepwalkers*, and describing it as "the first Stephen King story written specifically for the scream."

Released in 1992 during the renaissance in King films discussed in the previous chapter, *Sleepwalkers* did well, taking in more than $30 million at the box office, but, like *Maximum Overdrive*, it was, at its heart, a "chicken-circuit" picture. It tells the story of a mother and son, Mary and Charles Brady, the last survivors of a race of vampire-like creatures that feed off the life force of virgins and can be mortally wounded by cats. The film starts seriously, introducing challenging sequences of incest between the two, before shifting dramatically in tone after the first thirty minutes. At that point, Charles, who up until now has been a sensitive and sympathetic character, becomes a gurning lunatic. He attempts to murder Tanya Robertson, the girl he has been trying to woo, asking "exactly when did I begin to lose your trust?" before thrusting a pencil in a policeman's ear and shouting "Cop-Kebab!" From there, the film veers from horror to comedy to parody, featuring cameos from Clive Barker, John Landis, Joe Dante, Tobe Hooper, and King himself and a scene in which Mary kills a policeman by stabbing him with a corn cob, quipping, "No vegetables, no dessert." Yet, it also contains scenes of gore, including police captain Ron Perlman having his fingers bitten off and the sheriff being impaled on a picket fence.

Riding the wave of the popularity of *Pet Sematary* and *Misery*, the cinematic King Brand was strong enough in 1992 to sell *Sleepwalkers* on his name alone. While it was a major studio production, its horror-comic roots are tied to both *The Boogens* and to De Laurentiis's low-budget mid-1980s projects designed to make their money back on video. Thus, while *Shawshank* was a serious film overlooked in cinemas but successful in the home video market, the more significant relationship between King and that market emerged in the arena of a lower-budget, less prestigious form of horror filmmaking.

Shawshank was part of the second wave of King adaptations in the early 1990s, and by that time, the home video sector had expanded to such an extent that, on average, as Paul McDonald has pointed out, almost 39 percent of the revenues for the American film industry came from video, 14 percent more than from theatrical release. This is compared to 1980 when theatrical releases accounted for more than 50 percent of Hollywood's revenue (2007, 125–126). Furthermore, while rental dominated the home video sector in 1990, an increasing number of consumers were buying and collecting VHS tapes, alongside a smaller market of collectors of laserdiscs, a more expensive format for home viewing. This sell-through sector would eventually eclipse rental in the late 1990s with the advent of DVDs, which brought the added value features common to high-priced laserdiscs within the reach of the everyday consumer.

These shifts would lead from the kind of films De Laurentiis was producing, which hedged their bets and made money in cinemas and on VHS, to films that had either no or very limited theatrical runs and found circulation on home-viewing formats, and eventually to films that were never intended to be seen in theaters outside of the occasional screening at a specialist film festival. The rapidly evolving home-viewing market would create a space wherein not only was a mainstream but unsuccessful film like *Shawshank* able to find an audience, but also where filmmakers interested in King's work—or at least interested in exploiting it—could break away from the cinema, and from notions of the mainstream, to target what was a growing market for home-viewing horror among both horror fans and general audiences. The home-viewing sector thus saw the advent of a series of cheaper, mostly unofficial King sequels and franchises, alongside the occasional official original adaptation, that would together form a new strand to the cinematic Brand Stephen King.

HORRORS IN THE HOME: VHS AND THE HORROR GENRE

Videocassette recorders (VCRs) first became available at affordable prices to general consumers in the late 1970s. The idea of using a VCR to watch prerecorded videocassettes was secondary to the primary selling point, which was that consumers could record programs to be watched later, known in the industry as "time-shifting." The next few years saw the home-viewing market gradually standardize what was actually available for consumers to watch on their purchased or rented machines.

Initially, the Hollywood studios were hesitant to license their products for VHS (McDonald 2007, 114–115), and the result was that, in the United States, the primary pre-recorded material available to VHS consumers was not feature films but children's programs and pornography, while in the United Kingdom, a bewildering array of material found its way onto videotape, from infomercials such as *The Dulux Videoguide to Coloring Your Home* to public interest documentaries such as *The Story of Prince Charles and Lady Diana* (Kerekes and Slater 2000, 8–9).

Adding to this cornucopia was a particular focus on horror films. In the United Kingdom especially these included extreme European titles such as Sergio Garrone's *SS Experiment Camp* (1976), Lucio Fulci's *Zombie Flesh Eaters* (1979), Ruggero Deodato's *Cannibal Holocaust* (1980), as well as Sam Raimi's *The Evil Dead* (1981). The British Board of Film Censors (BBFC) took a strong stance on the violence in these films, requiring cuts to graphic content or banning them outright. Tobe Hooper's *The Texas Chainsaw Massacre* was banned because the BBFC felt that the issue was "the atmosphere of threat and impending violence" that could not be resolved through the cutting of certain sequences (Simkin 2012, 79–80). The same fate befell Wes Craven's *Last House on the Left*, along with a number of European exploitation titles. Banned from UK cinemas—or in the case of Fulci's and Raimi's films, released in censored versions—these films were able to circulate uncut via the then-unregulated video industry. Material that could not be seen in cinemas became accessible via VHS, and horror quickly found a new home on video. According to a survey carried out in the United Kingdom in 1983, "two percent of people who bought videocassettes and fifteen percent of those who rented 'chose horror titles'" (Kerekes and Slater 2000, 36), while the uncut VHS of *The Evil Dead* became the most rented tape in Britain that same year (Kendrick 2004, 160).

James Kendrick argues that in the United Kingdom, "the types of horror films that were popular tended to be of a B-Movie status" (160), and certainly a proportion were the more extreme fringes of the genre represented by the titles above. In the United Kingdom, many of these films would stir a moral panic in 1982–1983 about "video nasties" that resulted in the 1985 Video Recordings Act (VRA). This legislation mandated that all home video releases had to have a BBFC certificate and led to the withdrawal from video release of many of these more extreme titles. The moral panic, the VRA, and the banning of a number of particularly notorious films drove the market for horror underground and turned curious fans into collectors. As one UK horror fan said in the 1980s, "I think most collectors would like to own a full set of nasties . . . what self-respecting collector wouldn't want to?" (Kerekes and Slater 2000, 291).

It would be wrong, however, to assume that most VCR-owning Britons were watching Lucio Fulci films. The percentages involved in the survey cited by Kerekes and Slater suggest that the horror titles chosen by these viewers must have included mainstream horror films. Yet, while these "sanctioned" horror films passed by the BBFC made their way onto the shelves of video rental shops, the banned nasties passed onto the black market. Thus, from the outset, the VHS revolution in the United Kingdom not only provided a market for fans of mainstream horror, but also gave rise to a subcultural horror fandom of devotees, seeking out rare items on VHS and purchasing them, often at inflated prices.

In the United States, the situation was slightly different. As in the United Kingdom, horror films quickly found a popular niche in the market. As early as 1982, one of the pioneer independent video distributors in the United States, Andre Blay, head of Embassy Home Video, said in an interview that "it's easy to stay an independent if you find a niche such as horror . . . the types of films that have done well in home video, not at the box office" (Foti 1982a, 28). At this point, VHS tapes were generally priced high, around eighty dollars, meaning that the primary purchasers of VHS tapes in the United States were rental outlets, rather than home consumers. However, in 1982, Wizard Video released a number of horror films, including *I Spit on Your Grave* (1978), at lower prices ($49.95 or $54.95) because, as Wizard president Charles Band put it, "these films haven't been accessible to a wide audience, but they are horror films with a following . . . they sell" (Foti 1982b, 18).

Even as Wizard was acting, Hollywood studios were overcoming their wariness and embracing video. They not only started licensing their titles for home rental, but also tentatively began releasing a number of blockbuster titles for direct sale, again at these lower prices, a process that became known as "sell-through." As experiments such as those of Wizard suggested, there was a market for selling cheaper VHS tapes targeted at niche groups such as horror fans. So the question was whether the desire among the general public to purchase VHSs was large enough to warrant a similar release of a major film aimed at a wide consumer base.

Paramount first released a budget feature on VHS at the end of 1982. *Star Trek II: The Wrath of Khan* retailed at $39.95 and quickly became a best seller, attracting sales both from rental store owners and consumers. Paramount followed the *Wrath of Khan* success with other blockbuster titles, including *Raiders of the Lost Ark* (Segrave 1999, 197–198). The statistics were compelling. Paramount Home Video executive Robert Klingensmith reported in 1984 that 75 percent of the lower-priced *Raiders* tapes were being sold directly to consumers, while in the case of the higher-priced *Tootsie* (1982), also a substantial hit in cinemas, the figure was only 10 percent (Wasser 2001, 133). This kind of major mainstream product quickly came to dominate the US sell-through market.

As sell-through video in the United States was mostly mainstream Hollywood blockbusters, horror films, with a few exceptions, were found largely in rental rather than retail outlets in the mid-1980s, a situation that would continue into the 1990s. The exceptions were generally the kind of horror films that had already been successful with mainstream multiplex audiences. As Mark Bernard suggests, "During the VHS era violent, gory and low-budget horror was rarely for sale at major retailers. Videotapes of popular franchise films, such as *Friday the 13th* and *A Nightmare on Elm Street* series, might make it to retailers' shelves but for the most part, horror films . . . were relegated to rental outlets" (2015, 57). The rental market for horror in the United States was, however, booming. *Billboard* reported in 1985 that in the previous year, "horror movies accounted for 8 percent of the total video software dollar," while some video stores reported that horror films accounted for around 45 percent of their total rental turnover (Ciccolella 1985, HV3).

Furthermore, at the time that *A Nightmare on Elm Street* (1984) was released on home video in early 1985, the rental market was still dominant, with $3 billion spent in the United States on renting videos in 1986, compared to just $0.8 billion on buying sell-through tapes (McDonald 2007, 123). Therefore, while sell-through was growing, it was still a smaller market compared to that of rental, even though the product was primarily the most mainstream of Hollywood's output since that was what the studios were putting out at the lower prices. Despite this, however, one video store owner in North Carolina reported in 1985 that *A Nightmare on Elm Street* was both their top rental and their top sell-through title, even at $79.95 (Golden 1985, HV6), while Karen Yokel, a buyer for the Atlanta-based Video Warehouse chain, reported that in 1985 "more and more people are beginning to collect [horror] movies for their home libraries" (HV6).

In both the United Kingdom and the United States, therefore, the brief and anarchic early period of VHS saw horror films quickly become one of the major forces in rental, and this continued even after Hollywood embraced and quickly dominated the VHS sector. This relationship between home audiences and horror grew with the market in terms of both rental and sales until DVDs, the replacement for video in the 1990s, became one of the most important markets for both horror producers and fans. In addition, in the early years of video when the majority of VHS users were either renting movies or buying lower-priced blockbusters, the horror film fan also became a de facto specialized collector, seeking out films that were either banned and therefore sold underground, not available in the most mainstream retail outlets, or only for sale at high prices unlikely to be paid by the average consumer.

As specialized collectors of VHS tapes, horror fans were distinct from the purchasers of the mass-market blockbuster sell-through product, and also from the typical home collector who emerged in the mid-1980s. Consumers wishing to buy less popular fare gravitated toward the laserdisc format, which would become the principal home format for cinephile collectors until the advent of DVD in 1997. Arriving in 1984, laserdisc offered improved picture quality and sound and pioneered both the inclusion of additional features to accompany the film and the presentation of the film in its original aspect ratio at a time when tapes were routinely panned and scanned. The New York–based Criterion label led this initiative. Criterion's relationship with distributor Janus Films gave the label access to a library of classic European and art house titles, which were released in prestige packages with high-quality transfers, restored soundtracks, audio commentaries, and documentaries. The series was labeled the "Criterion Collection," and the first film to be released was Orson Welles's *Citizen Kane* (1941), which set the tone for the collection. The next release, *King Kong* (1933), was the first of the collection to include a commentary track. A publicity flyer for Criterion, which was included in the *Citizen Kane* disc and written by co-founder Robert Stein, stated that "our goal with this series is to extend the state-of-the art of the presentation of fine film works for home video. Future releases will bring to you screen classics produced with the same passionate concern for quality" (Stein 1984).

This concept of a collection of a canon of classic films, with an emphasis on the quality of the presentation and a high price for both the players and the discs, separated laserdisc from VHS and marked it as a collectors' medium. As Joan Hawkins points out (2000, 42), Criterion took an auteurist approach to its output, advertising that its versions presented the film as the director intended and working with directors and cinematographers on the transfers of more recent films. "In this way," Hawkins argues, "Criterion aligns itself with auteurist 'art' and . . . distances itself from the mainstream" (42). Hawkins further comments that the special edition Criterion laserdiscs, such as *Brazil* (1985), which retailed at $149 and contained the world premiere of Terry Gilliam's director's cut, "construct the home viewing environment as a sacrilized . . . space" (44), a place for serious, indeed reverential, viewing that re-creates (by being "as the director intended") or even supersedes (via the never-before-seen-director's cut) the theatrical experience.

Within the Criterion Collection there are relatively few contemporary American horror films, the main ones from the period under consideration in this book being De Palma's *Carrie*, Carpenter's *Halloween*, Demme's *The Silence of the Lambs*, and Coppola's *Bram Stoker's Dracula*. In keeping with Criterion standards, all four films maintain a stamp of authorship through the reputations of their respected directors, and all were also notable box-office and/or critical hits. So while *Halloween* was a low-budget and unexpected breakout success compared to the hybrid trans-generic constructed *Dracula*, all four films are fundamentally mainstream and auteur-led canonical examples of the horror genre. The same can be also said for Polanski's *Repulsion* and Cronenberg's *Dead Ringers* (1988), also horror films that encompass a level of authorial prestige.

This author-ized approach packaged home-viewing horror as art and was in direct contrast to the other end of the spectrum: the grainy VHS copies—often lower-generation bootleg dubs—of uncensored prints of films such as the video nasties that circulated in the United Kingdom. Yet, although the quality of these copies was often poor, the fact that these were uncensored also validated this notion of authorial authenticity. In the United Kingdom, for example, collectors sought out Lucio Fulci's *Zombie Flesh Eaters* not cut as the BBFC decided it should be seen, but uncensored as the director intended it, at least in terms of the content. In contrast to Criterion, quality was secondary to content, and "the very rawness of the image [became] both a signifier of the tape's outlaw status and a guarantor of its authenticity" (47). The "rawness" of the image reflects that of the film itself, with low production values but transgressive violent content often being part of a film's appeal. As such, grainy but uncut horror films on video became collectors items for horror fans much in the same way prestigiously restored cinema classics on laserdisc did for its fanbase. As Glyn Davis points out, "both cinephiles and, in their own fashion . . . the horror aficionado bring their own specific markers of quality to bear" (2008, 51).

"AUTHENTIC" AND "INAUTHENTIC" HORROR

The result of this was that VHS quickly became a site for a type of horror film that was transgressive, un-sanctioned, and therefore collectible. Barbara Klinger suggests that a theatrical release traditionally represents some form of legitimatization as a "bona fide" form of cinema (Walker 2014, 216). This is certainly true, for example, of De Palma's *Carrie*, which, with its auteurist vision and mainstream success, was ultimately released by Criterion as part of its canon of screen classics. It also connects, however, to Waller's description, discussed in chapter 1, of 1970s horror films like *Carrie* and *The Exorcist* being "acceptable and authorized," owing to their mainstream release, studio financing, and literary origins (1987a, 5). Yet, as discussed in chapter 2, as mainstream studio horror became increasingly cozy with the likes of *Psycho II* and *Poltergeist*, the link that emerged between video and more extreme forms of horror meant that home-viewing formats came to be a site for a subcultural horror fandom in which the concept of legitimization was turned on its head. According to Mark Jancovich, horror fans began to see films that had no theatrical release, or had been censored in theaters but were uncut on video, as a more "authentic" form of horror, as opposed to the mainstream "inauthentic horror" of the multiplexes (2000, 25). Jancovich argues that fans of the genre came to "privilege as 'real' and 'authentic' those films . . . whose circulation is usually restricted . . . and they do so specifically to define their own opposition to, or distinction from, what they define as inauthentic commercial products of a mainstream nature" (25).

As Matt Hills has argued, this opposition of authentic and inauthentic horror both derives from and fuels a subcultural horror fandom that attempts to "violate norms and regulations of the dominant national culture [and] depends on its treasured texts not being readily available outside the fan subculture" (2005, 102, 103). In the early years of home video, this subculture manifested, especially in the United Kingdom, as attempts to procure uncut copies of banned nasties by swapping them through ads in fanzines or buying them on the black market. However, a further aspect to the emergence of horror on VHS as a subcultural phenomena was the manner in which horror fans were demonized during this period. As James Kendrick has argued, the rhetoric around the video nasty debate sought to distinguish between normal, reasonable people who would naturally be offended by video violence, compared to, as the *Daily Mail* called them, "video sadists," with the result that "being offended by video nasties was rhetorically normalized; enjoying them in any fashion . . . coded one as deviant" (Kendrick 2004, 165). But, while it would be imprudent to suggest that no viewers of horror films, or indeed any film, ever exhibit deviant behavior, horror fans are not, as Mark Kermode argues, "a pack of marauding sadists hell bent on destruction" (1997, 51), but are, in fact, knowledgeable genre specialists who can "read aesthetically and thematically [while] non-fans appear to watch naively" (Hills 2005, 74). Hills concludes that in relation to horror, "fans" expressed pleasures that typically appear to be those of connoisseurship, which, in turn, "secures the distinctiveness of fan subcultural identity" (76). Like the auteurist horror entries to the Criterion Collection, collectors of banned VHS tapes sought out the works of Fulci and Deodato, with authenticity deriving not from the image quality but rather from the completeness of the copy, thus transposing Criterion's cinephilia into a subcultural form of horrorphilia.

In the United States, the situation was similar, although the origins were different. Since the late 1960s, cinemas had been regulated by the ratings system developed by the Motion Picture Association of America (MPAA). Beyond the R rating, which meant that anyone under seventeen years old was not admitted without a parent or guardian, was initially the X certificate, which was used both for films with content too strong for an R rating and for films that were not submitted to the Classification and Ratings Administration (CARA) to be rated. However, as Bernard points out, many cinemas refused to show X certificate films (the X category was replaced by NC-17 in 1990), and in reality "only pictures with CARA-approved ratings would be guaranteed easy passage through cinema distribution" (2015, 73). While home video releases adopted the ratings system, the same obstacles were not in place for material outside the sanctioned MPAA categories of U, PG, PG-13, and R. For example, many mall cinemas in the United States were not permitted to show X certificate films as a condition of their license (74, 75), a problem entirely avoided in the decentralized and independent video industry. Unlike in the United Kingdom, where, after the VRA, home video was more heavily controlled than cinema, in the United States, it was possible to release a film on video that had not been submitted to, or approved by, CARA. In order to distinguish them from X certificate films, which tended to imply pornography, these were issued as Unrated. Mostly these Unrated VHSs were versions of films that had been cut by CARA to achieve an R rating, released with that excised material reinstated. Therefore, in the United States, the kind of black market films of the United Kingdom could be distributed legally as Unrated, although in reality, the market was small and, as Bernard says, "the prices for 'Unrated' fare remained high," meaning that these films "attracted cult enthusiasts with the interest and the financial means" (82). While not illegal in the United States, as they were in the United Kingdom, these more extreme forms of horror still commanded a high price.

Thus, broadly speaking, the horror films that circulated on VHS in the early 1980s represented two ends of the genre. A subcultural fandom developed around material that was less sanctioned, far less accessible, and more likely to be purchased by fans at higher costs. The main selling point was the "authenticity" of seeing the director's own vision, which in turn often involved greater and more sustained violence and frequently was less concerned with the quality of the image. Alongside this was a more authorized and sanctioned mainstream product that was available through rental outlets and aimed at general audiences who had already had the chance to see them in cinemas.

The King adaptations of the early 1980s were, as has been argued, examples of mainstream multiplex horror, and the proximity of this first wave of King adaptations and the advent of video meant that some of these films began to enjoy a life on VHS. In the *Billboard* annual chart of 1984, *The Dead Zone* was the twentieth most-rented film of that year. It was also the number one horror title, followed by *Christine* at number twenty-seven, *Cujo* at forty-one, and *Children of the Corn* at fifty. The only two horror films in the top fifty most-rented films that were not King adaptations were *The Twilight Zone: The Movie* (1983) at twenty-five and *Psycho II* at thirty-nine. In the sell-through chart, *The Dead Zone* was again the best-selling horror film, this time at number forty-two. In the November 1985 issue, *Billboard* reported that the number one horror rental between 29 September 1984 and 28 September 1985 was *Firestarter*, with *A Nightmare on Elm Street* taking second place. *Christine* was number seven in the charts and *Children of the Corn*, number eight. One year later, all of these King titles had dropped from the *Billboard* rental chart from 17 August 1985 to 16 August 1986, with *A Nightmare on Elm Street* leading the horror rentals at number fifteen, followed by *Silver Bullet* at sixty-two, *A Nightmare on Elm Street 2* at seventy-three, and *Cat's Eye* at eighty-three.

Horror had all but vanished from the sales charts in the same period and so by the middle of 1986, all of the first wave of King films, with the exception of *Maximum Overdrive*, had made it onto the *Billboard* rental charts. In contrast, only one, *The Dead Zone*, made the sell-through chart. This seems to confirm that mainstream horror films, such as those branded Stephen King products, tended to be enjoyed by general viewers who were more likely to rent, rather than purchase, a tape.

Home-viewing formats represented not only a successful outlet for mainstream horror films, but also a market for those aimed more specifically at horror fans than at the multiplexes. These films were mostly cheaper to produce than mainstream fare and were often gorier and more explicit—sometimes extremely so, sometimes only a little. Yet, outside of the films produced by De Laurentiis, who picked up the rights via third parties, when it came to adapting Stephen King, cheapness was not an option because King routinely charged tens of thousands, sometimes hundreds of thousands, of dollars for the rights to film one of his novels. However, in 1987, with the King brand reputation at its lowest ebb after the failure of *Maximum Overdrive*, producer Richard Rubinstein decided that *Creepshow* had done well enough in cinemas and on VHS to warrant a sequel, the first to be produced for a King project. Talk of one had begun as early as 1983, but the project stalled for several years before New World Pictures expressed interest around 1986. The film was budgeted at only $3.5 million, and Romero decided to adapt King's stories into a screenplay and hand the reins to Michael Gornick, his director of photography on *Dawn of the Dead* and the original *Creepshow*.

As discussed in chapter 3, the mid-1980s was an era in which sequels and franchises dominated the horror genre, and *Creepshow 2* was therefore in keeping with the general trend of that genre, appearing in 1987 alongside the likes of *Evil Dead 2: Dead by Dawn*; *Hello Mary Lou: Prom Night II*; *House II: The Second Story*; as well as *A Nightmare on Elm Street 3* and *Howling III: The Marsupials*. The film did reasonably well, opening on just under nine hundred screens and taking in $14 million at the US box office in six weeks. It also outperformed the majority of the other horror sequels that year with the exception of *A Nightmare on Elm Street 3*.

Although King wrote the script for *Creepshow*, the sequel was only based on his stories. Nevertheless, it demonstrated that a sequel to a previous Brand Stephen King film success had box-office potential. More important was the fact that *Creepshow 2* made more money than any of the last three Stephen King-scripted adaptations, *Maximum Overdrive*, *Silver Bullet*, and *Cat's Eye*. As noted above, De Laurentiis embraced low-budget filmmaking with an eye to making profits on VHS more than in cinemas. *Overdrive*, however, had a budget of around $10 million, with *Silver Bullet* and *Cat's Eye* around $7 million each. Yet, while *Overdrive* failed to make its money back, the latter two did well enough to cover their costs in theaters. The tiny budget for *Creepshow 2* stretched the profits even further on even fewer screens, a little more than one thousand, showing that a Stephen King film did not need to be a big- or even medium-budget mainstream feature that proved to be a hit with a big audience, but could make money by being cheap enough to turn a quick profit in cinemas before finding a home on VHS.

Furthermore, *Creepshow 2* was inexpensive to produce not only because the production was done cheaply, but also because there was no need to pay King as Laurel Productions had acquired sequel rights with the original *Creepshow* deal. So its success not only demonstrated that there was a market for King sequels, but also that producing a sequel, the rights for which were already paid, was a means of keeping costs low and turning a profit even on a small cinema release. In this case, the film was sanctioned by King through his agreement to license the short stories to Rubinstein and through his relationship with Laurel Productions and George Romero. More generally, however, the exploitation of sequel rights did not require either King's involvement or his approval. This in turn would lead to the emergence of a substantial number of un-authorized King films.

Although *Creepshow 2* was low budget, it was still a mainstream product, focusing more on character than on shocks to entertain the audience, particularly in the first episode, "Old Chief Wood'nhead." Hollywood veterans George Kennedy and Dorothy Lamour play elderly shop owners killed by robbers, on whom the wooden Indian outside their store takes revenge. Tonally, the film largely avoids King's kind of humor, which had been rejected by audiences in *Maximum Overdrive*. With the exception of the animated wraparound story, which features Tom Savini as "The Creep," the sequel is more serious than even the original film, there being no equivalent to King's appearance as idiot bumpkin Jordy Verrill. In particular, "Old Chief Wood'nhead" is somber to the point of moving. Despite the focus on character, *Creepshow 2* had a few moments of gore, notably in the final story "The Hitchhiker" in which Tom Wright's hitchhiker appears in an increasingly bloody state as he is repeatedly run over and shot by Lois Chiles's businesswoman Annie Lansing. Also, in "The Raft," a mysterious waterborne oily blob terrorizes a group of teens on a raft in a lake. One of the swimmers is pulled through the raft's wooden slats, his leg broken and bent upright at an unnatural angle, and another has her face melted by the strange oil slick. Despite this, *Creepshow 2* is largely restrained in its imagery, and while it would introduce a particular strand of low-budget King-branded product, the film that followed it, *Graveyard Shift*, increased the humor, although not to *Maximum Overdrive* levels, and also added new and hitherto unseen levels of gore to the King brand.

King sold the rights to his short story, "Graveyard Shift," for $2,500 around the same time that Rubinstein was preparing *Pet Sematary* with Paramount. The rights were purchased by William J. Dunn, who had helped establish the Maine Film Commission in 1987. Using a script by John Esposito, Dunn offered the directing job to Ralph S. Singleton, who was a first-time feature director but an experienced producer at Paramount. Singleton was able to convince Paramount to invest in what was becoming a $10 million film and to give it a Halloween release (Wood 1990a, 8). *Graveyard Shift* took the money and ran, opening at number one by taking in $5 million in its first weekend and then quickly disappearing, making barely the same amount again over the next two weeks.

Despite an intriguing subtext about capitalism and the exploitation of workers, *Graveyard Shift* was *The Boogens* by another name, a cheerfully gory big mutant rat/bat movie. A group of mismatched and disgruntled workers in the Bachman mill, a textile factory, are coerced by the foreman to work nights to clear the factory of rats. The work takes them deeper into the sub-levels of the factory where they ultimately uncover a mutated form of rat. The film was branded as both a Stephen King product and a horror film, the trailer announcing "Stephen King invites you to venture deep inside the caverns below the old Bachman mill" and that "this is the new horror from the mind of Stephen King." It also foregrounded its horror credentials by casting Brad Dourif as the exterminator. Dourif was, as noted in the introduction, a cult figure in horror cinema as the voice of Chucky in *Child's Play* and in the role of the Gemini Killer in *The Exorcist III*.

While, as discussed in chapter 3, *Pet Sematary* was intended to be a departure from the blood and gore endemic to the horror genre in 1989 and had thus focused on creating a serious atmosphere of dread, *Graveyard Shift* moved in the other direction, offering a mixture of bloody deaths, rats and other creepy crawlies, and camp humor. As such, *Graveyard Shift* revels in its special effects. In one scene, Brogan, one of the members of the clean-up crew, walks into a web and finds his face covered with scuttling spiders. He reaches for the water hose, only to find he has picked up a severed arm with a rat gnawing on it. Another worker has his hand chewed off by the giant mutant rat/bat that lurks beneath the mill, and the villain of the piece, Foreman Warwick, is disemboweled. Finally, hero John Hall presses the rat/bat in a cotton picker in an extended, blood-soaked sequence. Offsetting the gore is Dourif's eye-rolling, exaggerated performance as the exterminator, and scenes such as the one where the rats escape drowning by standing on pieces of wood while the Beach Boys' "Surfin' Safari" plays. While building on the low-budget example of *Creepshow 2*, and to a lesser extent the De Laurentiis productions of 1984–1985, *Graveyard Shift* also crucially marks a turning point in King adaptations as a film that focuses upon gore in a way that none of the others, regardless of budget, had done prior to this point.

Though it was a very different product from *Pet Sematary*, *Graveyard Shift* was picked up by Paramount, keen to capitalize on the former's success.

Gallons of gore in Graveyard Shift *(1990)*.

Graveyard Shift grossed $11 million upon release. While *Creepshow 2* showed that there was a market for low-budget King sequels, *Graveyard Shift* proved that there was also one for an equally cheap but more explicit film, presenting a mixture of horror imagery alongside humor. In doing so, *Graveyard Shift* eschewed the kind of serious treatment of subject matter that categorized the majority of the mainstream films, but it also avoided the undermining silliness of *Maximum Overdrive*.

After *Graveyard Shift* made its money back, Paramount and Singleton turned to making a sequel to *Pet Sematary*, the first film to be based upon a premise of King's rather than on one of his stories. Paramount had acquired the sequel rights as part of the deal for the original film and approached both King and Rubinstein, neither of whom were interested. So the studio turned to writer Richard Outten who produced an entirely original story. No mention is made of King's name in the trailer or on the poster for the film, a decision that may have been influenced by the fact that, at the time of the film's release in August 1992, King was embroiled in the lawsuit with Allied Vision and New Line over *The Lawnmower Man*.

Pet Sematary II drew from the original by being set in the same town, some time after the first film concluded, and by having the dead come back to life after being interred in the burial ground. In keeping with the approach taken with *Graveyard Shift*, the sequel upped the violence from the original, replacing its dark and somber tone with a larger body count. Having been reborn in the Indian burial ground, Drew Gilbert's dog, Zowie, rips out the throat of Drew's abusive stepfather, the local sheriff who is seen at one point killing and skinning white rabbits. Meanwhile, at the local veterinarian's office, a dog savages and partially eats a group of kittens. Having himself been buried and resurrected, the sheriff then kills a high school bully by pushing a motorcycle tire into his face and revving the throttle, tearing off the boy's skin. The bully then returns and Jeff, the vet's son, pushes his fingers into his eyes, causing white pus to ooze from the sockets. While the emphasis shifts in the film from the loss of a child from the parent's perspective to the loss of a parent from the point of view of a child, the violence is the more noticeable change in the sequel, particularly that toward animals, which is treated far more seriously than the violence toward the human characters. The death of Zowie, for example, shot unnecessarily by the sheriff (while he is still human) is presented as far more horrifying than the scene in which the same sheriff, now reborn, kills the bully.

Although King was neither involved in nor associated with the film, and the sequel failed to emulate the performance of the original, *Pet Sematary II* nevertheless made $17 million at the US box office. This was more than *Creepshow 2* and was likely the result of at least a certain proportion of the audience who contributed to the huge success of the original *Pet Sematary* returning for the sequel. Given the difference in tone and violence, they may well have been disappointed, but ultimately, *Pet Sematary II*, along with *Creepshow 2* and *Graveyard Shift*, reinforced the notion that there was a market not only for sequels to King films but also for a more low-budget, less serious, gorier, and more exploitation-oriented form of film derived from King's work. These films, with their emphasis on visual effects, were aimed more at horror fans than the mainstream King films and were cheap enough to make back their production budgets in cinemas before tapping into the home-viewing market.

Moreover, while *Graveyard Shift* and *Creepshow 2* were King-branded products, *Pet Sematary II* was not. The producers drew not on King's name, but on the title. This marked a shift away from King himself and toward a title *associated* with King as the main selling point, even though the project had nothing to do with him. His non-involvement was not new since, as noted in chapter 2, the majority of King-branded products in 1983–1985 had no direct input from King, but were all nevertheless first-generation adaptations of King's work and, for the most part, were billed as *Stephen King's The Dead Zone* or *Stephen King's Firestarter*. In contrast, *Pet Sematary II* was the first horror film that is indirectly King branded by title association, and it set the stage for a new type of King product that drew on what Alan Jones refers to as "high audience title awareness" (Jones 1992, 14). These were entirely original projects that were also specifically horror films and were budgeted low enough to turn a profit from a brief cinema release and then VHS sales and rentals through the use of titles that were familiar enough to audiences to make them stand out on the horror shelves of rental stores. Following on from the new directions set by *Creepshow* and *Graveyard Shift*, *Pet Sematary II* became the template for a string of unauthorized and un-sanctioned Stephen King films that drew upon the King brand only by proxy.

First among these unsanctioned King films was a belated sequel to *Children of the Corn*, released in 1993. *Children of the Corn II: The Final Sacrifice* was produced by Trans-Atlantic Pictures, which had purchased the back catalogue of New World Pictures, including *Children of the Corn* and its sequel rights. As director David Price said, the main reason for making the film was financial. He noted that "a million-dollar film that makes $12 million is going to show a bigger profit than any $30 million film" (Goodson 1992, 13). *Children of the Corn* had the requisite "high audience title awareness" since, after disappearing from US cinemas after eight weeks, it was released on home video the following year and began to attract audiences, becoming, as noted above, the fiftieth most rented title of 1984 and the eighth most rented horror film between 1984 and 1985. The popularity of the film on home video led Bob and Harvey Weinstein of Miramax Films to announce in 1993 that the Trans-Atlantic sequel to *Children of the Corn* would be one of the two first films to be distributed by their newly formed horror subsidiary company, Dimension Films. The aim was to use the Dimension name specifically for the distribution of genre films, notably horror, and thus reap the benefits of the popularity of these films without sullying the prestige indie reputation that the Miramax brand had built for itself. Their first two projects were sequels, *Hellraiser III: Hell on Earth* (1992) and *Children of the Corn II: The Final Sacrifice*.

The Final Sacrifice begins shortly after the events of the first film in the town of Hemingford, near Gatlin where the children murdered their parents. The remaining children are fostered in Hemingford, and the emerging narrative features an investigative reporter, John Garrett, covering the Gatlin massacre. Meanwhile, the children are led back into murder by Micah, who is possessed by the spirit of He Who Walks Behind the Rows. Fritz Kiersch's original film, after the opening scene in which the parents are massacred, unfolds as a mystery in which the protagonists, Burt and Vicky, try to find out what happened in the town and to report the death of a small boy they have run over. The sequel maintains the Nebraskan setting and the central idea of two main characters with an antagonistic relationship: the dysfunctional Burt and Vicky in the original and Garrett and his son Danny in the sequel. The narrative, however, is structured much like a slasher film and, like *Graveyard Shift* and *Pet Sematary II*, is punctuated by regular deaths. First, a reporter and his cameraman are killed, the latter having his throat cut by the corn, while the former is impaled by a corn stalk. Shortly after, an old woman, who opposes the fostering of the children, is crushed to death under her house, while another member of the town bleeds to death from every orifice while in church. Eventually, Micah is killed, pulled into and shredded by a corn-harvesting machine in an echo of the rat/bat's end in *Graveyard Shift*. Unlike the suggestive violence of the original, the death scenes here make broad use of special makeup effects. As the reporter is impaled by a stalk of corn, the camera lingers as blood pours from his mouth and the open wound, and when Micah is dragged into the harvester a close-up shows his robes being torn before cutting to a shot of blood and entrails being ejected from the machine onto the ground.

In upping the gore and modeling its narrative along slasher lines, *The Final Sacrifice* set the tone for the *Children of the Corn* franchise to come. Like the original film, it was low budget, shot for less than $1 million in only twenty-three days. It was released in US cinemas in January 1993, at the tail end of the resurgence of the cinematic King brand discussed in the previous chapter, and some five months after Paramount had released *Pet Sematary II*. With Dimension's stated aim to focus on low-budget films that would have a small cinema release but make the majority of their money in the home, *Children of the Corn II* made a modest $6 million over two weeks in American cinemas, before being released on video, again by Paramount. The next sequel, *Children of the Corn III: Urban Harvest*, would also have a very limited cinema release in September 1995 before heading to video in July 1996.

Urban Harvest was followed by a virtually annual succession of sequels that were released directly to home video: *Children of the Corn IV: The Gathering* (1996); *Children of the Corn V: Fields of Terror* (1998); *Children of the Corn 666: Isaac's Return* (1999); *Children of the Corn: Revelation* (2001); and, much later, *Children of the Corn: Genesis* (2011). Unlike *Pet Sematary II*, each film included in the credits, as did parts II and III, that it was "based on the short story 'Children of the Corn' by Stephen King." Each stopped short, however, of naming the film, as did the original, as "Stephen King's *Children of the Corn*." As such, the primary branding is that of the title itself, each film drawing upon the example of the first sequel and using *Children of the Corn* with a subtitle. Following the format of *The Final Sacrifice*, each film is regularly punctuated by deaths, including, in *Urban Harvest*, a homeless man's eyes being penetrated by corn stalks and a woman having her faced burned off. The town doctor is cut in half by a gurney in *The Gathering*, and in *Fields of Ter-*

ror, David Carradine's head splits open down the middle from crown to chin and then shoots out flames that burn the face off Fred Williamson's sheriff. Despite this structural similarity, there is little or no continuity in narrative terms with the first film, nor indeed between the sequels themselves. So while *Urban Harvest* sets up a potentially ongoing narrative of "infected," adult-killing corn being exported around the world, none of the following films return to this story. The exceptions are *The Final Sacrifice*, which begins shortly after the first film ended, and the sixth film in the franchise, *Isaac's Return*, which sees John Franklin reprise his role as Isaac from the original film.

The remainder tell stand-alone stories linked only by the basic premise of creepy children threatening adults. Not all of them are even set in the corn fields of Nebraska, *Urban Harvest* being set in Chicago and *Revelation* in Omaha. That each film is a fresh take on the premise was a deliberate strategy by Dimension to keep the franchise going. For example, Ethan Wiley, writer and director of *Fields of Terror*, elected to build his story around the idea of the children of Gatlin being under the thrall of a cult leader, played by David Carradine. He said that "it's really been different filmmakers doing their own thing each time . . . there hasn't been a continuity so to speak . . . . So the best thing for me to do was to kind of ignore those other movies and go back to the original source. . . . I guess I have always had an interest or fascination with the mechanics of cults . . . and that was one thing the other films hadn't necessarily done" (Beeler 1998, 30). Likewise, Kari Skogland, director of *Isaac's Return*, was told by Dimension that "they wanted to make a slightly different, more unique horror film. . . . The mandate was to make a horror film that was smarter and cooler and more happening" (Scapperotti 1999, 58).

None of the films received many positive reviews, but they made money, first on VHS and then, from 1997, on DVD. The advent of DVD made the acquisition of high-quality copies laden, like laserdiscs, with additional extras both affordable and more available. Furthermore, more and more people were building film collections with the result that DVD "mainstreamed the type of collecting behavior normally reserved for 'cultish' audiences" (Bernard 2015, 58). In addition, DVD, with its lower prices, smaller production costs, and rapid uptake by consumers, led to a fusing of the high-quality product purchased by the Criterion connoisseur and the low-fi macabre films of the horror collector. So, for example, in 2004, Anchor Bay released the first three *Children of the Corn* films in a special edition three-disc box set, remastered for 5.1 sound and in new digital transfers. The first and second film also had audio commentaries by the directors and stars, with the original also including a specially shot documentary. The whole package was completed with a promotional booklet that states:

Home video has created many sequels that we might not have otherwise expected to see—by extending the life of a movie beyond the initial theatrical
release . . . video ensured that numerous films which failed to make much
impact at the box office would nonetheless become ubiquitous enough to
justify follow-ups, particularly as a large part of the video rental market
seemed to thrive on familiarity . . . . *Children of the Corn* had been a solid
renter for the best part of a decade . . . [the third film] plugged into the
cult surrounding the series, and its success more or less ensured a franchise
was born.

The booklet goes on to say that "twenty years on, *Children of the Corn* deserves reassessment as a movie and as a cultural phenomenon," thereby placing the film and the franchise firmly within the territory of the kind of classics
of cinema that Criterion first released in the mid-1980s.

Indeed, the fact that it was Anchor Bay that released this box set is significant. Not only was Anchor Bay partly owned by the Weinstein brothers,
as was Dimension, but also from the mid-1990s, the label began to special-
ize in DVD releases of horror titles. Drawing on the Criterion example, Anchor Bay included such canonical works as *Halloween* (and its sequels), but the
company also began to release fully restored versions of some of the more extreme horror titles that had been causes celebres in the 1980s, including works
by Lucio Fulci, such as *The New York Ripper* (1982); Sam Raimi's *Evil Dead*
(1981) and its sequels; and a number of horror classics by Dario Argento, released under the auteurist banner title of *The Dario Argento Collection*. In
many ways, the work of Anchor Bay brought together those earlier competing collectors' markets of the cinephiles and the horrorphiles, making the label's production of a *Children of the Corn* box set all the more important.

Similar treatment was given, albeit not by Anchor Bay, to the first film in
another franchise based on King's short story "The Mangler." In 1994, around
the time that the second wave of King adaptations was beginning to wane in
cinemas, director Tobe Hooper returned to King for the first time since the
1979 *Salem's Lot*. Hooper approached King about making a film version of
"The Mangler," promising that he would be faithful to the story and—ironically as it would turn out—that he wouldn't "turn the mangler into a virtual
reality machine" (Shapiro 1995, 20). King agreed, apparently working with
Hooper by offering comments and suggestions on some of the forty drafts of
the script (21). Finally, King saw the film and was "happy enough to lend his
name to the production" (20). The budget was again small, and the film was
shot in South Africa to take advantage of the exchange rate between the dollar and the rand. As Hooper points out, "South Africa suddenly became the
only place where I could stretch a moderate (under $10 million) budget into

"As gory as an R-rated movie can get": Strong violence in The Mangler *(1995).*

something. . . . I felt we could make a movie there that looked as if it cost $20 million" (22). New Line, which had produced Wes Craven's *Nightmare on Elm Street* series, released the film in the United States on 3 March, only three weeks before *Dolores Claiborne*. But unlike the latter, Hooper's film drew on the example of *Children of the Corn II*, *Pet Sematary II*, and particularly *Graveyard Shift* by appearing as a low-budget horror feature with a strong emphasis on gore. Hooper, who, thanks to *The Texas Chainsaw Massacre*, was an established director of strong, uncompromising horror, confirmed that "this is definitely gory . . . It's as gory as an R-rated movie can get" (22). So, for example, in the opening sequences, a woman is caught, drawn into the Mangler and crushed in a sequence very similar to those at the end of both *Graveyard Shift* and *Children of the Corn II*, the difference being that this is an innocent worker rather than a giant mutant killer rat/bat or He Who Walks Behind the Rows. Hooper lingers on the moment, first showing her arm being flattened, followed by an overhead shot of her halfway into the now-blood-soaked machine. As she is drawn in, blood sprays over the workers trying to help her, while her screams, and those of her coworkers, are joined by the sound of bones crunching and the rhythmic chopping sound of the Mangler itself. When the detective John Hunton visits the laundry, Hooper presents a series of close-up flashes of her mutilated body.

The fact that this is the opening of the film is significant. The gory demises of Micah and the rat/bat in *Children of the Corn II* and *Graveyard Shift* are reserved for the end of the films, the stories building up to this final cathartic scene of the destruction of the monster. In *The Mangler*, such violence is presented right at the outset and directed toward a perfectly innocent laundry worker, implying that there's more to come. The violence of this scene is indeed replicated and built upon later: first, when laundry owner Bill Gartley's protégé Lin Sue is sucked into the machine to be presented at the other end as just a face surrounded by a mass of bloody pulped flesh and then, when Gartley is knocked onto the machine and folded in three from the feet up.

The film was a disaster in cinemas, taking in a little more than $1 million at the US box office and disappearing after only a week, but, as John Kenneth Muir has pointed out, 1995 was "a terrible year for horror. The genre had hit hard times" (2005, 46). Hooper was not the only legendary horror director who failed that year. John Carpenter also struggled with *In the Mouth of Madness*, as did Wes Craven with *Vampire in Brooklyn*. Instead, the breakout hit of 1995 was David Fincher's *Se7en*, a dark brooding tale that, in keeping with the legacy of *Silence of the Lambs*, combined horror with an urban noir aesthetic and the narrative of a police procedural. It was therefore far more in keeping with the kind of hybridized mainstream direction that horror films, like those adapted from King's work, were taking at that time. While the various deadly sin-inspired deaths in *Se7en* are conceptually disturbing—as, for example, that of "Sloth," who is tied to a bed for an entire year—Fincher leaves the body horror mainly to the imagination. He does this either by having detectives Mills and Somerset narrate what actually happened, as in the case of Gluttony who is force-fed until he bursts, or by implying what happened, as in the case of Lust, where all that is seen is a photo of a razor-sharp strap-on and the trauma of the man forced to wear it during fatal intercourse. Although the huge and horrifically distorted body of the gluttony victim (created by Rob Bottin, who did the creature effects in *The Thing*) is seen both in the gothic confines of his dingy apartment and on a table under fluorescent lights in the coroner's lab, what is not shown are the events that killed him. Equally, at the end of the film, the audience is presented not with the sight of the head of the wife of Detective Mills in a cardboard box, but rather with Mills's reaction. *Se7en* is psychological, rather than visceral, horror, while, in contrast, *The Mangler*, for all its brooding and effective set design, had, as David Sterritt points out, "a propensity for gratuitous gore" that put "the picture way off limits for the squeamish" (1995, 14).

However, although *The Mangler* was too gory for mainstream cinema audiences, as John Kenneth Muir notes, the film was subsequently released in the United States on VHS and laserdisc in an Unrated director's cut, which, in fact, added gore, notably by extending the aforementioned initial scene in which the female worker is drawn into the machine, as well as Gartley's demise. Muir states that "it was in this secondary format that the film began to gain some adherents" (2002, 44), and this was evidently the intended strategy from the outset, with Hooper noting before the cinematic release that for horror fans "there will be the director's cut to contend with" (Shapiro 1995, 22). The draw of the grouping of Hooper, King, and Robert Englund, the cult star of *A Nightmare on Elm Street* (plus Ted Levine, who played serial killer Buffalo Bill in *Silence of the Lambs*) clearly had purchase among horror fans, and the release of the film as Hooper's own cut, replete with violence removed for cinemas, tapped into the home horror market. On one hand, it had the stamp of an authorial voice and authenticity that drew on the kind of prestige packaging of titles pioneered by Criterion on laserdisc, while on the other hand, it also offered the extra material deemed too "extreme" for mainstream cinema audiences.

Mark Bernard argues that when New Line Home Video, which released *The Mangler*, announced in 1990 an Unrated version of *A Nightmare on Elm Street 5: The Dream Child*, it marked "a major step towards the mainstream distribution of 'Unrated' exploitation films" (2015, 84). While, as noted above, the original *Nightmare* was both a mainstream horror film and a notable VHS success story, by the late 1980s, the franchise had reached a saturation point. The decision to release an Unrated version of the fifth film in the series therefore represented "an attempt to cultivate a new avenue of revenue" by tapping into "fan viewers . . . who were demanding more gore" (84–85). Following its own example, by repackaging *The Mangler* in terms of both authorial authenticity and extended violence, New Line was able to build a following for the film among horror fans in both home rental and sales, despite its box-office failure in a version for mainstream cinema audiences.

DISTINCTION AND DILUTION:
THE LOW-BUDGET BRAND STEPHEN KING

As a result of the extended life of *The Mangler* among horror fans on home-viewing formats, Barry Barnholtz produced a sequel, *The Mangler 2* (2002), released directly to DVD. Not only did the film bear no credit linking the film to King, but it also bore no relation to King's original premise or to Hooper's film. Instead, ironically considering Hooper's promise to King not to turn *The Mangler* into a virtual reality machine, it drew heavily on *The Lawnmower Man* in presenting a virtual cautionary tale in which a state-of-the-art security system in a prestigious high school is infected with a computer virus known as "The Mangler." The virus proceeds to kill the small group of student prefects and staff who remain at the school after the rest of the pupils have gone on a school trip.

The Mangler 2 was followed in 2005 by *The Mangler Reborn*, again produced by Barnholtz. This sequel links back to the original in a minimal fashion with old news clippings about the Blue Ribbon Laundry appearing under the opening credits. Washing machine repairman Hadley has purchased parts of the original Mangler and is putting it back together. The machine turns him into a zombie, and he is forced to feed it a regular supply of bodies in order to keep himself from decaying.

While *The Mangler 2* attempted a level of genre viability by casting Lance Henriksen from *Aliens* (1986) and *Near Dark* (1987) in the role of the school principal, both films, lacking any reference to King in either the credits or promotional material, were clearly drawing upon the same kind of title awareness that categorized the *Children of the Corn* franchise. Furthermore, both were low budget, to the extent that while the first sequel at least appears to have some sort of money behind it, *The Mangler Reborn* takes place almost entirely in a largely empty house and was reputedly made for as little as $85,000 (Von Doviak 2014, 293).

Both *The Mangler 2* and *The Mangler Reborn* represent a dilution of the cinematic Brand Stephen King. Hooper's film, for all its flaws, is well designed and executed as a horror film. Without a doubt, it is the goriest film to be produced from a King story. As such, in many ways, *The Mangler* represents the apotheosis of this particular type of low-budget King film, totally distinct from the bigger-budget mainstream product and, through the Unrated edition, aimed more at horror fans watching at home than multiplex cinemagoers. In contrast, while there are some imaginative death scenes in *The Mangler 2*—for example, a teacher's hair is caught in a (much smaller) mangler in the laundry room and a pupil is burned to death by scalding water—here, the violence is by comparison more implicit. Meanwhile, in *The Mangler Reborn*, aside from a brief sequence in which someone is fed to the machine, much of the violence is bloodless, with Hadley occasionally hitting someone over the head with a mallet. In practical terms, *The Mangler 2* draws upon the premise of *The Lawnmower Man*, while *The Mangler Reborn*, lacking even the tenuous genre links of an actor like Lance Henriksen, is a frankly witless piece, its ties to *The Mangler* name being its sole appeal.

Thus, *The Mangler* franchise exhibited a shift from a King-branded product, aligned also with the appeal of Hooper as director and Englund as star, toward a film the sole selling point of which is the title. The *Children of the Corn* franchise occasionally returned to King's original story and all the films are based on the premise of murderous religious rural children, and are thus at least connected to King. *The Mangler* sequels, however, are not.

A similar dilution can be found in the sequels to the TV movie based on King's short story "Sometimes They Come Back." The original, *Sometimes They Come Back* (1991), tells the story of Jim Norman, who returns to his home town to teach high school, having left as a child in the 1950s after his brother, Wayne, is killed by a gang of greasers, who shortly after are themselves killed. Jim's students start dying and are replaced by the greasers, returned from the grave to kill Jim and save themselves from hell. Like *The Mangler 2* and *The Mangler Reborn*, the first sequel, *Sometimes They Come Back . . . Again* (1996), was released directly to DVD and was also produced by Barry Barnholtz. It broadly retained the same idea as the first film, reworking some of the elements to keep it fresh. For instance, in the sequel, it is the protagonist's sister who is killed, rather than a brother. The second sequel, *Sometimes They Come Back . . . for More* (1998), like *The Mangler 2* and *The Mangler Reborn*, abandons King's premise entirely and tells the story of two immortal brothers, both sons of Satan, battling in the Arctic as one attempts to perform a ritual to raise their father.

There are a number of common factors to these franchise properties. The first is that they are low budget and designed to make their money back primarily or exclusively on home-viewing formats. The second is that they tend to be structured along slasher film lines and are punctuated by regular death scenes, which tend to be explicit—although not as much as those in *The Mangler* or *Graveyard Shift*. They use special makeup effects to present stabbings and burnings (*Children of the Corn III: Urban Harvest*), someone being cut to death by flying tarot cards (*Sometimes They Come Back . . . Again*) or having a huge scythe thrust through the back of one's head (*Children of the Corn IV: The Gathering*). The third common factor is that, with the exception of the original films in the franchise, they are relying on a familiar title to make them stand out on VHS/DVD rental and retail shelves.

In this respect, these franchises represent a contrast to the mainstream cinematic Brand Stephen King that downplays gore, is largely serious in tone, and builds story events around ordinary people with whom the audience can identify. In the franchise films, the characters tend to be ciphers, quick and easily identifiable types that fulfill their narrative function and then leave, die, or survive. The priest in *Children of the Corn: Genesis*, for example, has two functions. His small narrative purpose is to appear at an opportune moment to give the heroine some key information about her grandmother, the haunted apartment block in which she lives, and the relationship of both to He Who Walks Behind the Rows. Far more important is that the character provides an appearance for Michael Ironside, who played the head-exploding Darryl Revok in David Cronenberg's *Scanners* and thus brings an element of genre familiarity and commercial appeal to the project. This is also the main purpose of Lance Henriksen's appearance in *The Mangler 2*. In the *Children of the Corn* films, the younger cast members are creepy children, creepy children fodder, or the hero/heroine. A similar situation is in place in *The Man-*

gler 2, where the young cast members are there either to die or, in the case of the final girl, to survive. Rather than the narrative revolving around characters with psychological depth in real situations, these films echo the conventions of the slasher film, where the emphasis shifts to the story, with both protagonists and locations doing only what is necessary to advance the sequence of events toward the regular death scenes.

This is in direct opposition to King's own literary intentions. Discussing character in *On Writing*, King writes, "What happens to characters as a story progresses depends solely on what I discover about them as I go along—how they grow . . . . The best stories always end up being about people rather than the event, which is to say character-driven" (2000b, 151). In the *Night Shift* stories "Graveyard Shift," the original "Children of the Corn," and "The Mangler," characters draw in the reader by having the first words include the central character's name. Thus, "The Mangler" begins with "Officer Hunton got to the laundry just as the ambulance was leaving" (1978, 76); "Children of the Corn" with "Burt turned on the radio too loud" (237); and "Graveyard Shift" with "Two a.m. Friday. Hall was sitting on the bench by the elevator" (36). Similarly, in the original film of *Children of the Corn*, despite its difference from King's story, the characters of Burt and Vicky drive the narrative as they uncover the events that have taken place in Gatlin, while in *The Mangler*, the action unfolds through Ted Levine's Hunton and his concern for Gartley's niece Sherry. In "Graveyard Shift," the driver is the source of the underlying tension between Warwick, the foreman, and the drifter, Hall. In contrast, in *The Mangler 2*, although disgruntled teenager Jo is given a workaholic father to justify her uploading The Mangler virus into the school security system, all the other characters are there to be killed by the machine, much in the same way that most of the characters are there to be butchered by the children in the *Corn* franchise films. The movement from King as the selling point toward the title awareness of the franchise sees the engine that drives the story shift away from characters toward events embedded in and implied by the titles themselves. The result is that in contrast to the films discussed in the previous two chapters, these franchise properties primarily focus on the monstrous, the violent, and the supernatural—be it the children of the corn, The Mangler virus, or resurrected zombie-demon teenagers—and not on the world that is established beforehand.

These films are designed largely to make their money back through first VHS and then DVD rental and sales, with an emphasis on low budgets, event-driven narratives, and regular helpings of gore. Therefore, it is tempting to see them as tied to Jancovich's "authentic" form of horror, a breed apart from the "inauthentic" mainstream cinematic Brand Stephen King, because they do not attempt to mix horror with other conventions that cater to everyday cinemagoing audiences. These films do not emphasize the visual restraint that is an essential marker of the mainstream brand. One can argue that these are therefore films that are not afraid to be horror films, offering the gory thrills and chills wanted by the kind of fans of "authentic" horror discussed by Jancovich. While, as noted, from *Cujo* onward, the makers of the mainstream brand films took pains to distance themselves from general trends in horror cinema, particularly that of stalk and slash, these films happily embrace the conventions of the slasher film and thus connect far more closely with the prevailing trends of the genre.

One could also argue that by clearly marking themselves as horror, they appear to be more in keeping with the horror label that has formed an essential part of King's literary brand since the 1970s. Yet, at the same time, the absence of King's humor, as well as his painstaking focus on the details of everyday life and the development of rounded and identifiable characters, strongly evidences the lack of any sense of his literary style and preoccupations. While they may give audiences more by way of horror, the films sacrifice other elements. Therefore while unlike many of the mainstream adaptations they don't pretend *not* to be horror, they nevertheless fail to capture those hybrid elements that are the marker of King's success.

Emerging during the second wave of King films in the early 1990s, the low-budget films discussed in this chapter offer an alternative to the mainstream cinematic Brand Stephen King that draws upon different aspects of King's literary preoccupations. They represent the cinematic Brand Stephen King as horror exploitation film, aimed toward a subcultural horror fandom seeking a mixture of atmosphere, gore, and special effects, claiming additional legitimacy through the inclusion of genre figures like Hooper, Englund, Dourif, Ted Levine, Rubinstein, and King himself. Yet, as an alternative to the mainstream format of King adaptations, they were not alone. They appeared and developed at the same time as yet another significant type of King adaptation, which would take a very different approach to King's work—this time not in cinemas or VHS/DVD, but on broadcast television.

5 / STEPHEN KING AS TV HORROR

Any discussion of TV horror . . . would be incomplete without consideration of how the adaptation of King's work to television impacts upon our understanding of TV horror.

LORNA JOWETT AND STACEY ABBOTT, *TV HORROR: INVESTIGATING THE DARK SIDE OF THE SMALL SCREEN*

WRITING IN *DANSE MACABRE* IN 1981, KING DECLARED that the production-line nature of television meant that a TV writer had to have "the soul of a drone" and the ability to see writing as being "the mental equivalent of bucking crates of soda onto a Coca-Cola truck" (1981b, 213–214). In other words, writing for TV involved turning out scripts week after week in a production line that stifled creativity. Furthermore, he stated that because in TV "the financial stakes are enormous . . . television has become more and more cautious over the years," with the result that while working in TV, the horror writer is prevented "from bringing all of his or her powers to bear" (213–214). His stance toward television in 1981 may have been due to the failed proposal to turn his short story collection *Night Shift* into a *Twilight Zone*–style anthology series, with King as host, an idea that, as noted in chapter 2, collapsed due to issues with the networks' Standards and Practices. Disillusioned, King turned on TV as a medium for horror, declaring "the history of horror and fantasy on television is a short and tacky one" (239).

Over the years, King changed his view, a process that began after an eleven-year hiatus following the 1979 *Salem's Lot* when King first tentatively, then enthusiastically, embraced television, not only allowing a number of his novels and novellas to be adapted for the medium, but also taking a more active role in many of the projects than he had for the feature films, from writing the scripts to executive producing. Despite ongoing issues with Standards and Practices, TV became a second and, for a time, highly successful home for adaptations of his work, as miniseries, anthologies, TV movies, and long-form dramas.

On the audio commentary of his own adaptation for television of *The Shining* (1997), King comments that "the network giveth and the network taketh away." As mentioned earlier, what the network takes is his ability as a horror writer to bring all his powers to bear. On TV, the violence and the language in his stories has to be toned down in order to meet acceptable criteria for broadcast. However, in King's view, the network compensates by providing the time needed to tell the story and to allow the characters within it to be developed fully and to grow. A second crucial point in King's statement is his highlighting of the fact that it is the *network* that giveth and taketh. With only a few exceptions, such as the adaptation of his novella *Big Driver* (2014) for the cable channel Lifetime and the remake of *Salem's Lot* (2004) and the anthology series *Nightmares and Dreamscapes* (2006) for TNT, until 2015 King worked almost exclusively with major networks, notably CBS and ABC. His argument was that to work with a cable channel "would be like publishing a major novel with a small press. I have nothing at all against either small presses or cable TV, but if I work hard over a long period of time, I'd like a shot at the largest possible audience" (1999b, xii).

Therefore, in keeping with both his writing and the big-budget, studio-based adaptations, the essential aspect of King's TV projects is that they are designed for a mass, mainstream audience. As Jowett and Abbott point out, this presents something of a conundrum since horror is "generally perceived to appeal to a niche market" (2013, 72), yet King's objective on TV is to present his horror tales to as many people as possible in a format that they will enjoy. This chapter will argue that both the gift of time given by the networks and the corresponding restriction of violence have allowed the TV adaptations to tap into the emphasis within the literary brand Stephen King on character development and the establishing of a realistic and relatable world. This approach is a key element in making his work popular with general readers, and part of the initial success of adapting King's work for TV came from the fact that the TV adaptations focus on character and place and thus draw in a large mainstream network audience.

TERROR TELEVISION: CBS AND *SALEM'S LOT*

Indeed, character and time were at the heart of the response to the CBS production of *Salem's Lot*, the first foray of King's work into television. As noted in chapter 2, Warner Bros. optioned the book soon after its publication in 1975 and went through several screenwriters before Richard Kobritz persuaded the studio to let the TV department take it on as a three-hour miniseries (broadcast in two two-hour slots with commercials) and hired Paul Monash to write the screenplay (Earnshaw 2013, 16–18). Not only had Monash produced the adaptation of *Carrie* for the screen, he had also been a producer on the TV soap opera *Peyton Place*. Given King's stated opinion that *Salem's Lot* was Peyton Place with vampires, Monash was the ideal choice (Gagne 1980a, 31).

Tony Magistrale criticizes *Salem's Lot*, arguing that "the strengths of Hooper's film interpretation are unfortunately few" and that it "has not aged well even as a B-grade horror movie" (2003, 182). Magistrale only had access to a copy of the two-hour cut-down European movie version, which may explain his comment that the film "elects to stay within only the most superficial perimeters of the novel's basic plot" and that Tobe Hooper "fails to spend enough time and energy deepening and resolving either the film's plot or the fates of its central protagonists" (181). While the two-hour version sprints through the narrative events and pays scant attention to character, the longer miniseries takes time to develop not only the story's central protagonists but also some of the peripheral characters of the town, albeit not all who appear in King's book. In addition to the novel's principal players, including writer Ben Mears, his girlfriend Susan Norton, young Mark Petrie, teacher Jason Burke, and the vampire familiar Richard Straker, the miniseries also explores the affair between Bonnie Sawyer and real estate agent Larry Crockett—the man who sells a house to Straker and the vampire Kurt Barlow, thus inviting them into the town—and the subsequent revenge of her husband Cully. (In the book, Bonnie's affair is with another character, Cory Bryant.) The miniseries also highlights Constable Parkins Gillespie's investigations into Mears, Barlow, and Straker, all newly arrived in the Lot and therefore figures of suspicion. It also delves into the relationship between town drunk Weasel Phillips and landlady Eva Miller, the jealousy of Susan's ex-boyfriend (renamed Ned Tebbets), and the lonely life of gravedigger Mike Ryerson. Characters from the novel such as Dud Rogers, who lives in the town dump, abused mother Sandy McDougall, and her equally abused son Randy are omitted, while town doctor Jimmy Cody is merged with Susan's selectman father to become the composite character, Dr. Bill Norton. Therefore, while many of the characters in the novel are composited, dispensed with, or reduced in importance, those included in the miniseries (as opposed to the theatrical version) and played by accomplished character actors such as Elisha Cook Jr., Kenneth McMillan, and Geoffrey Lewis, are, in fact, given suitable time for the audience to get to know them.

Magistrale goes on to say that since the production of *Salem's Lot* in 1979, TV has "improved in its production approach to . . . portraying horror in general; and, as a consequence, certain King texts have translated better than others . . . producing quality work that transcends or at least manages better, 'the constraints of television'" (183). With this idea of "the constraints of television," Magistrale draws upon a point made by Michael Collings, who argues that it was these constraints—for example, "prohibitions against overt violence"—that meant that *Salem's Lot* was unable to take "the kind of innovative approach that would have made the film noteworthy against the backdrop of the hundreds of vampire films produced over nearly eight decades" (Collings 2006, 49–50). One of the elements of *Salem's Lot* criticized by Collings for its lack of innovation was the decision to change Barlow from the Dracula-inspired European gentleman of the novel into a mute monster copying the look of Max Schreck's Count Orlok from F. W. Murnau's *Nosferatu* (1922).

For Kobritz, the reason was one of timing. Airing in November 1979, *Salem's Lot* was in production shortly after Louis Jourdan had played the title role in the 1977 BBC *Count Dracula* and at the same time that Frank Langella was appearing in John Badham's film version, released in July 1979. Earlier that same year, in April, George Hamilton had appeared in the comedy *Love at First Bite* (1979), spoofing both Langella (who had played the role on Broadway before recreating it in Badham's film) and Bela Lugosi. In the late 1970s, the predominant cinematic image of the vampire was therefore one of a sophisticated European aristocrat, exactly in keeping with King's take on Barlow. Furthermore, this particular vision of the count was attractive (Jourdan), seductive and romantic (Langella), or parodic (Hamilton), with the result that, in Gregory Waller's words, the aristocratic count had been "defanged" in such a way as to suggest that "the undead pose no threat to the modern world" (1986, 233).

Determined to avoid this depiction, Kobritz argued that there was no advantage in "going back to Frank Langella and George Hamilton where you had that loquacious, smarmy . . . seductive vampire." Instead, he sought to portray the vampire as "the essence of evil" and so he "went back to *Nosferatu*" (Earnshaw 2013, 179). It was not only Collings who criticized Kobritz's choice. King also argued that by going back to Murnau's vision, which itself had recently been reworked on film by Werner Herzog in his own version of *Nosferatu the Vampyre* (1979), Kobritz showed "a certain bankruptcy in originality . . . this is the third time that make up has been used, and I think they could have been more original" (32–33). Yet, for all that Kobritz's decision may have been derivative, neither version of *Nosferatu* would have been as familiar to American audiences in 1979 as Langella's or Hamilton's take on the vampire.

Furthermore, while Collings and King may argue that Kobritz and Hooper's film was not as innovative as it could have been in terms of vampiric representation, Kobritz's intention was clearly to be original in terms of tele-visual style and the representation of TV horror. In hiring Tobe Hooper, Kobritz was seeking a director who "has never directed television" and "who is visual, who knows how to tell it in terms of camera, not in terms of dialogue, or not in terms of conventional camera coverage." Kobritz had two hard-and-fast rules for his directors: "I don't want a zoom lens on that camera . . . and I want to keep that camera moving. That's unfortunately become the way of television, so what I try to do is a small feature" (122–124).

The anti-televisual style insisted upon by Kobritz was not just an affectation. Restricted by Standards and Practices from showing scenes of violence, Kobritz and Hooper sought to use aesthetics to make sure that *Salem's Lot* "deals in scares instead of blood" (132) and envisaged the film as "a relentless mood piece where the threat of violence—rather than a killing every few minutes—sustained terror" (50). This idea of a horror "mood" is in keeping stylistically with the trend of TV horror in the 1970s, a period described by John Kenneth Muir as one in which "terror television truly came into its own" (2001, 1). For Muir, TV horror in the 1970s became more violent and darker in look and tone as "the fun, brightly-colored, action-packed and optimistic TV visions of the 1960s . . . were . . . superseded by violent, dark, grim programming such as *Night Gallery*." Muir argues that this "turn towards darkness" was responding to "a shift in the national mood" as a result of images on TV of Vietnam and civil rights violence, which meant that "for the first time Americans were aware of a darker world, and television reflected this shift in perspective" (2).

Although in the early 1970s standards for the depiction of violence on TV were comparatively relaxed, leading, in the wake of series like *Night Gallery* (1970–1973), to this proliferation of violent scenes and both thematic and aesthetic darkness, Muir claims that "the networks cleaned up their act" (2) with the result that when *Salem's Lot* came to be made, Standards and Practices was taking a tougher line. In deciding to focus upon projecting a darker mood rather than explicit scenes of death, Hooper was the ideal director, having made *The Texas Chainsaw Massacre*, which, as noted in chapter 4, was banned in the United Kingdom because of the whole tone of the film rather than because of specific scenes of violence. For instance, when Pam, one of the group of terrorized teenagers, enters the isolated farmhouse of the cannibalistic family in the film, she finds a dusty room strewn with bones and chicken feathers, in which there is a couch made from a human skeleton, hanging mobiles crafted from hands and skulls, and a live chicken in a cage. The imagery is shocking, but more disturbing than the individual images themselves is the depraved, insane collage they present in a series of distorted close-ups accom-

"A rotting, sick appearance": The Marsten House in Tobe Hooper's Salem's Lot *(1979).*

panied by a screeching and discordant musical score and the relentless frightened clucking of the chicken.

In creating the interior of the Marsten House for *Salem's Lot*, production designer Mort Rabinowitz worked with Hooper to present it as similarly having "a rotting, sick appearance almost as if . . . we were looking into the body, the heart of the vampire" (Earnshaw 2013, 56). With rubbish and feathers everywhere and damp oozing from the walls, the interior of the house represents, as it did in *Chainsaw*, "a house of horrors . . . I don't mean with ghosts and that, I mean the dirtiest, filthiest house you've ever seen" (126). When Susan enters the house, she, like Pam, sees a place that is beyond horrible. While the interior of the Marsten House is not as disturbing as that in *Chainsaw*, nor is it presented in the same way as a series of increasingly uncanny and distressing close-ups, it nevertheless brings the shocking set design and tonal terror of Hooper's film to TV.

Equally eerie are the two memorable sequences where first Ralphie and then Danny Glick appear as vampires floating outside the windows of Danny's room and Mark Petrie's room, respectively. In these sequences, there is no violence to speak of. Ralphie's attack on Danny freeze-frames a split-second before he bites his brother, while Mark repels Danny with a cross. But the floating children and strangely billowing smoke are nevertheless highly effective uncanny moments, as is the sight of vampiric Mike Ryerson, with bright glowing eyes, gently rocking in a chair and hissing at Jason Burke, "I'll see you sleep like the dead teacher." While Collings may consider that *Salem's Lot* lacked innovation in terms of its representation of vampires, tonally it reflected the approach to TV horror in the 1970s outlined by Muir, emphasizing mood, style, and mise-en-scène. This, in turn, led the miniseries to become what writer Paul Monash, according to Kobritz, described as "a benchmark in television horror" (196) that "pushed the boundaries of what was acceptable on television much further than anyone has ever seen" (16).

Right from the outset therefore, the relationship between King and television was important to both parties. It would be another eleven years before his work would again appear on television in the miniseries format, but, ultimately, King's name would, at least through the 1990s, become an annual lynchpin in the TV horror genre in numerous projects, which, like *Salem's Lot*, pushed the boundaries of what was acceptable on network TV.

HORROR FOR THE MASSES:
THE ABC STEPHEN KING MINISERIES

In the late 1980s, ABC and Lorimar Telepictures announced that they would be producing a seven-hour miniseries based on King's 1986 best-seller *IT*, to be directed by George Romero (Wood 1990b, 9). With a first print run in hardcover of 860,000 copies (Collings 1987, 42), *IT* was one of King's biggest-selling novels, spending more than thirty weeks on the *New York Times* best-seller lists between September 1986 and April 1987. It was also his longest novel at that time, which may explain why King sold the rights to ABC for television, rather than for theatrical release. The decision might also be explained by the fact that the rights were sold during the fallow period for King horror adaptations, after *Maximum Overdrive* and before the success of *Pet Sematary*. During this period, Glenn Lovell stated that "King's stock in Hollywood is down. His name no longer assures box office success" (Herron 1988, 224). King dourly noted that he was not optimistic about *IT* ever making it to the screen, saying in an interview in 1989 that "ABC is one of the networks that still has a fairly strong censorship code . . . I thought when they offered to buy it, 'This will probably never get made'" (Von Doviak 2014, 231). It certainly did not get made by Romero, who left the project and was replaced by Tommy Lee Wallace, who had directed *Halloween III: Season of the Witch* (1982), and several episodes of the revived *Twilight Zone* TV series for CBS (Wood 1990b, 9).

Wallace took over a script that had been written by Lawrence D. Cohen, who had adapted *Carrie* for De Palma. Cohen simplified the complex structure of King's novel, which tells the story of the Losers Club, a group of children in the Maine town of Derry who, in 1958, face and defeat an amorphous evil force, known only as "IT," that lurks beneath the town and preys on children. IT has been hidden beneath Derry for centuries, emerging every twenty-seven years or so to feed. The entity has gradually poisoned the town, so that the adults who live there are incapable of seeing the suffering of their kids. The unfolding narrative is interspersed with a contemporary story set in 1985, in which IT rises once more and now adult members of the Losers Club must return to Derry to face IT again and fulfill a promise they made in 1958. While King's book shifts back and forth between the action in the 1950s and that of the 1980s, Cohen reworked the story for the miniseries, cut down to four hours in two parts, so that the first night focused on the 1950s, while at the same time bringing the adults together in the 1980s. The second part dealt with the confrontation between IT and the adults in the present day.

In addition to the restructuring, Cohen also changed the nature of IT itself, a decision not dissimilar to that of Kobritz in relation to the vampire Barlow in *Salem's Lot*. In the novel, IT appears in various guises, drawing upon the fears of the children of the Losers Club. To Ben Hanscom, IT appears as Boris Karloff in *The Mummy* (1932), to Eddie Kaspbrak as the Creature from the Black Lagoon and as a leper, to Mike Hanlon as a monstrous bird, and to Richie Tozier as the werewolf from *I Was a Teenage Werewolf* (1957). Cohen instead presents IT in a more consistent form, adopting the first and principal face that IT wears in King's book, that of Pennywise the Dancing Clown. Unlike the novel, which opens in 1958 with the death of Bill Denbrough's brother George at the hands of Pennywise, the series first glimpses the clown in the present, hiding behind sheets drying on a clothesline. A girl on a tricycle sees a smiling clown who greets her with a friendly "Hi!" The sequence then goes into slow motion and the smile fades on the little girl's face as she sees the clown again, this time looking threatening. The scene then cuts to a point-of-view shot from the clown's perspective, pushing through the sheets toward the girl with a roar as the screen fades to black. Mike Hanlon, the one member of the Losers Club to stay in Derry, visits the scene of the girl's disappearance, finds George's picture, and calls Bill, who then remembers his brother, prompting the first flashback to 1958 and the catalyst for the story, George's death.

George's murder plays out similarly in both the book and the miniseries, but with crucial differences. His paper boat drops down a storm drain and when he reaches for it, the little boy is surprised to find a clown staring at him from the drain, offering him both his boat and a balloon. After some banter in which George tells the clown he is not supposed to talk to strangers, Pennywise side-steps the prohibition by introducing himself. George reaches for his boat, and as King describes in the novel:

> the clown seized his arm. And George saw the clown's face change. What he saw then was terrible enough to make his worst imaginings of the thing in the cellar [George is scared of the cellar, to which he had to go to fetch paraffin to seal the paper boat] look like sweet dreams; what he saw destroyed his sanity in one clawing stroke. . . . George craned his neck away from that final blackness and began to scream into the rain, to scream mindlessly . . . . The left side of George's slicker was now bright red. Blood flowed into the stormdrain from the tattered hole where his left arm had been. A knob of bone, horribly bright, peeked through the torn cloth. (1986b, 22)

The miniseries diverges from King's description in two key ways. First, it shows neither the blood nor the white bone sticking out of George's slicker where his arm had once been, leaving the nature of the damage inflicted on George to the imagination. In the case of Pennywise, however, the opposite takes place. King leaves his description of how the clown's face changes deliberately vague, asking the readers to delve into their own imagination to envisage what could make a six-year-old boy lose his sanity in an instant. The miniseries instead offers a specific image of Pennywise's face first contorting in anger as he says his signature line, "You'll float, too!" and then transforming in a close-up that highlights a row of razor-sharp fangs. His face moves forward as if to bite the camera before a freeze-frame that then dissolves to an image of George's coffin.

As played by Tim Curry, Pennywise, with his Brooklyn accent and leering delivery—"Oh, yes, they float, Georgie, they float"—suggests all kinds of potential horrors, both vicious and sexual, but suggest is all he does. The violence that is explicit in King's novel becomes implicit while the distorted face of Pennywise, which is not described in the book, becomes personified in the shape of a scary well-played clown with razor-sharp teeth. When approaching the miniseries, Wallace was certain that the gore would have to be eliminated. He said, "You can imagine that Standards and Practices . . . wants to go light on the gore and rotting flesh, those kind of things" (Wood 1990b, 10). However, one of the long-standing taboos of Standards and Practices, raised in 1979 when CBS adapted *Salem's Lot*, was the issue of placing children in danger. Such endangerment is the premise of the 1950s narrative, and to avoid that would have effectively made King's novel unfilmable for TV. However, as Wallace reported, "In terms of children being in mortal jeop-

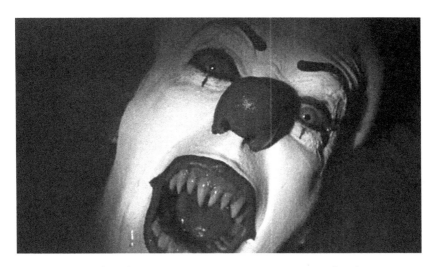

The face of terror: Pennywise the Dancing Clown in IT *(1990).*

ardy, they've been very supportive of the way it's told. After seeing dailies, they've come to have some confidence in the filmmakers" (Wood 1990b, 10).

The implication behind Wallace's account is that when Standards and Practices saw how he was approaching the scenes of children in danger, they agreed to allow the premise of the miniseries to stand. One could imagine, however, that ABC had already agreed to some sort of relaxation of standards in advance, since if Standards and Practices was going to object to such scenes on principle, the entire project would have been scrapped before any money had been spent. Scott Von Doviak suggests that in part this relaxation was due to the great success of the first season of David Lynch and Mark Frost's surrealism-inflected TV drama *Twin Peaks*, which aired on ABC from April to May 1990. He argues that *IT* benefitted from ABC's "deep dive into a pool of weirdness" with a series that "pushed the envelope . . . in its portrayal of graphic violence" (2014, 232). However, certainly in its first season, *Twin Peaks* was not particularly graphic, and, the principal shocking imagery in the series was the frank depiction of the corpse of Laura Palmer, the murdered homecoming queen. Arguably, the most violent moment in the first season is when Agent Cooper pulls a small square of paper, on which is printed the letter *R*, from under the fingernail of Laura's corpse in the morgue. While the representation of forensic body horror in series like *CSI* (2000–2015), *Bones* (2005–2017), and *Dexter* (2006–2013) (see Brown and Abbott 2010) is now commonplace within mainstream TV, the lingering gaze at Laura's body was both challenging and unflinching, pre-dating the extended autopsy sequences in the British crime drama *Prime Suspect* (1991) that Deborah Jermyn suggests "broke new ground . . . in opening up the spaces of the autopsy room and forensic labs" (2010, 74). Similar to *Salem's Lot*, *Twin Peaks* also pushed the envelope in terms of tone—in this case, one of strange surrealism, which lent the entire series an uncanny air that brought both humor and a sense of uncertainty to the action (see Jowett and Abbott 2013, 159–166).

Another key horror element in *Twin Peaks* came in the form of Bob, the supernatural spirit who possesses Laura's father Leland and kills her. Lorna Jowett calls Bob "the spirit of menace," arguing that "his unkempt appearance and grimacing at the camera offers a style of performance in keeping with *Twin Peaks*'s melodrama and excess" (2015, 223). With his long hair, denim-clad frame, and wild eyes, Bob becomes the personification of an uncanny and nebulous evil. Crawling and snarling, he appears sporadically but lurks behind the narrative as a pervasive threatening presence. As Jowett puts it, Bob "gets relatively few minutes of screen time but is extremely memorable" (233), and the same is true for Pennywise in *IT*. In *Twin Peaks*, Sheriff Truman suggests to Agent Cooper that maybe Bob is simply "the evil that men do." Cooper argues against this, but there is no doubt that it is around the figure of Bob that the lurking evil behind the façade of Twin Peaks coalesces. In this respect, Bob is both horrific and comforting: a frightening image of evil, but arguably, as Cooper suggests, in this personified form, evil is far less disturbing than the idea that Leland Palmer raped and murdered his own teenage daughter.

Predating *Twin Peaks*, *Salem's Lot* is a similar mood piece, combining atmosphere with memorable horror set pieces—such as the vampiric Glick boys at the windows—and a visually striking central monster embodying evil in NosferBarlow. *IT* also contains stand-alone horror moments comparable to those in *Salem's Lot*. These include the scene where the adult Losers Club members open fortune cookies to find, among other things, the fetus of a small bird and a staring eyeball. More significant, however, are two scenes involving blood spatter. In 1958, Bev, a member of the Losers Club who lives with her abusive father, looks into her bathroom sink after hearing a child speak to her from the pipe. A balloon emerges from the drain and bursts, showering the sink with blood. Adults in Derry are blind to children's suffering, so Bev's father cannot see the blood. He touches the sink, smearing the blood over his hands before touching—in a way that implies abuse—Bev's shoulder and face. In 1985, another member of the club, Ritchie, upon arriving in Derry as an adult, sees Pennywise in the town library. The clown releases hundreds of balloons, which again burst, showering the unknowing patrons, and a horrified Ritchie, with gore.

Beyond these, and other similar moments, *IT* focuses its scares and horror impact primarily in the figure of Pennywise, rather than developing a mood in the same manner as *Salem's Lot*. The scene of George's death effectively set the template for the way in which the ABC King miniseries would approach the horror of the author's work. Violence, gore, and swearing were removed or reduced, as indeed were the atmospheric tone and gothic visuals that Hooper brought to *Salem's Lot*. In their place was a competent visual style that captured the action. But what was primarily drawn out in these subsequent miniseries were the ongoing narrative events involving a group of well-rounded characters, coupled with a sense of the personification of evil as an elemental force that is seductive without being overtly sexual and powerful without being entirely undefeatable.

ABC aired *IT* during the November sweeps week and it was a resounding success. The first part aired on Sunday, November 18, 1990, and drew more than 17 million viewers with the second part on the following Tuesday drawing 19 million. More importantly, King was happy enough with the result that he agreed to give ABC the opportunity to finally bring *The Stand* to the screen (Von Doviak 2014, 242), the adaptation of which would be the most successful of the ABC miniseries and would draw upon the same conventions as *IT* in terms of visual style, character focus, and a central personification of evil.

In 1990, after years in development at Laurel Productions, with Richard Rubinstein and George Romero struggling to produce either a viable script or financial backing, *The Stand* was back on their roster of upcoming film productions, owing mainly to the fact that *Pet Sematary* had shown that a King project could still find a large audience (Wood 1994, 20). Once again Romero was to direct, but still the long-promised feature film proved problematic. As with *Pet Sematary* and *IT*, Romero left before shooting began, the official reason being "scheduling conflicts" (21). Although King had always been skeptical about the possibility of *The Stand* on TV, arguing that "advertisers don't want to sponsor the end of the world" (20), the success of *IT* made a televisual adaptation viable. Further, Rubinstein was finally convinced that a deal with ABC was worth it to ensure that the project finally got off the ground, saying "it was the choice of a miniseries, not getting the film made at all, or simply struggling for another ten years to find financing" (21).

King decided if it was going to happen, he wanted to take control of the project, arguing that "because the book has always been important to a lot of fans, and because the book has been important to me . . . I thought, if I'm going to do this, let me jump in the whole way. I'll do the script. I'll stick with it down the line. I'll make the revisions . . . I'll executive produce" (Beeler 1994b, 25). Part of that role involved director approval, and with Romero gone, King turned to the director of *Sleepwalkers*, Mick Garris.

With an eye on both attracting a mainstream audience and placating Standards and Practices, Garris and King exercised restraint, particularly in visualizing the apocalypse created by the unleashing of the superflu known as "Captain Trips," which kills most of the world's population. As Michael Beeler notes, "Ultimately, some concessions were made . . . the foul language was toned down considerably and most of the sex, blood and gore was taken off stage. Also, interesting to note, there was a major reduction of snot," because, as King noted dryly, the "Standards and Practices people said, 'there's a lot of mucus in this book'" (26). King describes the terminally ill soldier Charles Campion upon his arrival at Hap's gas station in Arnette, Texas: "His nose was running freely . . . the man on the floor grunted and then began to cough, racking chainlike explosions that sent heavy mucus spraying from his mouth in long and ropy splatters" (King 1978, 9). His wife and child are already dead, "their necks had swelled up like inner tubes and the flesh there was a purple-black color, like a bruise . . . Thick mucus had run from their noses and was now clotted there. Flies buzzed around them, lighting in the mucus, crawling in and out of their open mouths" (8). The miniseries conveys the level of Campion's infected lungs by off-camera sound, cutting to a close-up of Gary Sinise's Stu Redman watching as the dying man noisily coughs up phlegm. The camera also offers only a glimpse in silhouette of the wife and child, shooting through the dark car so that the focus of the shot is on one of Hap's buddies looking through the window and turning away to retch.

As with the opening of *IT*, the explicit detail is gone, but through the use of sound and the actors' performances, the implication still remains for the audience to imagine. Also in keeping with *IT*, the presentation of supernatural horror in *The Stand* coalesces around a single adversarial figure—in this case, Randall Flagg, the "walkin' dude," King's version of the devil or evil personified, played by Jamey Sheridan. In the novel, Flagg's face, like that of Pennywise, is kept deliberately vague, described by King merely as dark and grinning, and the miniseries begins with a similar representation. Flagg is first glimpsed in a vision that deaf mute Nick Andros has of Mother Abigail, the kindly old woman to whom the good survivors flock. Backlit, Flagg appears standing in silhouette in Mother Abigail's cornfield, eyes and mouth glowing red. His next appearance is on the road in Arizona in a sequence that hides his face but hints at his identity. In his cowboy boots, blue jeans, and denim jacket, he kills a deer with a gesture. The sequence is intercut with that of a doomsday preacher in New York City, warning people that the "Dark Man" is closer now. Across the miles, Flagg hears the preacher, now saying, "He's here, the monster's here, the Dark Man's here," and with a flash of his red eyes, he stops the preacher's heart, the series cutting back to New York where the preacher sinks to the ground. When Flagg is finally seen, releasing imprisoned criminal Lloyd Henreid, who will become his right-hand man, Sheridan plays up the grin that King describes, projecting Flagg as having a mischievous gleam in his eye and an unshakeable confidence in his power.

With Flagg positioned as the bogeyman, Captain Trips is portrayed less as a horror destroying the world and more as a disease destroying people. Part One of the miniseries focuses on the deaths of peripheral characters who are important to the main players, including Fran Goldsmith's father, Larry Underwood's mother, and Stu's friends from Hap's gas station. Rather than showing rotting corpses clogging the streets as King describes in the novel, the miniseries depicts the horror of the outbreak through seeing recognizable individuals die. It also comes through the imposition of martial law by the state, including sealing off Arnette. This is coordinated by General Starkey. Following King's novel, Starkey is holed up in a control room, gradually going mad, in part because of his obsession with the image on a monitor of a quarantined dead lab technician with his face in a bowl of soup. In keeping with the concept of depicting unimaginable global destruction through the personal, Starkey, as played by the instantly recognizable Ed Harris, is the image of the powerless US government, his inability to prevent an unprecedented loss of life encapsulated in his frustrated desire to simply lift that technician's head out of his congealing lunch.

Apocalyptic loss of life is dealt with through personal character tragedy, but, as with *IT*, the true evil horror of the piece is embodied in the image of a sole perpetrator, who is ultimately defeated. As the series develops over four parts, Flagg is increasingly human in his personification, becoming a kind of corrupt mob boss, relaxing in a luxurious penthouse as the bad people who have flocked to him create chaos in Las Vegas. By the finale, he is further reduced to a Vegas showman, performing light-show magic tricks before crowds in the streets, but powerless to stop both the crazed pyromaniac Trashcan Man from bringing an A-bomb into the city and Mother Abigail from manifesting as a Hand of God that sets the bomb off. As soon as Trash reveals what he has brought, half of Flagg's followers run for the hills, leaving him on stage weakly protesting, "Come back. Come back, you cowards." Through this focus on Flagg as a powerful but fallible evil, the horror of the apocalyptic premise of *The Stand* is somewhat muted. Although most of the people in the world die at the start of the miniseries, by the end, the main evil of the story is just a conjuror with a bad hairdo who is easily defeated. Likewise, while Derry at the end of *IT* may still be full of adults who beat their children or are indifferent to the suffering of young people, the spider that personifies IT's evil is vanquished. The most conceptually disturbing elements are reduced in favor of a simpler and more resolvable conflict between good people and a bad force, an idea that draws on King's literary brand.

Yet, these conflicts are presented as horror. NosferBarlow and the floating Glick boys are genuinely chilling, just as are Pennywise and Randall Flagg with his scarecrow face, glowing eyes, and confident grin. It is true that *The Stand* does not encourage the viewer to imagine the stench of millions of rotting bodies in the way Hooper suggests we consider the smell of the feather-strewn interior of the Marsten House, but what these adaptations have in common is that they present, as King's novels do, decent ordinary folk first threatened by, and then overcoming, a malevolent force.

In this respect, what seems to be so successful about these ABC adaptations, in terms of both attracting and sustaining audiences, is that they tap precisely into those aspects of King's writing that, as I argue in chapter 1, make his work so successful. Horror is depicted less as stand-alone visuals and more through the viewpoint of characters whom the audience comes to know through the extended length of the miniseries and with whom they can come to identify. This, in turn, allows for the development of the human drama within the natural world, an essential aspect of King's appeal, meaning the monster is not so much a threat to the audience as it is a threat to the characters about whom the audience cares. The ABC miniseries were able to capture that element of King's writing. As Randall Larsen notes, "by spending a little more time with his characters we get to know more about them and, consequently, care more for them. As a result the horrors they face become more real" (1985, 103–104).

The same holds true for King's only original screenplay for ABC, *Storm of the Century*, broadcast in 1999. Once again, a small community—this time, that of Little Tall Island off the coast of Maine—is terrorized by an implacable and malevolent force in the form of Andre Linoge (his surname is an anagram of legion). Linoge has the power to see the sins of the townsfolk, turn them against one another, and drive them to suicide by appearing in their dreams. He finally reveals that what he wants is one of their children to be his heir, and if the townspeople don't supply one, he will make them walk into the sea. As played by Colm Feore, Linoge is, like Randall Flagg, seen on occasion in a monstrous guise (either with glowing red eyes or as a haggard old man of unimaginable age), but more often in human form, sitting implacably in his jail cell like Hannibal Lecter in *Silence of the Lambs*. When he first appears, he walks up to the home of elderly Martha Clarendon and as she opens the door, he spouts crazy catchphrases ("Born in sin. Come on in!") before killing her with his cane and sitting down to drink her tea. It is only in his second appearance, still sitting in Martha's chair, that his supernatural nature is exposed, as he opens his eyes to reveal they are completely black. This is intercut with scenes establishing both the pleasantness of the community and the stolid main character, Constable Mike Anderson (Tim Daly), as he is called to the local daycare center to help a child with her head stuck in the bannisters. Shown to be both supernatural and monstrous, Linoge is presented as an uncanny threat, an enigmatic outsider who *knows* things about people and wants something but won't tell them what. When his need is revealed, the horror of the story comes from presenting the townspeople's appalling response to the terrible choice they have to make. This community of people, whom the audience have come to know and with whom they have been encouraged to identify, actually agrees to allow him to take a child.

Such thematic consistencies are also visible in *The Tommyknockers*, which was aired by ABC between *IT* and *The Stand*. After *IT*, ABC wanted *The Stand* for the May sweeps in 1993, but it was unlikely to be ready, so the network instead rushed *The Tommyknockers* into production. Like *Storm of the Century*, *The Tommyknockers* tells the story of a Maine community, Haven, being threatened and torn apart. This time, though, the people are possessed by a power emanating from a buried alien spacecraft uncovered by local writer Bobbi Anderson. Science fiction rather than horror, *The Tommyknockers* is King's homage to Jack Finney's *The Body Snatchers* by way of *Salem's Lot*. Once again, a dark force gradually warps and amplifies the sins of the townsfolk and must be resisted by a damaged hero. Unlike Ben Mears in *Salem's Lot*, traumatized by childhood memories, Jim "Gard" Gardner, Bobbi's partner in *The Tommyknockers*, is, like Jack Torrance in *The Shining*, a recovering alcoholic, an alter-ego for King, who, in 1987 when the book was written, was at the height of his addictions (Rogak 2009, 154–155). Not only was the lead character an addict, but also the entire novel becomes a metaphor for addiction as the townspeople become increasingly enamored of the power they draw from the spaceship—the ability, for example, to make all kinds of new technological devices—despite the visible way in which it ravages their bodies, such as making their teeth fall out.

For the adaptation, ABC turned again to Lawrence D. Cohen, who once more reduced some of the darker imagery of King's book. For instance, in the novel, when Gardner goes into Bobbi's shed and finds it full of alien technology, King highlights his discovery that Bobbi's beloved dog, Peter, is not dead, as he thought, but has in fact been turned into a living battery.

Peter had somehow been hung up on posts in two old galvanized steel shower cabinets . . . the entire top of the dog's skull had been peeled away; dozens of . . . cords ran out of Peter's exposed and pulsing brain. Peter's eyes, free of cataracts, turned towards Gard. He whined . . . Peter's fur had fallen out in patches. His hindquarters appeared to be collapsing in on themselves. His legs moved through the liquid in long lazy sweeps, as if in his dreams he was running away. (1987, 423–424)

In the miniseries, Peter is still hooked up as a battery, but his skull has not been exposed, and while his legs are moving dreamily, the physical damage that King describes is not seen. Whereas in the novel Gard, after killing Bobbi, puts Peter out of his misery by setting fire to the shed and burning him alive, in the miniseries, Gard is able to appeal to the last spark of Bobbi left in her possessed body and brings her humanity back. At that point, she runs to the shed and rescues Peter, while Gard pilots the spaceship away from Haven. In the TV version, this results in all the townsfolk being cured, whereas in the novel, they all die. The majority perish in a huge forest fire caused by Gard piloting the Tommyknockers' spaceship out of the ground. Of those left, some kill themselves, while others are killed by the army. The remainder, now mad, are taken for study by The Shop, where they too die. It is a very bleak ending for a writer in whose tales good normally triumphs over evil.

Cohen therefore stripped away not just the physical torture of Peter, but also other things, such as Gard's copious nosebleeds and his violent tendencies when he drinks. In addition, Cohen removed the nihilism of the novel, in which addiction is insurmountable and punishable by death. What is left is the core premise, as well as many of the incidents and characters of the novel, which come together to tell a tale, like *Salem's Lot* and *Storm of the Century*, of a town taken over by a malevolent force. In *IT*, *The Tommyknockers*, and, indeed, *The Stand*, this force is ultimately defeated by the actions of either an individual or a group of particularly brave souls. In *Storm of the Century*, the force wins, while the ending of *Salem's Lot* is more ambiguous. Ben and Mark Petrie kill Barlow and set fire to the town, destroying, it is suggested, most of the vampires. They are, however, still on the run at the end, found in Mexico by a vampiric Susan Norton, whom they stake before moving on because, as Ben says, "there'll be others."

What *The Tommyknockers* miniseries lacks, in comparison with *Salem's Lot* and particularly *IT*, is a central personified figure of evil, the aliens only appearing at the very end. Instead, *The Tommyknockers* focuses upon the characters of Haven, from vampy post office worker Nancy Voss, to parents Bryant and Marie Brown, whose son Davey is inadvertently sent to the Tommyknockers' home planet by his older brother Hilley. The miniseries presents the townspeople's gradual dehumanization through the eyes of those who resist, like Gard, Hilley's grandfather Ev, and Sheriff Merrill, who are puzzled by Bryant and Marie caring less and less about their missing boy. To this, director John Power adds atmosphere by using the uncanny green glow of the Tommyknockers' power, contrasting it with the bright daytime scenes of the town. Gradually, through the proliferation of the green-light spouting inventions and the increasingly pallid and ill-looking townsfolk, the visuals become progressively sickly and strange, reaching their height of brightness and horror in the green luminescence of the interior of the shed and the revelation of the alien power source.

King was more ambivalent about *The Tommyknockers* than he was about *IT*, declaring it to be "adequate" and saying, "I liked *The Tommyknockers* a little bit less . . . . But I thought they did a pretty decent job with a book that wasn't top drawer to begin with" (Beeler 1994b, 26). The miniseries was, however, a ratings winner. The *Los Angeles Times* reported that the first part was ranked fourth for primetime viewing in the May sweeps (Margulies 1993). This is despite the fact that it softened aspects of King's novel, was science fiction rather than horror, was based on a novel generally considered to be one of his weakest, and was broadcast only a month after *The Dark Half* flopped in cinemas across the United States, a sign, as discussed in chapter 3, that the King renaissance in cinemas launched by *Pet Sematary* was on the wane.

In cinemas, 1994 saw only the release of *The Shawshank Redemption*, which was neither branded a Stephen King project nor successful at the box office. In contrast, on TV, the King-branded *The Stand* was an even bigger hit than *IT* or *The Tommyknockers* for ABC, with all four parts broadcast in a single week on Sunday, Monday, Wednesday, and Thursday, each achieving around 19 million viewers and dominating the Nielsen ratings. This made *The Stand* the highest-rated miniseries on ABC since *North and South, Book II* in 1986 (Margulies 1994). As Mick Garris later joked, "It's great having the most successful miniseries of the last dozen years or so. In 1994, after the Oscars, the top four rated shows on television were *The Stand, The Stand, The Stand*, and *The Stand*" (Szebin 1997a, 20). It was sold on King's name and the associated event status of a sweeps weeks ABC King miniseries and, as producer Richard Rubinstein suggested, the long road to its final emergence also allowed for the build up of a huge potential audience. "I think," he said, "the book has had its fans consistently since it was first published in 1978. . . . It was Steve's best-selling backlist book in all the years between the first edition and the republishing in '89 of the second. I think it's cumulatively his best-selling book of all time and that's what's driving this film" (Beeler 1994a, 8). In 1994, after a decline in cinemas and growth on TV, the visual Stephen King brand had redefined its success in terms of the miniseries.

THE ABC KING MINISERIES IN DECLINE

The ABC follow-up to *The Stand* in May 1995 was a much smaller affair. *The Langoliers* was a two-part adaptation of his novella from the 1990 collection *Four Past Midnight*. Although less well known as a story than *IT* and *The Stand*, and arguably less so than *The Tommyknockers*, *The Langoliers*, Parts

One and Two, still ranked fourth for their respective weeks, drawing upward of 17 million viewers (Von Doviak 2014, 248). With such consistent numbers, King was offered by ABC the chance to do whatever he wanted, and so he took the opportunity to re-adapt *The Shining*, this time his way. ABC apparently paid Kubrick, who owned both sequel and remake rights, a large sum of money to proceed, and Kubrick also insisted that King stop complaining about his film, which he dutifully did until Kubrick's death (Von Doviak 2014, 296). So *The Shining* proceeded with King in full creative control, not only writing the script but also getting Mick Garris to direct.

The miniseries returned to King's novel and reinstated many of the things that, to King's dismay, had been removed in Kubrick's version, including the moving topiary animals, Jack's obsession with the historical news clippings about the Overlook in the basement, and the creeping boiler pressure that ultimately destroys the hotel. Most importantly, King reworked the characters of Jack and Wendy Torrance to his original conception. As played by Rebecca De Mornay, Wendy is a strong and independent woman, more than capable of standing up to Jack, contrasting with Shelley Duvall's more helpless and hysterical interpretation of the role. Most significantly, Stephen Weber's Jack is, in contrast to Nicholson's characterization, a fundamentally decent man who is corrupted by both the hotel and by his alcohol addiction. As adapted by King, *The Shining* is consistent with the ABC Stephen King format, in which horror elements are still important, but less so than the characters and their emotional journeys. As Frederick Szebin points out, "*The Shining* is a character-driven story at its core" in which "carefully chosen special effects . . . enhance the drama of the characters' plight" (1997a, 20). This is especially important in a story where, unlike the sprawling cast of *The Stand*, the majority of the miniseries focuses upon only the three main characters, isolated in the snowbound hotel. King approached the project precisely in this way, saying it was "about a haunted hotel but also a story about a haunted marriage. The two things should work together. The reality of that abusive relationship should enhance and make the ghost story more frightening than it is" (Barron 1997, 18). The slow buildup of the characters pays off in the final sequences where Jack, fully possessed by the hotel, beats Wendy with a roque mallet and then stalks Danny through the halls, telling him he has to "come out and take your medicine." While the ghosts of the Overlook Hotel have come to life by this point, as King envisages it, they are of secondary importance to the emotional impact of Jack's final descent into the abusive husband and father he has struggled not to be.

King was thoroughly involved in the project, even going so far as to publish "Before the Play," a prologue to the novel, in *TV Guide* the week the show aired (1997, 22–25, 49–57). With a strong cast and King's emphatic participation, *The Shining* seemed set to be another winner for ABC, but this did not prove to be the case. Of all the ABC King miniseries, *The Shining* tips the balance between character drama and supernatural horror. While King's novels almost always focus on setting up the reality of the characters and the world in order to draw the audience into the supernatural events as they unfold, the miniseries tend to play up the horror elements from the start: *IT* opens with the attack by Pennywise on the young girl, Part One of *The Stand* focuses on the plague and introduces Flagg, and the citizens of Haven begin to transform early on in *The Tommyknockers*. The opening part of *The Shining*, however, is almost entirely character based—so much so that Garris was uneasy, stating, "*The Shining* is sort of like winding the clock for the first two hours: we're just laying the groundwork for what's to come. It makes me a little nervous to not have as much 'play' in part one . . . part one is definitely the most quiet part" (Szebin 1997b, 29).

The opening Sunday night episode came in fourth after *A Match Made in Heaven*, a TV movie on CBS starring Olympia Dukakis; the first network showing of the movie *The River Wild* (1994), starring Meryl Streep; and *The X-Files* (1993–2002, 2016). ABC was confident that *The Shining*, like the previous King miniseries, would increase the audiences on subsequent nights, and it did on Monday, before the concluding part lost out to *ER* and *Seinfeld* on Thursday (Williams 1997). Arguably, *The Shining* fell between the expectations of the literary brand Stephen King and that of the cinematic/televisual brand. Deliberately faithful to the novel, and with the emphasis on character development before bringing in the horror, *The Shining* delivered more or less exactly what the novel does, but audiences responded less enthusiastically to the shift away from horror toward character drama compared to the other miniseries. In this respect, the branding of King adaptations across both film and TV primarily as horror worked against it. Like *The Tommyknockers*, *The Shining* is predominantly a story about addiction, but whereas in the miniseries of *The Tommyknockers*, this is the subtext to a science-fiction story about alien influences that manifest early in the plot, in King's adaptation of *The Shining*, the supernatural elements of the hotel remain secondary to the marital drama. Furthermore, one could argue that although King wanted to see the novel adapted faithfully, for general audiences the miniseries was more remake than adaptation. While *The Stand* was the long-awaited adaptation of a book that had been read by millions, Kubrick's *The Shining* was already out there for audiences to enjoy, thus making King's version more of a project of niche interest subject to comparisons with a film that, by 1997, was an acknowledged classic.

Storm of the Century fared even worse, garnering lower ratings than any of the previous miniseries and suffering the indignity of having its closing episode broadcast against George Clooney's final appearance on *ER*. ABC's relationship with King continued into the twenty-first century with one original screenplay, *Rose Red* (2002), and *Kingdom Hospital* (2004), King's adaptation of a Danish TV miniseries, *Riget*, produced by Lars von Trier. Neither performed well: *Rose Red* had a strong start, but viewing figures dropped for the subsequent parts, while *Kingdom Hospital* was a disaster, hemorrhaging viewers over the course of its fifteen weeks (Von Doviak 2014, 255, 272). Inspired as much by *Twin Peaks* as von Trier's original, *Kingdom Hospital* was an uneasy mix of drama, humor, and surrealist imagery, opening with the character of Peter Rickman being hit and almost killed—Stephen King style—by a truck and then being visited at the side of the road by a giant talking anteater who claims to be the god Antubis, a guardian of the path between life and death. While the narrative built slowly over the first few episodes, as it had in *The Shining*, audiences evidently lost patience, leaving King to surmise that the reason for what he called "this el floppo" was that "we were asking viewers to give us a week or two, maybe three, and that was more time than most were willing to give" (Von Doviak 2014, 272). King's final project with ABC, a 2006 adaptation of his novel *Desperation*, again directed by Garris, was another ratings failure, not even making the Nielsen top 20 (262).

With the exception of *Desperation*, none of the miniseries that followed *The Shining* were adaptations of a King book and so they lacked the connection to a best-selling novel that had evidently helped acquire huge viewing figures for the likes of *The Stand* and *IT*. Instead, they were sold purely on King's name as the master of horror and there was already evidence that King's name alone, without a corresponding book title, was not a sufficient draw for TV audiences. In 1991, after the success of *IT*, King and CBS worked together on a series called *Stephen King's Golden Years*. This was another original screenplay, drawn from an undeveloped idea for a novel. King was inspired to write the series after seeing the success of *Twin Peaks*. He told the *New York Times* "up until *Twin Peaks* came on . . . the only sort of continuing drama that TV understood was soap opera . . . David Lynch gave them that. But he turned the whole idea . . . inside out like a sock" (Applebome 1991).

Golden Years revolved around a typically ordinary blue-collar King character thrust into extraordinary and unnatural circumstances. Seventy-year-old Harlan Williams, a janitor at a military research lab, is exposed to chemicals that start making him younger. He goes on the run, and while dealing with the consequences of his reversed aging, particularly in regard to his relationship with his wife, is pursued by agents of The Shop.

It was written as a seven-part series, the first five of which were scripted by King, and the finale was left open for a second season. Poor ratings meant that no second season appeared. As a limited series, there was no recognizable slot for the show on CBS. The traditional network model in the early 1990s was for a series to run between twenty-two and twenty-four episodes in order to give the networks "enough content to fill the nine-month season that ran between September and May" and to also hit the spring and autumn sweeps weeks (Adalian 2015). The result was that CBS aired *Golden Years* over the summer, traditionally an off-peak period for TV drama. As a limited series in 1991, *Golden Years* was unable to flourish in what was a largely inflexible network programming structure, a situation not helped by the fact that this was an original story so that the title, despite including King's name, was unfamiliar to audiences.

The lack of an existing best seller, as noted above, also affected the ratings for *Rose Red* and *Kingdom Hospital*. However, another key reason for the decline in audiences for these later post-millennial series was the fact that, as Jowett and Abbott point out, the 1990s in particular saw a "widespread move away from the notion of *broad*casting of programming for the largest audience possible . . . towards *narrow*casting" and the targeting of niche products to specific markets (2013, 6). Networks like Fox, Showtime, the WB, and UPN invested in serial dramas in order to build loyal audiences, and following the global success of *The X-Files*, horror became a key part of this strategy. The WB fostered its audience with Joss Whedon's *Buffy the Vampire Slayer* (1997–2003), at least until the show moved to UPN after season five, and *Buffy* spin-off *Angel* (1999–2004), while Showtime did the same with *Dexter* (see Johnson 2005, 106–107, and Brown 2010, 159–162). These were shows that, similar to King's work, used horror tropes, but in what Matt Hills refers to as a format of "generic and discursive hybridity" designed to appeal to mainstream audiences and "horror/dark fantasy fans" (2005, 126–127). They often contained imagery that was the equal of, or even gorier than, anything to be found in King's made-for-TV work, but these shows presented such visuals within a mixed generic coding. *The X-Files*, for example, was part police procedural drama, part science fiction, and part horror, with conspiracy narratives of alien invasion appearing alongside monsters of the week, such as the legendary deformed and inbred family of the fourth season episode "Home." All of this circled around the heart of the series, which was the developing relationship between the two central protagonists, FBI agents Mulder and Scully. *Buffy* mixed horror with comedy and high-school melodrama, with Buffy and her "Scooby Gang" of fellow vampire hunters battling romantic and coming-of-age issues as often as they did the legions of the undead. *Dexter* embedded hybridity in its very premise about a police blood-spatter analyst who is also a serial killer by night.

In all these shows, the focus was on character rather than on scares, drawing the audiences in as King's miniseries had done, but this time not over two, three, or four nights, but rather over the many weeks and years afforded by multiple seasons. Robin Nelson suggests that these shows were part of a general shift in the 1990s toward the primacy of the long-running series, and this was particularly noticeable within the genre of TV horror (1997). Nelson also suggests that this in turn saw an increasing emphasis on the importance of the writer-producer or showrunner, referred to by Roberta Pearson as "the hyphenate" (2005), particularly in the case of Chris Carter of *The X-Files* and Joss Whedon of *Buffy* and *Angel*, which in turn saw the decline in significance of, in Nelson's words, the "authored, literary tradition of the playwright" (1997, 26). In short, the impetus of the kind of hybrid, character-driven horror stories that King told shifted away from the event TV format of the sweeps miniseries toward the appointment-to-view format of the long-running drama, while the concept of creative authorship moved away from the writer and executive producer toward the creator-writer-director. Far from having the "soul of a drone" and writing scripts like "bucking crates of soda," these creative figures worked with teams of writers to produce ever more intelligent, thoughtful, and complex unfolding dramatic arcs.

This is demonstrated by the fact that in 1997, King provided a script for an episode of *The X-Files*, titled "Chinga" (10:5). At that time, *The X-Files* was at the peak of its success, reaching its highest season average rating of 12.1 (Brown 2013, 13), and so the marriage of Fox's horror hybrid juggernaut and the master of the macabre would have seemed to be ideal. Yet, according to King, when he submitted his script, Carter "came back to me and said, 'This isn't what we wanted'" (Von Doviak 2014, 218). Carter ended up rewriting King's script so that, according to director Kim Manners, "there was very little of Stephen King left in it . . . [it] was really one of Chris's scripts" (Hurwitz and Knowles 2008, 121). King's premise, about an evil doll that possesses the mind of an autistic girl and commits murders remains, but ultimately King was unable to write the established Mulder-Scully voices and Carter reworked his script to such an extent that he and King shared the writing credit.

Less than a year after ABC aired his cherished remake of *The Shining*, King was rewritten by the man who, by 1998, had taken over the mantle of the master of TV horror. This may explain why, in the 2000s, projects sold on King's name alone like *Rose Red* and *Kingdom Hospital* failed to sustain their viewers. In the pre-*X-Files* and -*Buffy* era, the legacy of enormous and beloved best sellers like *IT* and *The Stand* made King a standout horror name on television, but in the mid- to late 1990s Chris Carter, and later Joss Whedon, took his crown. *Buffy*, for example, first aired in March 1997, just a month before *The Shining* and would go on to achieve the status of a "cultural phenomenon that epitomized trends in the production and reception of commercial television" (Levine and Parks 2007, 2).

Both *The X-Files* and *Buffy* embody the movement in TV horror away from adaptations and the miniseries format toward hybridized long-running series led by showrunners rather than writers. Furthermore, both *Buffy* and *The X-Files*, and later *Angel*, pushed the boundaries of what was acceptable on television in terms of horror, and they did so not entirely through explicit imagery—although it was there—but rather by tying violent events to characters. While this reflected what King and ABC had been doing in the miniseries of the 1990s, the level of explicitness was raised along with the level of the character identification, now built up over multiple seasons. In the second season of *Buffy*, the vampire Angel, who is ensouled and with whom Buffy is in love, becomes evil after sleeping with Buffy, the result of a gypsy curse that should he ever know perfect happiness, his soul will be lost. His irredeemable nature is cemented when he kills Jenny Calendar, a regular recurring character and former girlfriend of Buffy's mentor, Rupert Giles ("Passion," 2:17). As Rhonda Wilcox has pointed out, this marked "the first instance of a Whedon trademark, the death of a character in whom the audience is invested" (Wilcox 2012, 103). This was a strategic decision on Whedon's part, first, because "we needed to kill somebody because we needed to tell the audience that not everything is safe," and second, because "we wanted to show that—No, Angel isn't just pretending to be evil" (108). Angel kills Jenny by breaking her neck, and this takes place in shadow with merely the sound of what he does emphasized. The sequence lacks not only prolonged physical violence but also any sense of anticipation, since it occurs quickly and Angel's decision to kill her is almost casually taken. Instead, the episode dwells upon the emotional trauma wrought by Jenny's death, as Giles finds her body laid out on his bed, surrounded by rose petals, with opera playing in the background. Angel taunts Giles with an image of a relationship that can now never be, and the sequence plays out wordlessly, focused on the shock evident on Giles's face, which in turn encourages the audience to address their own reaction to losing someone they cared about without warning. The scene is constructed so that the horror comes out of a sense of identification with the people on screen.

Toward the end of the sixth season, *Buffy* pushed the boundaries even further by having Willow, a principal character, turn evil and murder Warren, leader of a group of three teens known as the "Troika," who has shot her lover, Tara ("Villains," 6:20). Unusually for an antagonist in the series, Warren is not a vampire or demon, but a man. Bound by his arms in a cruciform pose, Willow uses her powers of witchcraft to slowly drive a bullet through Warren's chest, before flaying him alive with a wave of her hand. Cut for syndicated daytime broadcasts, this sequence is explicit but only briefly so, conforming to what Stacey Abbott calls "the glimpse" of body horror, which, she

Warren is flayed alive: A "glimpse" of body-horror
in Buffy the Vampire Slayer *(1997–2003).*

argues, is potentially as disturbing as explicit, lingering horror in the context of prime-time TV, where "we don't expect to see graphic displays" (2009, 54). More importantly, while the quick moment of Warren's demise is viscerally shocking, the sequence is emotionally harrowing, as Willow, one of the most sympathetic characters, crosses the same line that Angel did four years earlier, and it is the emotional impact that lingers far longer than Warren's violent death. As with Jenny Calendar, the power of the moment derives from being seen through the eyes of other characters, as Buffy, with friends Xander and Anya, stares with horror, not at the sight of Warren's body, but at what has become of her friend. "Willow," asks Buffy helplessly, "What did you do?" Later, Willow's witchcraft-fueled rampage reaches the point where she is capable of destroying the world, and it is not through action that she is stopped, but rather through a character moment as childhood friend Xander offers himself in sacrifice and finally allows her to overcome her rage and confront the pain of Tara's loss.

The experiments of *Buffy* in extending the limits of both physical and emotional violence, first on the youth-oriented WB and subsequently on UPN, appeared alongside the rise of largely uncensored television on pay cable channels like HBO and Showtime. Series with strong violence, language, and sexual content like *The Sopranos* (1999–2007) and *Sex and the City* (1998–2004) on HBO paved the way for Showtime to experiment with more extreme horror content by developing, with Mick Garris, the anthology series *Masters of Horror* (2005–2007). An auteur-led show, with episodes directed by horror legends such as John Carpenter, Dario Argento, and Joe Dante, *Masters* brought, as Donato Totaro notes, some of "the most outrageously intense, violent, sexual, controversial and political horror images to television screens" (2010, 87). When it aired in August 2006, *Desperation* looked weak and tame compared to the December 2005 finale of "John Carpenter's Cigarette Burns," from the first season of *Masters of Horror*, which featured an old man feeding his own intestines into a film projector. *Masters of Horror*, followed by series such as *True Blood* (2008–2014), *The Walking Dead*, and *American Horror Story* (2011–), went on to conclusively prove that graphic violence can work on TV. At the same time, series such as *Supernatural* (2005–) combine ever-intensifying character identification with imagery every bit as frightening as Pennywise or Randall Flagg to the younger audiences of the CW network, formed in 2006 by a merger of the WB and UPN, the former homes of *Buffy* and *Angel*.

The result was that from the late 1990s, King's brand of mainstream horror on TV became increasingly outdated, both in terms of the low levels of horror imagery and of the short miniseries format. The element that worked best in King's writing, the creation of relatable characters within a hyper-realistic world into which the supernatural intruded, became part of the lexicon of hybrid horror shows like *Buffy* and *The X-Files* and later in more explicit horror series like *The Walking Dead*, which served up character-driven drama alongside hitherto unforeseeably graphic images of zombie-related death.

Furthermore, *The Walking Dead* is part of a trend within American serial television moving away from the standard 22–24 episode seasons of *Buffy* and *The X-Files* and toward 12–13 episodes or fewer. Led primarily by HBO again with *The Sopranos* and *Sex and the City*, and later *Game of Thrones* (2011–), others quickly adopted the fewer-episode format. While in 1991 a short season for *Golden Years* meant that CBS had to schedule it for the summer because there was nowhere else for it to go, in the new millennia, cable channels, according to Charlie Collier, president of AMC, were "not competing on the same cadence as broadcast with regards to sweeps" so that "length of series was subordinate to putting your programming in . . . a window, no matter what the length, where . . . our storytelling could stand out" (Adalian 2015). The result was the audiences became, according to Josef Adalian, "trained . . . to live with just 13 episodes of their favorite shows" (2015) and this in turn allowed for more consistency of quality, as series had longer lead-in times and less hectic shooting schedules. By the end of the first decade of the twenty-first century, it was common on US television for a season to last thirteen or even ten episodes and for the target audience to loyally tune in weekly on a regular basis. The shorter-run series effectively replaced the miniseries as an alternative format to the traditional twenty-two-episode season just as the niche but loyal viewership replaced the huge viewing figures of the network era as the primary goal of the horror or fantasy series.

FROM MINISERIES TO SERIES: *THE DEAD ZONE* (2002–2007) AND *HAVEN* (2010–2015)

The new format allowed more time than the miniseries for character development, and so it was not surprising that during the course of this shift in broadcast practices, King's work would be adapted for the thirteen-episode format, first in 2002 with *The Dead Zone* on the USA Network (although over the course of its six seasons, the number of episodes ranged from eleven to nineteen per season), then in 2010 with *Haven* on Syfy, and finally on CBS in 2013 with *Under the Dome*.

The Dead Zone billed itself in the opening credits as being "based on characters from the Stephen King novel," and the first episode follows the book, opening with the prologue of Johnny Smith having a vision after hitting his head on the ice while skating. As in the novel, the action then jumps forward twenty years to find Johnny and Sarah Bracknell visiting a fair and Johnny winning at the wheel of fortune. The series downplays the supernatural and horror elements included in both the novel and the Cronenberg film. For example, in the book, in a scene missing from the Cronenberg film, Johnny's win at the wheel is couched in unsettling terms. The events are told largely from Sarah's perspective. She is feeling increasingly ill from eating a bad hotdog, and at one point, she sees Johnny looking ever stranger: "it seemed to her (although it might have been the sickness, which was now rolling through her belly in gripping, peristaltic waves) that his eyes were almost black. Jekyll and Hyde, she thought, and was suddenly, senselessly afraid of him" (1979, 40). In the series, Johnny's success at the wheel, though unusual, is presented simply as a montage of him winning and carries no supernatural overtones. Likewise, his first vision after waking, of the nurse's young child trapped in a burning house, is dramatic rather than disturbing. In contrast to the cold and deadpan delivery of Christopher Walken in the same scene in the film, Anthony Michael Hall shouts to the nurse that it's not too late. Most significantly, in the series, the younger, Vietnamese Dr. Tran replaces Dr. Weizak, and instead of Johnny seeing a vision of Weizak's mother escaping Nazi Germany, he sees Tran's mother during the fall of Saigon, where, it was believed, she was killed. Johnny tells Tran his mother is alive, and this is followed by a scene in which Tran goes to Saigon and is reunited with his mother. The event is updated from World War II to Vietnam so that the action of the series can take place in the present day. More importantly, while Weizak is appalled by Johnny's vision and unable to reconcile with his mother—suggesting that Johnny's vision and the knowledge it brings are painful for Weizak—in the TV series, Johnny's visions are seen as a force for good. Indeed, although in the book, the film, and the series, Johnny is ridiculed and mistrusted, in the series, he is not left alone to deal with his new gift. Instead, he is supported by his physiotherapist, Bruce Lewis, whose optimistic outlook helps prevent Johnny from being isolated and lonely, as he is in both the novel and the film. The shift in tone that Lewis brings is made explicit in the second season episode "Zion" (2:12), where Johnny has a vision of what his life would be like had Lewis not been part of it, and as presented, that life looks remarkably like Johnny's life in the novel and in Cronenberg's film.

Because Johnny is surrounded—as was Buffy—by a support group of other characters, the series, in keeping with the approach of *Buffy*, emphasizes character, and so major narrative events from the novel are reimagined as personal dramas. Sarah is now married to Sheriff Bannerman, and their child is Johnny's child. As in the novel, Bannerman is investigating a series of murders, but in the series, the relationship between Bannerman and Johnny is reworked to be equally personal and professional, their mutual desire to catch the killer existing alongside their rivalry over Sarah, who vacillates between the two men. When Greg Stillson is introduced in the final episode of the first season, he is not just a crazed politician, about whom Johnny happens to hear. Instead, the relationship between them is also personalized. A sequence is added in which Stillson and Johnny meet as children, just a few weeks after Johnny's fall on the ice, and in the present, Stillson is being supported by the Reverend Purdy, Johnny's legal guardian and the man who took care of his mother after his accident. Furthermore, when Johnny wakes from his coma after the car accident, the first thing he says is "something's wrong." At that point, in the first episode, we are led to believe this links to his vision of the nurse's daughter trapped in the flames, but it is revealed in the first season finale that this is the exact moment that Stillson is sworn into office as mayor and it is to this that Johnny refers. Thus, the battle to come between Stillson and Johnny is presented as both personal and predetermined.

The series also moderates other, darker aspects of King's novel and the Cronenberg film. The killer that Johnny and Bannerman investigate is the Bangor Strangler, whose method of killing is less bloody than that of the Castle Rock Killer. When Johnny has a vision of the Strangler in Bannerman's office, there is no sense of the lasting physical or mental torments that the visions exert on him in the film. While he is pained by the experience, he quickly recovers enough to go to dinner with Bannerman and Sarah, where he has another vision, this time of a young boy in the diner having hot coffee spilled on his head, which he is able to avert without discomfort. The Bangor Strangler turns out to be Frank Dodd—the Castle Rock Killer of the novel and film—but this time Dodd shoots himself rather than slitting his throat or impaling himself on scissors ("What It Seems," 1:2). Ultimately, the series draws upon the format of *The X-Files* and *Buffy*, intertwining stand-alone vision-of-the-week episodes with longer arc narratives, such as that of Stillson, all tied together by character drama, such as the love triangle of Johnny, Sarah, and Bannerman (and later Johnny, Sarah, and Stillson). By the end of the second episode, *The Dead Zone* retained little of King's original work beyond the premise, but although the show was cancelled after its sixth season, leaving the narrative unresolved, the very fact that it lasted so long demonstrated that a Stephen King series on TV could be successful.

The Dead Zone had no input from King, nor did the next attempt to craft King's work into a long-running series. Even compared to *The Dead Zone*, *Haven* had a tenuous relationship to its source material, a short book called *The Colorado Kid*. The novel is not supernatural. Two old reporters for the newspaper on a small island off the coast of Maine recount to a young recruit the tale of a body found on the beach in 1980. The dead man has no identification and died from choking on a chunk of fish. A year later, the man is identified as a resident of Colorado, who inexplicably managed to get from his home state to Maine in under five hours. The mystery is never explained. *Haven* took this premise and, rather like *The Lawnmower Man*, fashioned a completely different story around it, one drawing heavily, and self-consciously, on *The X-Files* with its tale of an FBI agent who comes to the town of Haven and finds herself investigating a series of supernatural phenomena. These events, known as "The Troubles," seem to emanate from the townsfolk, who exhibit strange powers triggered by emotional stress. The link to King's novel comes from the fact that the resurgence of The Troubles is connected to the discovery of the body of the Colorado Kid back in 1985. The show has multiple and regular references to King's work, such as The Troubles recurring on a regular basis like the reappearance of IT in Derry—a town also mentioned in the series—and the appearance of a "thinny," a weak spot between worlds that allows people to pass through, which also appears in *The Talisman* (1984). These, however, appear more as homages to King, making *Haven* essentially an *X-Files* narrative drawing broadly from King's universe, rather than a formal adaptation. Yet, after *The Dead Zone* went off the air in 2007, the arrival of *Haven* in 2010 once again demonstrated that a King premise could be reworked for a series, and the next time this was proposed, King decided to take a more active role.

KING AND CBS GO *UNDER THE DOME* (2013–2015)

Immediately after its publication in 2009, the rights to King's *Under the Dome* were purchased by Steven Spielberg's Amblin Entertainment. A lengthy political satire, King's novel involved the inhabitants of the town of Chester's Mill being cut off from the rest of the world when an enormous transparent dome suddenly lands on them from nowhere. Arguably more so than any other of King's novels, *Under the Dome* most clearly demonstrates King's principal preoccupations and appeal. The reason for the dome's existence is a McGuffin in the novel. It is revealed through the discovery of the generator of the dome that extra-terrestrial children, known as "leatherheads," placed it over the town as a kind of ant farm, so they can observe what happens to living beings when captured. This is precisely what King is interested in doing, isolating a group of people with some form of supernatural occurrence and watching what happens next, and he has demonstrated this interest throughout his career with stories like "The Mist," *The Langoliers*, *Salem's Lot*, *Needful Things*, and *Dreamcatcher*. As a result, *Under the Dome* focuses not on the science-fiction elements of the dome, but on the people of Chester's Mill and how they react to the problems it brings. While the dome creates the situation, it is not the main catalyst of the sequence of events in the novel. Rather, events are put in motion by the actions of the corrupt town selectman and used car salesman "Big Jim" Rennie, whom King based on Vice President Dick Cheney (Memmott 2013). Rennie takes over the town, forming a militia made up of cronies and sowing panic among the townspeople. He orchestrates a riot at the Food City supermarket by insisting that it be closed and its contents rationed. As the townspeople gather, Rennie pays a couple of them to throw rocks and thus start a violent panic, on the grounds that the threat of anarchy will mean the people of the town will be less resistant to his increased police force. Not only does Rennie cause a food shortage, but he is also responsible for a lack of heating oil, having stolen and hoarded tanks from the municipal buildings in order to power his methamphetamine manufacturing operation. Rennie's meth cook, known as "The Chef," becomes increasingly paranoid through sampling his own product, prompting Rennie to try to take back the lab, using his militia. However, The Chef blows up himself, the meth, and all the petroleum, leading to a catastrophic conflagration that poisons the air and kills most of the residents under the dome.

Showrunner Brian K. Vaughan and Showtime informed King that they would be reworking the rationale for the dome's existence, something with which King agreed. In his view, he presented a scenario that was perfect for a book, which has a finite number of pages. Therefore, in his version of the story, the dome is down for only a week, but for the producers, the aim was to create a long-running series. So, as King notes in the documentary on the DVD of the first season, the idea was that the dome could be down for weeks, even months, because "if people like the show it won't have to end after x number of pages. They can come back to Chester's Mill week after week."

As I have argued elsewhere (Brown 2017), part of the process of adapting the novel into a long-format series was to make the reason for the dome more complex and mysterious and to add more depth and complexity to the characters. In the novel, the fact that the dome is an ant farm cover placed by aliens is discovered about halfway through and not really questioned after that, but in the series, the nature of the dome evolves through several season-long mysteries. In Season One, the enigma of the dome revolves around the discovery of an egg inside a smaller minidome that can be touched by no one except four teenagers known as the "four hands." When the dome is touched, an avatar of one of the teenagers, Joe, appears and says, "The monarch will be crowned." Ostensibly suggesting that somewhere in Chester's Mill is a person who will be crowned king or queen by the dome, this statement is rendered ambiguous by the fact that monarch butterflies are seen congregating on the surface of the dome. In the second season, the mystery shifts to the sudden arrival of a woman, Melanie, one of a previous group of four hands who found the egg in 1988 and who was later murdered. Behind her old high school locker is a tunnel leading to caves, at the end of which is a seemingly bottomless pit that leads outside the dome. At the end of Season Two, Melanie leads the people of Chester's Mill into similar tunnels and, apparently, to freedom. This turns out to be a lie, since it is revealed at the start of Season Three that they are not outside the dome but still in the tunnels, cocooned under the town. When they break free, a new character, Christine Price, becomes their leader. It is finally established that the dome is extraterrestrial in origin and that the townspeople are to be transformed into an alien race, which will be protected under the dome from the Armageddon to be wrought by an alien force.

This reworking of the dome's rationale allows for its explanation to be revealed gradually, creating a mystery that is sufficiently enigmatic to be not only extended but also revised and reworked. The same is true of the characters. King's characters in the novel only have seven days to act and so change very little. His usual approach to characterization, most evident in *The Stand*, is to portray characters, for the most part, as mainly good or bad from the outset, and in *Under the Dome*, with few exceptions, they are placed into categories at the start and then stay that way—although, as Jennifer Miller argues, they are not all entirely black and white, but retain some shades of gray (2015, 17). For example, short order cook and ex-soldier Barbie, who leads the good faction, at one time colluded in the torture of a prisoner in Fallujah. Barbie leads the good characters along with journalist Julia Shumway, doctor Rusty Everett, and teenagers Joe, Norrie, and Benny, while Big Jim, his son Junior, and the weak-willed first selectman Andy Saunders lead the bad faction.

In the series, the characters are given greater shades of gray. Barbie becomes a debt collector who kills Julia's husband just before the dome comes down. Junior is not, as in the novel, a brain tumor-induced psychopath who kills his girlfriend Angie at the start. In the series, he is still disturbed, kidnapping Angie and holding her in the bomb shelter belonging to his father, Big Jim. He allows himself to be used by the likes of Big Jim and Christine Price, even going so far as to attempt to sacrifice the children of Chester's Mill to the dome. But he is presented less as someone openly murderous and more as a confused and disturbed young man who becomes "generally speaking, a productive member of Chester's Mill society" (Watkins 2015, 33–34). In his role as a police officer, he mostly helps more than hinders, is distraught when he discovers that his mother is not dead, as he believed, and he both rejects and loves his father. Of all of the characters, Big Jim is given the most depth and shading. King writes him as a born-again despot. In the series, he is capable of murder and always plays the angle that will be to his advantage, but he also loves Junior and much of what he does in the series is more to protect his son than to help himself.

Although *Under the Dome* is science fiction rather than horror, the changes made from the book epitomize the transition in TV horror since the mid-1990s. *Under the Dome* is a very typical King novel, using a supernatural premise to place his ordinary characters in a world rendered strange by inexplicable forces, then examining how they react, thus providing a hybrid of character drama and generic tropes. As the first long-running drama series to be made from King's work with his input and approval, *Under the Dome* represents a significant shift in the adaptation of King's work for television. With an eye on a long run, *Under the Dome*, almost uniquely in the Stephen King canon, was able to open up King's original story, rather than close aspects of it in order to fit a prescribed length. Whereas in 1979, *Salem's Lot* cut characters in order to squeeze the narrative into three hours, *Under the Dome*, like *Haven* and *The Dead Zone*, was able to add characters not in the original story. As unofficial adaptations, *The Dead Zone* and *Haven* are effectively their own series, using King's text as a starting point for something entirely new. Nevertheless, King's input into *Under the Dome* and his support of the changes made are significant. While the results are then arguably less faithful to the original work than even Kubrick's *The Shining*, the TV series *Under the Dome* manages to capture the spirit of King's novel, with his blessing. Once again, the swearing is removed and some of the more violent scenes are toned down, but the thirteen-episode multi-season arc of *Under the Dome* presents King's premise and characters with heretofore unprecedented time to grow, blending the kind of character development and identification that made events in *Buffy the Vampire Slayer* so significant with King's own literary preoccupations of ordinary people in an extraordinary setting.

Dwindling audiences meant that *Under the Dome* was cancelled by CBS in 2015 after three seasons. Despite this, it represents an important development in adapting King's work through the merging of his literary preoccupations, the mainstream ABC miniseries of the 1990s, and the structural shift in TV horror away from the miniseries and the writer to the long- and then short-format series and the showrunner that finally overtook the work of King and ABC as the main format for horror on TV. The result is a series that keeps the majority of the elements of this new structural paradigm, but returns to the ABC projects by being sold once more on King's name—and that of Spielberg as producer—rather than on that of the showrunner Brian K. Vaughan. As I have argued elsewhere (Brown 2017), as a summer series on network TV with a shorter number of episodes than the standard network run, *Under the Dome* demonstrates the way in which the programming of genre TV has changed since *Stephen King's Golden Years* in 1991. It also demonstrates that, despite the demise in popularity of the miniseries adaptations in the early years of the twenty-first century, King's name still has drawing power. The success of *Under the Dome*, while short lived, not only created a new dramatic paradigm for King adaptations—the long-format series—it also served to reinvigorate interest in adapting King's work, leading to yet another renaissance across both film and television. Finally, with its focus on science fiction rather than horror tropes, *Under the Dome* served to shift the perception of the adapted Brand Stephen King in the public imagination, leading to a number of emerging new projects that are not directly associated with horror, a movement in keeping with a change in King's own literary preoccupations in the second decade of the twenty-first century.

The TV adaptations represent a shift in the balance between tropes of horror and character and place identification that is the hallmark of King's hybrid literary success. Beginning with *Salem's Lot*, TV prohibited filmmakers from replicating the scenes of horror and violence in King's books, but gave them the time to develop the relationship between the audience and the people onscreen that gave an emotional weight to the supernatural threats they ultimately faced. The eventual transition of these adaptations from miniseries to long-running serial drama, coming in response to changes in viewing habits and industry practice, placed character ever more central, with the result that *Under the Dome*, which is in many ways among the least faithful adaptations of a King novel, captures that elusive "King-ness" in a way that the faithful film version of *Firestarter* does not. While the history of King adaptations in cinemas is largely a cyclical one of boom-and-bust, his relationship with TV has been much more sustained since the airing of *IT* in 1990, and his relationship to the TV horror genre has been more straightforward than his relationship to cinematic horror. For a time in the 1990s, adaptations of his novels defined TV horror as, namely, literary event TV miniseries, before shows like *The X-Files* and *Buffy* shifted the impetus toward long-running serial drama. Despite disappointments with original screenplays like *Storm of the Century* and *Rose Red*, a new adaptation of an already best-selling Stephen King novel still retained cultural capital and audience appeal and was thus a relatively safe investment. CBS therefore embraced *Under the Dome* as a project for new industry initiatives, such as the shorter season and the summer broadcast.

In 1981, King could perhaps argue that the history of TV horror was short and tacky, but his own relationship with that medium since 1990 has proved to be anything but. Indeed, despite its cancellation after only three seasons, *Under the Dome* demonstrated that it was possible after forty years to approach adapting a King novel in a completely new way, jettisoning much of its concept and plotting, yet still capturing its spirit. More importantly, the arrival of the series *Under the Dome* and the fact that its first season was a ratings success made King's name bankable once more, leading to a new surge of adaptations across both film and TV that, at the time of writing, is just beginning to emerge.

Conclusion / THE FUTURE IS ALSO HISTORY:

THE CONTEMPORARY EVOLUTION

OF BRAND STEPHEN KING

Why would it be hard? Because the past doesn't want to be changed?
Something doesn't want it changed. I'm pretty sure of that.

JAKE EPPING AND AL TEMPLETON, *11/22/63* BY STEPHEN KING

THIS BOOK HAS ARGUED THAT, BEGINNING WITH DE PALMA'S *Carrie*, the cinematic and televisual Brand Stephen King has largely existed within the horror genre. In cinema, the Brand has distanced itself from the genre as it existed at any given time by downplaying violence and gore in order to attract a wider, mainstream audience. On television, the Brand has similarly aimed for broad appeal, avoiding the excesses of the likes of *Masters of Horror* and *The Walking Dead* that were made possible by cable networks. Instead, it has been attached to the major networks and their sweeps weeks audiences, delivering horror suitable for the masses. With the exception of the more violent low-budget films that drew more heavily on the tropes of the slasher film and were aimed mainly at the home market, the Brand can be categorized as, in Waller's words, an "acceptable and authorized" form of horror for general audiences (1987a, 5).

In the 1970s, such "acceptable" films were, like *The Exorcist* and *Carrie*, well-made and intelligent movies that did not compromise on horror visuals. As the genre shifted in the early 1980s, first toward and then away from the bloodletting of stalk, slash, and body horror, the concept of mainstream horror became increasingly "cozy." It was toward this form that the Brand Stephen King gravitated in its first wave, and there it remained, occupying a middle ground between mainstream audiences and horror fans. As King explored the genres of fantasy and psychological thriller in the 1990s, the adaptations also shifted into thriller territory, concealing their connections to King in order to lure audiences by avoiding the link to horror that was implied by his name. Also hiding their King credentials were the adaptations of his non-horror stories, some of which went on to become among the most respected of the films. Either through adherence or denial, the cinematic and televisual Brand Stephen King was tied not only to the horror genre, but also to a specifically mainstream form of it, existing between the prestige projects denying their creator and the gorier, low-budget movies cheerfully flaunting him.

Under the Dome, however, ushered in a new era for Brand Stephen King on film and TV. The successful first season opened up the Brand in a number of ways. Clearly branded as King, the series was nevertheless science fiction, rather than horror, and as a character-driven drama in the vein of *Lost* (2004–2010), it allowed the focus on place and people—an essential part of King's literary brand—to take center stage. Here was an adaptation in which the central conceit was merely a means to get a group of people stuck in a strange and pressured situation. Through its transition to a long format, the series broke the hegemony of concepts of fidelity. *Under the Dome* adapted the spirit, rather than the letter, of King, creating both new possibilities and a new impetus.

The next King book to appear on the small screen was his 2011 novel, *11/22/63*. In 2016, the American online platform Hulu streamed an adaptation of the book (the title undergoing a slight format change to *11.22.63*), comprising eight hour-long episodes, which aired in the United Kingdom on Fox. In the story, Jake Epping, a high school teacher from Maine, travels back in time to 1958 via a portal found in the back room of a diner owned by his friend, Al Templeton. Dying of cancer, Al asks Jake to assume the task he originally set himself: to save John F. Kennedy from assassination. Like *Under the Dome*, *11.22.63* consisted of a best-selling book, King's name, and a high-profile executive producer—this time not Spielberg but J. J. Abrams who, before taking over both the *Star Trek* and *Star Wars* franchises, had made his name in television through the spy-fi series *Alias* (2001–2006) and then as the brains behind *Lost*. Also like *Under the Dome*, *11/22/63* and its adaptation were not a horror story, but rather a character drama with a science-fiction element—in this case, time travel. However, as with the leatherheads in the novel of *Under the Dome*, the portal in both the book and series of *11/22/63* is merely a means to an end. The real objective is to consider the question: What would you do if you could change the past? More importantly, it is to bask in the nostalgic glow of the late 1950s and early 1960s, the era of King's teenage years to which he frequently returns—for example, with the Losers Club in *IT* and the four friends in *The Body*.

While principally science fiction, *11/22/63* contains a horror element in both the novel and the adaptation: the depiction of the resistance of time itself. As quoted above, Al tells Jake that the past actively struggles against change, and a number of scenes draw upon horror tropes as time pushes back. An Episode One sequence in which Jake is attacked by hundreds of bugs in a dingy basement echoes the final story, "They're Creeping Up on You," in *Creepshow* ("The Rabbit Hole"). In the same episode, he is almost run over while using a phone booth. He tries to call his father, but is unable to properly connect, instead hearing garbled and unearthly sounds coming from the receiver, as if he has connected to another dimension. Walking away, he changes his mind, and as he turns back, a car smashes the booth, appearing without warning from the left of frame. Horror traditions are also evoked in the final episode vision of the apocalyptic world that Jake finds after having saved Kennedy. Returning to the present, he finds a ruined America populated by a scattering of survivors, a country blighted and destroyed by some kind of undefined war in the mid-1970s.

These are, however, isolated moments, and even the science-fiction aspect of time travel takes a back seat for much of both the novel and the series. Overall, the main thrust of the story in both media is part investigative thriller, as Jake shadows Lee Harvey Oswald to determine if he really killed Kennedy, and part love story, as he romances school librarian Sadie Dunhill. The emotional climax is not the revelation of the alternate present that Jake finds upon his return, but rather when he, after going back into the past and "resetting" the present world to its original state, finds the now elderly Sadie, who does not know him, and dances with her. Jake is trapped between a life in the past that will affect the future and a life of solitude in the present, once again connecting, as do the series *The Dead Zone* and *Under the Dome*, a genre conceit with personal character drama.

The series *11.22.63* is part of a new renaissance of King adaptations driven partially by the success of the first series of *Under the Dome*, which once again demonstrated that a King project could be an attractive option. This re-emergence of confidence in King was also aided by the publicity surrounding the attempt to transfer his *Dark Tower* saga to the big screen, which predated but then developed alongside *Under the Dome* and *11.22.63*. Abrams had originally been linked to an adaptation, but in 2010, NBC Universal announced that director Ron Howard and his producing partner Brian Grazer had devised an ambitious trans-media concept to include three feature films interspersed with two TV series. Universal eventually dropped the project a year later due to budgetary concerns, and in early 2012, Warner Bros. expressed an interest but then passed, leaving *The Dark Tower* in limbo (Kit 2015). However, the ambition of the project and the level of media discussion about it prompted the revival of interest in King adaptations, so that in 2013, the year *Under the Dome* premiered, Abrams announced *11.22.63* (Jackson 2014).

The period between Abrams's announcement and the release of *11.22.63* also saw the appearance of three more projects. The most high-profile production was a new theatrical version of *Carrie* (2013), which starred Chloe Grace Moretz, who, at sixteen, was closer to Carrie's age than the twenty-six-year-old Sissy Spacek had been in De Palma's film. Updating the visual effects with CGI and relying upon strong central performances by Moretz and Julianne Moore, the film did well, earning $16 million in its opening weekend. A year later came the straight-to-DVD *Mercy* (2014), based on King's short story "Gramma" from *Skeleton Crew* (1985). The year 2014 also saw two adaptations from the collection *Full Dark, No Stars* (2010), one of King's bleakest works. *A Good Marriage*, a tale about a woman who realizes her husband of many years is a serial killer, had a limited theatrical release in October and was simultaneously made available via online on-demand platforms, while the rape revenge tale, *Big Driver*, also aired in October, on Lifetime.

None of these projects found a significant audience in the way that the remake of *Carrie* did, but *11.22.63* was heavily promoted and generated a great deal of interest, with the result that even before it aired in 2016, more King adaptations were already in the works. The first of these was the delayed adaptation of his 2006 apocalyptic horror novel *Cell*, which finished filming in 2014 and finally had a video-on-demand release followed by a very limited theatrical run in the summer of 2016. The summer of 2017 saw the release of *The Dark Tower*, now only a single film that, while it draws elements from King's saga, is more a continuation of the story rather than an adaptation. *The Dark Tower* is directed by Nikolaj Arcel and stars Idris Elba as Roland Deschain and Matthew McConaughey as his nemesis Walter, the Man in Black. In addition, Part One of a two-part theatrical version of *IT*, directed by Andres Muschietti, is scheduled for a 2017 release, and also filming for the cable channel Spike is a ten-part TV drama based on *The Mist* and for Netflix, a version of both *Gerald's Game* and *1922*, another novella from *Full Dark, No Stars*. Among other projects in development are a TV series based on King's recent *Mr. Mercedes* trilogy (2014–2016), produced by David E. Kelley, who created *LA Law* (1986–1994), and a cinema adaptation of *Revival* (2014) by Josh Boone, who put aside his previous project, a theatrical adaptation of *The Stand*, in order to develop it. Finally, Abrams and King are collaborating on an anthology series called *Castle Rock*.

As in the early 1980s and the early 1990s, King is big among producers once more. Yet, there is a distinct difference in this current crop of projects. Besides the *Carrie* remake, of those already released or at least completed, only *Mercy* and *Cell* are what one might call, to once again quote Peter Straub, "immediately classifiable horror" (2000, ix). In King's novel *Cell*, a mysterious pulse sent through mobile phone signals turns the majority of people into violent, animalistic killers ruled by a hive mind. The adaptation is clearly positioned as horror, in part through the connection of mass mindless hordes of violent people to zombies, which, as Stacey Abbott points out, have undergone a renaissance so that "21st century cinema now positions the zombie as a central member of the canon of classic big screen monsters" (2016, 93). It also marks itself as horror by reuniting John Cusack and Samuel L. Jackson, the stars of *1408*, the adaptation of a King short story (as discussed in chapter 3). A much smaller production, released straight to DVD, *Mercy* is the story of two boys who look after their ailing grandmother and find she has supernatural powers. This is also identifiable as a horror film. Not only does it star Chandler Riggs, who plays Carl in *The Walking Dead*, but it was also produced by Jason Blum for his Blumhouse Productions, which specializes in horror films, such as *Paranormal Activity* (2007) and *Insidious* (2010).

In contrast, both *Under the Dome* and *11.22.63* connect more closely to science fiction, and while *A Good Marriage* and *Big Driver* are both arguably horror stories, given their bleak subject matter, the monsters and the threat they pose are entirely human, coming as they do from a collection that, in Neil Gaiman's words, "tends to avoid or downplay the supernatural" to focus on "stories of retribution and complicity" (2010). Thus, although the stories are horrific, they do not draw upon the supernatural elements associated with King in relation to the horror genre. Furthermore, both stories are narrated from the perspective of female characters: Darcy in *A Good Marriage* and Tess in *Big Driver*, echoing the trilogy of female character-based psychological thrillers from the 1990s, *Dolores Claiborne*, *Gerald's Game*, and *Rose Madder*. Finally, as depictions of cat-and-mouse games between the central female protagonists and their male nemesis, these works fall more closely within the thriller genre than horror.

While the canon of King adaptations has traditionally, like the current crop, included horror, psychological thrillers, science fiction, and magical realist tales, the difference between this contemporary spate of adaptations and previous ones is that, with the exception of *Mercy*, *IT*, and *Carrie*, all these projects, across film and TV, highlight King's name in the publicity. *IT* and *Carrie* are slightly different in that the films are sold, in a manner similar to *Children of the Corn*, on their title awareness. The teaser poster for *Carrie* showed a close-up of Moretz's face, covered in blood, with the tagline, "You will know her name," and the title, playing upon awareness of Carrie as both a name and a brand associated with horror. Equally, the poster for *IT* merely depicts a boy in a yellow rainslicker, the face of Pennywise partially hidden behind a balloon, the title, and the tagline "You'll Float, Too." These posters are designed with the idea that audiences are already aware of the projects, either through the books or previous adaptations. As for the others, whereas the adaptation of the psychological drama *Dolores Claiborne* avoided overt references to King, *Big Driver* conspicuously displayed its connection to his story, while the poster for the other adaptation from *Full Dark, No Stars* billed it as *Stephen King's A Good Marriage*. This is despite the fact that, unlike *Under the Dome* and *11/22/63, Full Dark* did not make the number one slot on the *New York Times* best-seller list and, like *The Body* and *The Shawshank Redemption, Big Driver* and *A Good Marriage* were titles of novellas within a book and thus likely to be less familiar to general audiences than the title of the book itself.

In addition, it is important to note the enormous publicity, including extended coverage in *Entertainment Weekly* in July 2016, surrounding the production of *The Dark Tower*. With its quest narrative in a setting of a mythical and magical world seemingly derived from our own, this is not only a fantasy story in the vein of J. R. R. Tolkien's *The Lord of the Rings* or George R. R. Martin's *A Song of Ice and Fire* (1996–), but also one of King's least-read works, even among his Constant Readers. Yet, despite this, King's name has been prominent in all the production reports although notably not on the poster.

Together, these examples indicate that the cinematic and televisual Brand Stephen King is changing in the current resurgence. In the ever-present tension between King as a popular writer and sellable name and King as a writer only of horror tales of consequently limited appeal, it seems that, in the mid-2010s, there is both an acknowledgment that he is more than simply the master of the macabre and an acceptance by producers that as a writer, he is increasingly seen this way. Consequently, the cinematic and televisual Brand Stephen King is expanding to include non-horror adaptations like *11.22.63* and *Big Driver* that freely broadcast their King connection.

This undoubtedly reflects a shift in the popular perception of King as a writer. For all that he has been labeled a horror author throughout his career, regardless of the nature of his actual stories, the fact that he is no longer solely a writer of horror is now undeniable. *Full Dark, No Stars, 11/22/63, Revival,* and the *Mr. Mercedes* trilogy demonstrate that since the publication of *Cell,* King's writing has emphatically moved away from any concept of being "immediately classifiable horror fiction" and, arguably, from being horror at all, even if one were to accept that, early on, this was King's staple genre.

The exception to this shift is the sequel to *The Shining, Doctor Sleep* (2013), which, not surprisingly, contains strong supernatural horror overtones in its tale of grown-up Dan Torrance, the boy from *The Shining*, and his battle with the True Knot, a group of semi-immortal gypsies who live off the life force, known as "steam," of children. This book aside, the majority of his recent works feature mainly human monsters, and when they do invoke the supernatural, as in the example of resistant time in *11/22/63*, it takes a backseat. Even in *Doctor Sleep*, Dan Torrance follows in his father's footsteps into alcoholism and abusive behavior, and the novel becomes a metaphor for addiction and recovery as the True Knot is presented as a group of steam addicts, traveling the country for a fix. The same focus on addiction underpins *Revival*, as two men—one addicted to heroin, the other to hate, revenge, and experimentation with electricity—cross paths over forty years. As noted, both *Under the Dome* and *11/22/63* are science-fiction-inflected character studies, while *Full Dark, No Stars* explores the dark side of humanity with its stories of rape, murder, and revenge. King's most sustained recent narrative is the three-part detective series: *Mr. Mercedes, Finders Keepers* (2015), and *End of Watch* (2016). That the central character, Bill Hodges, is first a retired cop and then head of his own detective agency, plus the fact that *Mr. Mercedes* won the 2014 Goodreads Choice Award for Best Mystery and Thriller, shows that these are police thrillers more in keeping with the likes of James Patterson than Stephen King.

In the last ten years, it has become evident that King has embraced the thriller and shifted away from horror and monsters. Still, all these books maintain his consistent focus on place and character. Just as *11/22/63* is as much about Jake's love affair with Sadie as it is about saving JFK, and *Revival* and *Doctor Sleep* are about men battling addiction, the *Mr. Mercedes* trilogy is about two damaged people, suicidal Bill Hodges and the traumatized (and possibly autistic) Holly Gibney, learning to re-enter society and trust another person, while killer Brady Hartsfield increasingly pushes himself into isolation.

The cinematic and televisual Brand Stephen King has responded to this shift in King's own literary brand, adapting his new material and promoting his name, thereby breaking the hegemony of the association with the cinematic and televisual horror genres that Brand Stephen King adaptations have maintained since *Carrie* and *Salem's Lot*. At the same time, however, as Al suggests in *11/22/63*, the past is pushing back. Alongside new adaptations like *Mr. Mercedes, A Good Marriage*, and *The Dark Tower* (which is not a new literary work but is a new adaptation), the current resurgence of interest in King also includes a thread that is turning back to the horror genre and to his literary and visual heritage, offering new versions of iconic horror stories, including *Carrie, IT, The Stand*, and *The Mist*, updated on screen for a new generation. This revival of the cinematic and televisual Brand Stephen King is therefore simultaneously embracing the new, non-horror, literary Stephen King brand that has emerged post-*Cell*, while at the same time resisting the change, *11/22/63*-style, and delving into the past to revisit the "classic" horror King of old.

IT, produced by Warner Bros., was to be directed by Cary Fukanaga, who had gained wide acclaim for his thoughtful and intelligent approach to Series One of *True Detective* (2014) at HBO. Fukanaga left over creative differences, the details of which are unclear. Possibly he was planning to take the same cerebral, philosophical, and surrealist approach to *IT* that he did to the detective genre, while Warners was apparently looking for something a little more traditional. After Fukanaga left, the studio cut the budget; hired Muschietti, whose previous credits included the horror film *Mama* (2013); and shifted the project to, as Brent McKnight puts it, "their more genre-centric offshoot New Line" (2015).

The Mist meanwhile is produced by Dimension TV, which also adapted Wes Craven's *Scream* (2015) for the small screen. It is a "reimagination" of King's work, which tells the story of a "seemingly innocuous mist that seeps into a small town and creates havoc" (Gennis 2017, Prudom 2016). The fact that the narrative is opened up beyond the supermarket/strip mall setting of King's original to include an entire town and that the cast list consists largely of characters not in the novella or previous film confirms that the conception of *The Mist* draws upon the example of *Under the Dome* (Evry 2016). It remains to be seen whether the genre focus will therefore be more science fiction than horror, but character drama will undoubtedly play a significant part, though whether *The Mist* extends beyond a single season, only time will tell.

Finally, although it is currently shelved, writer-director Josh Boone's version of *The Stand*, originally written as a single three-hour film and then extended at the request of Warner Bros. into a multi-film project, was conceived by Boone as an R-rated horror story (Jagernauth 2014). In an interview with *Nightmare Magazine*, Boone describes his vision as "attempting to revive the idea of the elevated horror film—movies like *The Exorcist*, *Rosemary's Baby*, *The Shining* . . . an event movie . . . *The Godfather* of post-apocalyptic epics" (Morton 2016).

For all that the current cycle of adaptations seems to be shifting the territory of the cinematic and televisual Brand Stephen King away from horror in line with his contemporary writing, it is significant that Boone, a lifelong fan of King books but also an avid viewer of the adaptations, should once again be referencing the prestigious literary horror films of the 1970s that spawned King's popular success. Boone goes on to say that, in relation to what he calls the "elevated" horror film, "the 1980s really killed this idea because studios realized you could make horror films for dirt cheap and make a killing" (Morton 2016). Despite the DVD revolution that brought a large number of direct-to-home horror films, of which *Mercy* and, to a certain extent, *Cell* and *A Good Marriage* are also examples, the current crop of forthcoming titles post-*Carrie* remake and *Under the Dome* are all, horror or not, pitched as major, big-budget prestige projects. Thus, in keeping with the ABC King miniseries, *The Stand*, in Boone's estimation, is "an event." Similar rhetoric is being used for *The Mist*, destined to be Spike's first scripted series in more than ten years and described by Harvey Weinstein as a "signature show" (Andreeva, 2016).

Whether across film or television, the connection of King, horror, and adaptation therefore still holds within it the concepts of the event, of prestige, and thus of the potential for popular success in mainstream multiplex venues for *IT* and *The Stand* or on cable TV for *The Mist*. In horror terms, this denotation of a King adaptation as "prestige" also serves as a marker of distinction not only as "quality" (and therefore in Waller's phrase "acceptable") horror, but also as different from standard horror fare.

What the current situation demonstrates is that there remains, despite all the evidence of the diminishing returns of past cycles in the early 1980s and 1990s, an abiding confidence within the industry for the appeal of both Stephen King stories and the King name as brand for film and TV audiences. Within this new cycle, some projects will succeed critically and/or commercially and some will fail, but what will be different is that, unlike in the past, they will not be either King-branded horror films or non-King branded non-horrors like *The Shawshank Redemption* or *Dolores Claiborne*. Instead, despite crossing genres into fantasy, science fiction, horror, and psychological drama, more of them will be branded as King. As chapter one discussed, his overwhelming and sustained popularity effectively created his own literary brand based on his themes, language, and style. The result was that, in essence, from a literary perspective as a designated writer of horror, King has existed outside the conventions of the genre, his writing in effect becoming the sub-genre known as "Stephen King." The adaptations, divorced from those consistent stylistic and thematic traits and relying mainly on King's name as a specifically cinematic or televisual brand, struggled to find a place within horror on film or TV, representing as they do a particularly mainstream form of the genre, even within the subculture of straight-to-DVD movies.

The fact that the contemporary cycle of adaptations is both shedding genre connections and delving into the back catalogue demonstrates that this connection with the mainstream appears to be unshakeable. Furthermore, that the new cycle includes new versions of previously adapted works signals an embracing and acknowledging of King not just as the author of new stories, but also as the creator of modern horror classics worthy of revival. As a writer of best sellers, for the studios, networks, and producers, King still represents a high-profile brand and therefore possible breakout success. Whether the new cycle of films and shows finally breaks the hegemony of the horror connection or not, this notion of both prestige and the potential to attract large audiences remains the very core of the cinematic and televisual Brand Stephen King.

SELECTED TV AND FILMOGRAPHY

FILMS

Alien (1979), dir. Ridley Scott, US/UK
Alligator (1980), dir. Lewis Teague, US
The Amityville Horror (1979), dir. Stuart Rosenberg, US
Apt Pupil (1998), dir. Brian Singer, US
Audrey Rose (1977), dir. Robert Wise, US
Black Christmas (1974), dir. Bob Clark, Canada
Bloody Birthday (1981), dir. Ed Hunt, US
Body Snatchers (1993), dir. Abel Ferrara, US
The Boogens (1981), dir. James L. Conway, US
Bram Stoker's Dracula (1992), dir. Francis Ford Coppola, US
The Brood (1979), dir. David Cronenberg, Canada
Cannibal Holocaust (1980), dir. Ruggero Deodato, Italy
Carrie (1976), dir. Brian De Palma, US
Carrie (2013), dir. Kimberly Peirce, US
Cat's Eye (1985), dir. Lewis Teague, US
Cell (2016), dir. Tod Williams, US
Children of the Corn (1984), dir. Fritz Kiersch, US
Children of the Corn II: The Final Sacrifice (1992), dir. David F. Price, US
Children of the Corn III: Urban Harvest (1995), dir. James D. R. Hickox, US
Children of the Corn IV: The Gathering (1996), dir. Greg Spence, US
Children of the Corn V: Fields of Terror (1998), dir. Ethan Wiley, US
Children of the Corn 666: Isaac's Return (1999), dir. Kari Skogland, US
Children of the Corn: Revelation (2001), dir. Guy Magar, Canada
Children of the Corn: Genesis (2011), dir. Joel Soisson, US
Christine (1983), dir. John Carpenter, US
Creepshow (1982), dir. George A. Romero, US
Creepshow 2 (1987), dir. Michael Gornick, US
Cujo (1983), dir. Lewis Teague, US

The Dark Half (1993), dir. George A. Romero, US

The Dark Tower (2017), dir. Nikolaj Arcel, US

Dark Water (2002), dir. Hideo Nakata, Japan

Dark Water (2005), dir. Walter Salles, US

Dawn of the Dead (1979), dir. George A. Romero, US

Dawn of the Dead (2004), dir. Zack Snyder, US/Canada/Japan/France

The Dead Zone (1983), dir. David Cronenberg, US

Dolores Claiborne (1995), dir. Taylor Hackford, US

Dracula (1979), dir. John Badham, US/UK

Dreamcatcher (2003), dir. Lawrence Kasdan, US

The Entity (1982), dir. Sidney J. Furie, US

E.T. the Extra-Terrestrial (1982), dir. Steven Spielberg, US

The Evil Dead (1981), dir. Sam Raimi, US

The Exorcist (1973), dir. William Friedkin, US

The Exorcist III (1990), dir. William Peter Blatty, US

Final Exam (1981), dir. Jimmy Huston, US

Firestarter (1984), dir. Mark L. Lester, US

Flatliners (1990), dir. Joel Schumacher, US

1408 (2007), dir. Mikael Hafstrom, US

The French Connection (1971), dir. William Friedkin, US

Friday the 13th (1980), dir. Sean S. Cunningham, US

Full Circle (1977), dir. Richard Loncraine, Canada/UK

Ghost Story (1981), dir. John Irvin, US

A Good Marriage (2014), dir. Peter Askin, US

Graveyard Shift (1990), dir. Ralph S. Singleton, US

The Green Mile (1999), dir. Frank Darabont, US

Halloween (1978), dir. John Carpenter, US

Halloween (2007), dir. Rob Zombie, US

Halloween III: Season of the Witch (1982), dir. Tommy Lee Wallace, US

Happy Birthday to Me (1981), dir. J. Lee Thompson, Canada

The Haunting (1999), dir. Jan de Bont, US

Hearts in Atlantis (2001), dir. Scott Hicks, US

Hostel II (2007), dir. Eli Roth, US/Czech Republic/Italy/Iceland/Slovenia

House of Wax (2005), dir. Jaume Collet-Serra, US/Australia

The House on Haunted Hill (1999), dir. William Malone, US

The House on Sorority Row (1983), dir. Mark Rosman, US

I Spit on Your Grave (1978), dir. Meir Zarchi, US

Insidious (2010), dir. James Wan, UK/US

In the Mouth of Madness (1994), dir. John Carpenter, US

IT (Part One) (2017), dir. Andres Muschietti, US

Jacob's Ladder (1990), dir. Adrian Lyne, US

Jurassic Park (1993), dir. Steven Spielberg, US

The Keep (1983), dir. Michael Mann, US/UK

The Last House on the Left (1972), dir. Wes Craven, US

The Last House on the Left (2009), dir. Dennis Iliadis, US

The Lawnmower Man (1992), dir. Brett Leonard, US/UK/Japan

Love at First Bite (1979), dir. Stan Dragoti, US

The Mangler (1995), dir. Tobe Hooper, US/South Africa/Australia/UK

The Mangler 2 (2002), dir. Michael Hamilton-Wright, Canada

The Mangler Reborn (2005), dirs. Matt Cunningham and Erik Gardner, US

Mary Shelley's Frankenstein (1994), dir. Kenneth Branagh, US/Japan

Maximum Overdrive (1986), dir. Stephen King, US

Mercy (2014), dir. Peter Cornwell, US

Misery (1990), dir. Rob Reiner, US

The Mist (2007), dir. Frank Darabont, US

The Mummy (1999), dir. Stephen Sommers, US

My Bloody Valentine (1981), dir. George Mihalka, Canada

Needful Things (1993), dir. Fraser Heston, US

The New York Ripper (1982), dir. Lucio Fulci, Italy

Night of the Living Dead (1968), dir. George A. Romero, US

Night School (1981), dir. Kenneth Hughes, US

A Nightmare on Elm Street (1984), dir. Wes Craven, US

Nosferatu (1922), dir. F. W. Murnau, Germany

Nosferatu the Vampyre (1979), dir. Werner Herzog, Germany

Obsession (1976), dir. Brian De Palma, US

The Omen (1976), dir. Richard Donner, UK/US

The Other (1972), dir. Robert Mulligan, US

Paranormal Activity (2007), dir. Oren Peli, US

Peeping Tom (1960), dir. Michael Powell, UK

Pet Sematary (1989), dir. Mary Lambert, US

Pet Sematary II (1992), dir. Mary Lambert, US

Poltergeist (1982), dir. Tobe Hooper, US

Prom Night (1980), dir. Paul Lynch, Canada

Psycho (1960), dir. Alfred Hitchcock, US

Psycho II (1983), dir. Richard Franklin, US

The Puppet Masters (1994), dir. Stuart Orme, US

Rabid (1977), dir. David Cronenberg, Canada

The Ring (2002), dir. Gore Verbinski, US/Japan

Ringu (1998), dir. Hideo Nakata, Japan

Rosemary's Baby (1968), dir. Roman Polanski, US

The Running Man (1987), dir. Paul Michael Glaser, US

Scanners (1981), dir. David Cronenberg, Canada

Scream (1996), dir. Wes Craven, US

Secret Window (2004), dir. David Koepp, US

Se7en (1995), dir. David Fincher, US

The Shawshank Redemption (1994), dir. Frank Darabont, US

The Shining (1980), dir. Stanley Kubrick, US/UK

Shivers (1975), dir. David Cronenberg, Canada

The Silence of the Lambs (1991), dir. Jonathan Demme, US
Silver Bullet (1985), dir. Daniel Attias, US/Netherlands
Sleepwalkers (1992), dir. Mick Garris, US
Something Wicked This Way Comes (1983), dir. Jack Clayton, US
Sometimes They Come Back . . . Again (1996), dir. Adam Grossman, US
Sometimes They Come Back . . . for More (1998), dir. Daniel Berk, US
Spasms (1983), dir. William Fruet, Canada
SS Experiment Camp (1976), dir. Sergio Garrone, Italy
Stand by Me (1986), dir. Rob Reiner, US
Star Trek II: The Wrath of Khan (1982), dir. Nicholas Meyer, US
The Survivor (1981), dir. David Hemmings, UK
Tales from the Darkside: The Movie (1990), dir. John Harrison, US
The Texas Chainsaw Massacre (1974), dir. Tobe Hooper, US
The Texas Chainsaw Massacre (2003), dir. Marcus Nispel, US
The Thing (1982), dir. John Carpenter, US
Thinner (1996), dir. Tom Holland, US
13 Ghosts (2001), dir. Steve Beck, US/Canada
Vampire in Brooklyn (1995), dir. Wes Craven, US
Videodrome (1983), dir. David Cronenberg, Canada
When a Stranger Calls (1979), dir. Fred Walton, US/Canada
Wolf (1994), dir. Mike Nichols, US
Zombie Flesh Eaters (1979), dir. Lucio Fulci, Italy

TV MINISERIES AND SERIES

American Horror Story (2011–), FX
Angel (1999–2004), WB
Bag of Bones (2011), dir. Mick Garris, A&E
Big Driver (2014), dir. Mikael Salomon, Lifetime
Bones (2005–2017), Fox
Buffy the Vampire Slayer (1997–2001), WB; (2001–2003), UPN
Count Dracula (1977), dir. Philip Saville, BBC
CSI: Crime Scene Investigation (2000–2015), CBS
The Dead Zone (2002–2007), USA Network
Desperation (2006), dir. Mick Garris, ABC
Dexter (2006–2013), Showtime
11.22.63 (2016), Hulu
Freddy's Nightmares (1988–1990), syndication
Haven (2010–2015), Syfy
IT (1990), dir. Tommy Lee Wallace, ABC
Kingdom Hospital (2004), dir. Craig R. Baxley, ABC
The Langoliers (1995), dir. Tom Holland, ABC
Lost (2004–2010), ABC

Masters of Horror (2005–2007), Showtime
The Mist (2017), Spike
Night Gallery (1969–1973), ABC
Nightmares and Dreamscapes (2006), TNT
The Night Stalker (1972), dir. John Llewellyn Moxey, ABC
The Night Strangler (1973), dir. Dan Curtis, ABC
Peyton Place (1964–1969), ABC
Prime Suspect (1991), Granada
Rose Red (2002), dir. Craig R. Baxley, ABC
Salem's Lot (1979), dir. Tobe Hooper, CBS
Salem's Lot (2004), dir. Mikael Salomon, TNT
Shawshank: The Redeeming Feature (2001), dir. Andrew Abbott, Channel Four
The Shining (1997), dir. Mick Garris, ABC
Sometimes They Come Back (1991), dir. Tom McLoughlin, CBS
The Stand (1994), dir. Mick Garris, ABC
Stephen King's Golden Years (1991), CBS
Storm of the Century (1999), dir. Craig R. Baxley, ABC
Supernatural (2005–2006), The WB; (2006–), CW
The Tommyknockers (1993), dir. John Power, ABC
Trucks (1997), dir. Chris Thomson, USA Network
The Turn of the Screw (1974), dir. Dan Curtis, ABC
The Twilight Zone (1959–1964, 1985–1989), CBS
Twin Peaks (1990–1991, 2017), ABC/Showtime
Under the Dome (2013–2015), CBS
The Walking Dead (2010–), AMC
The X-Files (1993–2002, 2016), Fox

REFERENCES

Abbott, S. 2007. *Celluloid Vampires*. Austin: University of Texas Press.

———. 2009. *Angel*. Detroit: Wayne State University Press.

———. 2010a. "David Cronenberg." In *Fifty Key Figures in Science Fiction*, ed. M. Bould, A. Roberts, and S. Vint, 56–61. London: Routledge.

———. 2010b. "High Concept Thrills and Chills: The Horror Blockbuster." In *Horror Zone*, ed. I. Conrich, 27–44. London: I. B. Tauris.

———. 2016. *Undead Apocalypse: Vampires and Zombies in the 21st Century*. Edinburgh: Edinburgh University Press.

Adalian, J. 2015. "10 Episodes Is the New 13 (Was the New 22)." *Vulture*, 12 June. www.vulture.com/2015/06/10-episodes-is-the-new-13-was-the-new-22.html#.

Alegre, S. M. 2001. "Nightmares of Childhood: The Child and the Monster in Four Novels by Stephen King." *Atlantis*, 23:1, pp. 105–114.

Andreeva, N. 2016. "*The Mist* Stephen King Adaptation Gets Series Order at Spike." *Deadline*. 14 April. http://deadline.com/2016/04/the-mist-stephen-king-tv-series-spike-1201737493/.

Anon. 1979a. "Monster Invasion." *Fangoria* 1, pp. 62–65.

Anon. 1979b. "Romero, King Team Up 'Big Time Fear.'" *Cinefantastique* 9:3/4, Spring, p. 78.

Anon. 1994. *The Shawshank Redemption*. Empire. www.empireonline.com/reviews/reviewcomplete.asp?DVDID=3903.

Anon. 2007. "Room Service." *Starburst* 353, pp. 96–100.

Anon. 2008. "The 500 Greatest Movies of All Time." *Empire*. www.empireonline.com/movies/features/500-greatest-movies/.

Applebome, P. 1991. "TV Gets a New Poltergeist: Stephen King." *New York Times*, 14 July. www.nytimes.com/1991/07/14/arts/television-tv-gets-a-new-poltergeist-stephen-king.html?pagewanted=all.

Arnold, G. 1982. "The Shape of Thing Redone." *Washington Post*, 25 June.

Barron, F. 1997. "Stephen King on *The Shining*." *Cinefantastique* 28:11, May, p. 18.

Barthes, R. 1967. "The Death of the Author." *Aspen*, pp. 5–6.

Beeler, M. 1994a. "*The Stand.*" *Cinefantastique* 25:2, April, pp. 8–23.

———. 1994b. "Stephen King: *The Stand.*" *Cinefantastique* 25:3, June, pp. 24–31.

———. 1998. "Fields of Terror." *Cinefantastique* 30:4, August, pp. 30–31.

Bernard, M. 2015. *Selling the Splat Pack: The DVD Revolution and the American Horror Film*. Edinburgh: Edinburgh University Press.

Bianculli, D. 1993. "Smits and Helgenberger Nail Down Fine Performances in ABC's *The Tommyknockers.*" *Baltimore Sun*, 8 May. http://articles.baltimoresun .com/1993–05–08/features/1993128105_1_tommyknockers-allyce-beasley-rube -goldberg.

Billson, A. 1997. *The Thing*. London: BFI.

Blair, I. 1995. "Back in the Swing." *Film and Video* 12:4, April, pp. 70–71, 74–75.

Brod, D. 1987. "See Arnie Run! See Arnie Kill!" *Fangoria* 7:69, December, pp. 48–50, 68.

Brophy, P. 1986. "Horrality: The Textuality of Contemporary Horror Films." *Screen* 27:1, pp. 2–13.

Brosnan, J. 1983. "*Poltergeist.*" *Starburst* 62, October, pp. 10–11.

Brown, S. 2010. "Cult Channels: Showtime, FX and Cult TV." In *The Cult TV Book*, ed. S. Abbott, 155–162. London: I. B. Tauris.

———. 2013, "Memento Mori: The Slow Death of *The X-Files.*" *Science Fiction Film and Television* 6:1, Spring, pp. 7–22.

———. 2014. "The Golden Years of Stephen King." 14 March. http://cstonline.tv /the-golden-years-of-stephen-king.

———. 2017. "Alternate Versions of the Same Reality: Adapting *Under the Dome* as a SF TV Series." *Science Fiction Film and Television* 10:2 Summer, 267–283.

Brown, S., and S. Abbott. 2010. "The Art of Sp(l)atter: Body Horror in *Dexter.*" In *Dexter: Investigating Cutting Edge Television*, ed. D. Howard, 189–204. London: I. B. Tauris.

Browning, M. 2009. *Stephen King on the Big Screen*. Bristol: Intellect.

———. 2011. *Stephen King on the Small Screen*. Bristol: Intellect.

Carroll, N. 1990. *The Philosophy of Horror*. London: Routledge.

Church, D. 2006. "Return of the Repressed. Notes on the American Horror Film (1991–2006)." *Offscreen*, 10:10. http://offscreen.com/view/return_of_the_repressed.

Ciccolella, C. 1985. "How to Sell Horror as a Year-Round Traffic Builder." *Billboard*, 2 November, p. HV3.

Collings, M. 1985. *The Many Facets of Stephen King*. Mercer Island, WA: Starmont House.

———. 1987. *The Stephen King Phenomenon*. Mercer Island, WA: Starmont House.

———. 2006. *The Films of Stephen King*. Rockville, MD: Wildside Press.

Conrich, I. 2010. "The *Friday the 13th* Films and the Cultural Function of a Modern Grand Guignol." In *Horror Zone*, ed. I. Conrich, 173–188. London: I. B. Tauris.

Corrigan, T., ed. 2012. *Film and Literature: An Introduction and Reader*, 2nd ed. London: Routledge.

Crawford, G. W. 1985. "Stephen King's American Gothic." In *Discovering Stephen King*, ed. D. Schweitzer, 41–45. Mercer Island, WA: Starmont House.

Crawley, T. 1983. "Dee Wallace and Man's Best Friend." *Starburst* 64, December, pp. 24–28.

Creed, B. 1993. *The Monstrous Feminine: Film, Feminism, Psychoanalysis.* London: Routledge.

Davis, G. 2008. "A Taste for *Leeches!* DVDs, Audience Configurations, and Generic Hybridity." In *Film and Television After DVD,* ed. J. Bennett and T. Brown, 45–62. London: Routledge.

Davis, J. P. 1994. *Stephen King's America.* Bowling Green, OH: Bowling Green State University Press.

Dika, V. 1987. "The Stalker Film, 1978–81." In *American Horrors: Essays on the Modern American Horror Film,* ed. G. Waller, 86–101. Chicago: University of Illinois Press.

Earnshaw, T., ed. 2013. *Tobe Hooper's* Salem's Lot: *Studies in the Horror Film.* Lakewood, CO: Centipede Press.

Ebert, R. 1998. *"Apt Pupil." Siskel and Ebert.* www.youtube.com/watch?v =IgIJ8ms6HEA.

———. 2003. *Dreamcatcher.* www.rogerebert.com/reviews/dreamcatcher-2003.

Edwards, P. 1983. *The Thing. Starburst* 62, October, pp. 22–23.

———. 1984. *The Dead Zone. Starburst* 70, June, pp. 40–41.

Edwards, S. 1988. *"Apt Pupil*: A Lesson in Terror from Stephen King." *Film Review,* June, p. 6.

Egan, J. 1987. *"The Dark Tower*: Stephen King's Gothic Western." In *The Gothic World of Stephen King: Landscape of Nightmares,* ed. G. Hoppenstand and R. B. Browne, 95–106. Bowling Green, OH: Bowling Green State University Press.

Evry, M. 2016. *"The Mist* TV Series Cast Announced by Spike." *Comingsoon.net.* 14 July. www.comingsoon.net/tv/news/702287-full-cast-announced-for-spikes -the-mist-tv-series.

Falsetto, M. 2001. *Stanley Kubrick: A Narrative and Stylistic Analysis.* Westport, CT: Praeger.

Farrow, B., and F. Avingola. 1992. "Legal Storm Brews as King Disowns *The Lawnmower Man.*" *Screen International* 860, 5 June, p. 4.

Ferrante, A. 1998. *"Apt Pupil*: A Lesson in Fear." *Fangoria* 178, November, pp. 66–69, 92.

Fletcher, J. 1988. "Stephen King: The Limits of Fear." In *Reign of Fear: The Fiction and Film of Stephen King (1982–1989),* ed. D. Herron, vii–xv. London: Pan Books.

Flood, Alison. 2013. *"Joyland* by Stephen King–Review." *Guardian,* 22 June. www .theguardian.com/books/2013/jun/22/joyland-stephen-king-review.

Foti, L. 1982a. "Andre Blay Speaks His Mind," *Billboard,* 18 September, pp. 6, 28.

———. 1982b. "Lower Prices Spur Video Sales." *Billboard,* 2 September, pp. 15, 18.

Frost, R. 2015. "A Different Breed: Stephen King's Serial Killers." In *Stephen King's Contemporary Classics: Reflections on the Modern Master of Horror,* ed. P. Simpson and P. McAleer, 117–132. London: Rowman and Littlefield.

Gagne, P. 1980a. "One of the Best Horror Films that Has Ever Been Made for Television: An Interview with Stephen King." *Famous Monsters of Filmland* 162 and 164, February and May. Reprinted in Earnshaw, T. ed. 2013. *Tobe Hooper's Salem's Lot: Studies in the Horror Film*, 29–43. Lakewood, CO: Centipede Press.

———. 1980b. "Stephen King." *Cinefantastique* 10:1, p. 34.

———. 1982a. *Creepshow, Cinefantastique* 12:1, February, pp. 16–21.

———. 1982b. *Creepshow. Cinefantastique* 13:1, September/October, pp. 16–35.

Gaiman, N. 2010. "*Full Dark, No Stars* by Stephen King–Review." *Guardian*, 5 November. www.theguardian.com/books/2010/nov/05/full-dark-stephen-king-review.

Garrett, D. 2007. "Proyas to Direct Universal's *Dracula.*" *Variety*, 10 July. http://variety.com/2007/film/news/proyas-to-direct-universal-s-dracula-2-1117968320/.

Gennis, S. 2017. "Spike's *The Mist* Series Is a 'Reimagination' Not a Remake." *TV Guide*, 13 January. www.tvguide.com/news/spike-the-mist/.

Goddu, T. A. 1997. *Gothic America: Narrative, History and Nation*. New York: Columbia University Press.

———. 2007. "American Gothic." In *The Routledge Companion to Gothic*, ed. C. Spooner and E. McEvoy, 63–72. New York: Routledge.

Goldsmith, J. 2007. "Now Playing: *The Mist.*" *Creative Screenwriting* 14:6, November/December, pp. 26–28.

Golden, M. 1985. "Retail Dominates But More Sales Follow Lower Prices." *Billboard*, 2 November, pp. HV3, HV6–7.

Goodson, W. W. 1992. Stephen King: *Children of the Corn II. Cinefantastique* 23:4. December, p. 13.

Grant, B. K., ed. 1996a. *The Dread of Difference: Gender and the Horror Film*. Austin: University of Texas Press.

———, ed. 1996b. *Planks of Reason: Essays on the Horror Film*. Lanham, MD: Scarecrow Press.

———. 2004. "Disorder in the Universe: John Carpenter and the Question of Genre." In *The Cinema of John Carpenter: The Technique of Terror*, ed. I. Conrich and D. Woods, 10–20. London: Wallflower Press.

Hantke, S. 2010. "They Don't Make 'Em Like They Used To." In *American Horror Film: The Genre at the Turn of the Millennium*, ed. S. Hantke, vii–xxxii. Jackson: University Press of Mississippi.

Hatlen, B. 1988. "King and the American Dream: Alienation, Competition and Community in *Rage* and *The Long Walk.*" In *Reign of Fear: The Fiction and Film of Stephen King (1982–1989)*, ed. D. Herron, 19–50. London: Pan Books.

Hawkins, J. 2000. *Cutting Edge: Art Horror and the Horrific Avant Garde*. Minneapolis: University of Minnesota Press.

Hendrix, G. 2013. "The Great Stephen King Reread: *Needful Things.*" www.tor.com/2013/10/30/the-great-stephen-king-reread-needful-things/.

Herron, D. 1985. "The Biggest Horror Fan of Them All." In *Discovering Stephen King*, ed. D. Schweitzer, 26–40. Mercer Island, WA: Starmont House.

———. 1988. "The Summation." In *Reign of Fear: The Fiction and Film of Stephen King (1982–1989)*, ed. D. Herron, 209–247. London: Pan Books.

Hervey, B. 2008. *The Night of the Living Dead*. London: BFI.

Hillier, J. 1993. *The New Hollywood*. London: Studio Vista.

Hills, M. 2005. *The Pleasures of Horror*. London: Continuum.

———. 2010. "Mainstream Cult." In *The Cult TV Book*, ed. S. Abbott, 67–73. London: I. B. Tauris.

Hollows, J. 2003. "The Masculinity of Cult." In *Defining Cult Movies*, ed. M. Jancovich, A. L. Reboll, and J. Stringer, 35–53. Manchester: Manchester University Press.

Hoppenstand, G. 2011. "On Stephen King." In *Critical Insights: Stephen King*, ed. G. Hoppenstand, 2–7. Pasadena, CA: Salem Press.

Hoppenstand, G., and R. Browne. 1987. "The Horror of It All: Stephen King and the Landscape of the American Nightmare." In *The Gothic World of Stephen King: Landscape of Nightmares*, ed. G. Hoppenstand and R. B. Browne, 1–19. Bowling Green, OH: Bowling Green State University Press.

Horsting, J. 1983. "*Cujo*: Director Lewis Teague Reveals the Difficulties of Adapting the Best-Selling Novel for the Screen." *Fantastic Films* 36, November, pp. 40–43, 46.

Hughes, D. 1990, "Dead Pets Society," *Starburst* 137, January, pp. 11–13.

Hurwitz, M., and C. Knowles. 2008. *The Complete X-Files: Behind the Series, the Myths, and the Movies*. New York: Insight.

Hutcheon, L. 2006. *A Theory of Adaptation*. London: Routledge.

Indick, B. 1985. "What Makes Him So Scary?" In *Discovering Stephen King*, ed. D. Schweitzer, 9–14. Mercer Island, WA: Starmont House.

Jackson, M. 2014. "Stephen King and J. J. Abrams Team Up for *11/22/63* Miniseries Event." *Blastr*. 22 September. www.blastr.com/2014-9-22/stephen-king-and-jj-abrams-team-112263-miniseries-event.

Jagernauth, K. 2014. "Director Josh Boone Says *The Stand* Will Now Be a Four-Movie Event 'With a Cast that Will Blow People's Minds.'" *Indiewire*. 21 November. www.indiewire.com/2014/11/director-josh-boone-says-the-stand-will-now-be-a-four-movie-event-with-a-cast-that-will-blow-peoples-minds-269864/.

Jancovich, M. 1992. *Horror*. London: B. T. Batsford.

———. 2000. "'A Real Shocker': Authenticity, Genre and the Struggle for Distinction." *Continuum* 14:1, pp. 23–35.

———. 2002. "Genre and the Audience: Genre Classification and Cultural Distinctions in the Marketing of *The Silence of the Lambs*." In *Horror: The Film Reader*, ed. M. Jancovich, 151–161. London: Routledge.

Jancovich, M., and N. Hunt. 2004. "The Mainstream, Distinction and Cult TV." In *Cult Television*, ed. S. Gwenllian-Jones and R. Pearson, 27–44. Minneapolis: University of Minnesota Press.

Jeffords, S. 1994. *Hard Bodies: Hollywood Masculinity in the Reagan Era*. New York: Rutgers University Press.

Jenkins, J. 2014. "Fantasy in Fiction: The Double-Edged Sword." In *Stephen King's Modern Macabre: Essays on the Later Works*, ed. P. McAleer and M. Perry, 10–23. Jefferson, NC: McFarland.

Jermyn, D. 2010. *Prime Suspect*. London: BFI.

Johnson, Catherine. 2005. *Telefantasy*. London: BFI.

Jones, A. 1983. "A *Starburst* Interview with Anthony Perkins." *Starburst* 63, October, pp. 12–15.

———. 1984a. "*Children of the Corn*." *Starburst* 72, August, pp. 16–20.

———. 1984b. "*Firestarter*." *Starburst* 72, August, p. 8.

———. 1985. "*Cat's Eye*." *Starburst* 84, August, p. 15.

———. 1992. "Bob Keen's Hell on Earth." *Starburst* 165, August, pp. 12–15.

———. 1999. "Genesis of Terror: Brandon Boyce, *Apt Pupil* Screenwriter," *Shivers* 67, July, pp. 30–32.

Jowett, L. 2015. "Nightmare in Red? Twin Peaks Parody, Homage, Intertextuality and Mashup." In *Return to Twin Peaks: New Approaches to Materiality, Theory, and Genre on Television*, ed. J. Weinstock and C. Spooner, 211–228. Basingstoke, UK: Palgrave.

Jowett, L., and S. Abbott. 2013. *TV Horror: Investigating the Dark Side of the Small Screen*. London: I. B. Tauris.

Kaye, D. 2007. "Two Writers: *1408*." *Fangoria* 265, August, pp. 66–71.

Kelley, B. 1976. "*Carrie*." *Cinefantastique* 5:3, Winter, p. 20.

Kendrick, J. 2004. "A Nasty Situation: Social Panics, Transnationalism, and the Video Nasty." In *Horror Film: Creating and Marketing Fear*, ed. S. Hantke, 153–172. Jackson: University Press of Mississippi.

Kerekes, D., and D. Slater. 2000. *See No Evil: Banned Films and Video Controversy*. Manchester, UK: Headpress.

Kermode, M. 1997. *The Exorcist*. London: BFI.

———. 2003. *The Shawshank Redemption*. London: BFI.

Kit, B. 2015. "Stephen King's *Dark Tower* Alive Again, Lands at Sony." *Hollywood Reporter*, 10 April. www.hollywoodreporter.com/heat-vision/stephen-kings-dark-tower-alive-787758.

Kristeva, J. 1982. *Powers of Horror: An Essay on Abjection*. New York: Columbia University Press.

Larson, R. 1985. "*Cycle of the Werewolf* and the Moral Tradition of Horror." In *Discovering Stephen King*, ed. D. Schweitzer, 102–108. Mercer Island, WA: Starmont House.

Lehmann-Haupt, C., and N. Rich. 2006. "Stephen King: The Art of Fiction," no. 189, *Paris Review* 178. www.theparisreview.org/interviews/5653/the-art-of-fiction-no-189-stephen-king.

Levine, E., and L. Parks. 2007. "Introduction." In *Undead TV: Essays on* Buffy the Vampire Slayer, ed. E. Levine and L. Parks, 1–15. Durham, NC: Duke University Press.

Leyman, C. 1993a. "*The Dark Half*: Horror Meister George Romero Films Timothy Hutton as King's Jekyll and Hyde." *Cinefantastique* 24:1, June, pp. 16–17, 19–20.

———. 1993b. "*The Dark Half*: Stephen King, Maine's Master of the Macabre on the Production of his Horror Bestseller." *Cinefantastique* 24:1, June, p. 21.

Lloyd, A. 1993. *The Films of Stephen King*. London: Brown Books.

Longwell, T. 2003. "Dreamweaver: Genre Master Lawrence Kasdan Takes Plunge into the Realm of Horror with *Dreamcatcher.*" *Cinefantastique* 35:2, April/May, pp. 20–23, 76–77.

Magistrale, T. 1988. *Landscape of Fear: Stephen King's American Gothic.* Bowling Green, OH: Bowling Green State University Press.

———. 2003. *Hollywood's Stephen King.* New York: Palgrave McMillan.

———. 2012. *The Films of Stephen King: From* Carrie *to* The Mist. New York: Palgrave McMillan.

Margulies, L. 1993. "TV Ratings: Stephen King's *Tommyknockers* Pushes ABC to Top." *Los Angeles Times,* 12 May. http://articles.latimes.com/1993–05–12/entertainment/ca-34260_1_stephen-king.

———. 1994. "TV Ratings: Stephen King Miniseries Stands Alone." *Los Angeles Times,* 18 May. http://articles.latimes.com/1994–05–18/entertainment/ca-59201 _1_stephen-king.

Mathijs, E., and J. Sexton. 2011. "Cult Horror Cinema." In *Cult Cinema: An Introduction,* ed. E. Mathijs and J. Sexton, 194–204. Oxford, UK: Blackwell.

Matthews, T. 2005. "The End of Innocence: *Stand by Me* 19 Years Later." *Creative Screenwriting* 12:5, September, pp. 69–73.

McAleer, P., and M. Perry, eds. 2014. *Stephen King's Modern Macabre: Essays on the Later Works.* Jefferson NC: McFarland.

McCarty, J. 1984. *Splatter Movies: Breaking the Last Taboo.* Kent, UK: Columbus Books.

McDonald, P. 2007. *Video and DVD Industries.* London: BFI Palgrave.

McFarlane, B., ed. 1996. *Novel to Film: An Introduction to the Theory of Adaptation.* Oxford, UK: Clarendon Press.

McKnight, B. 2015. "Stephen King's *IT* Back on Track with New Horror Director." *Cinemablend.* www.cinemablend.com/new/Stephen-King-It-Back-Track-With -Horror-Director-72628.html.

Memmott, C. 2013. "Age-Old Conflicts Bubble Up *Under the Dome.*" *USA Today,* 23 June. www.usatoday.com/story/life/tv/2013/06/23/under-the-dome-stephen -king-lost/2110397/.

Miller, J. 2015. "A Tale of Ambiguous Morality: Narrative Technique in *Under the Dome.*" In *Stephen King's Contemporary Classics: Reflections on the Modern Master of Horror,* ed. P. Simpson and P. McAleer, 13–26. London: Rowman and Littlefield.

Morton, L. 2016. "Interview—Josh Boone." *Nightmare Magazine* 42, March. www .nightmare-magazine.com/nonfiction/interview-josh-boone/.

Muir, J. K. 2001. *Terror Television: American Series 1970–1999,* Vol. 1. New York: McFarland.

———. 2002. *Eaten Alive at Chainsaw Massacre: The Films of Tobe Hooper.* New York: McFarland.

———. 2005. *The Films of John Carpenter.* New York: McFarland.

———. 2011. *Horror Films of the 1990s.* New York: McFarland.

Murray, S. 2012. *The Adaptation Industry: The Cultural Economy of Contemporary Literary Adaptation.* London: Routledge.

Naremore, J. 1995–1996. "American Film Noir: The History of an Idea." *Film Quarterly* 49:2, Winter, pp. 12–28.

———, ed. 2000. *Film Adaptation*. New York: Rutgers.

Neale, S. 1995. "Questions of Genre." In *Film Genre Reader II*, ed. B. K. Grant, 159–186. Austin: University of Texas Press.

Nelson, R. 1997. *TV Drama in Transition*. Basingstoke: McMillan.

Newhouse, T. 1987. "A Blind Date with Disaster: Adolescent Revolt in the Fiction of Stephen King." In *The Gothic World of Stephen King: Landscape of Nightmares*, ed. G. Hoppenstand and R. B. Browne, 49–55. Bowling Green, OH: Bowling Green State University Press.

Newman, K. 2011. *Nightmare Movies: Horror on Screen since the 1960s*. London: Bloomsbury.

Nicholls, P. 1984. *Fantastic Cinema: An Illustrated Survey*. London: Ebury Press.

Notkin, D. 1990. "Stephen King: Horror and Humanity for Our Time." In *Fear Itself: The Horror Fiction of Stephen King (1976–1982)*, ed. T. Underwood and C. Miller, 131–144. London: Pan.

Owens, J. 2006. "The Once and Future Stephen King." Powell's City of Books. www.powells.com/post/interviews/the-once-and-future-stephen-king.

Palko, A. 2011. "Stephen King's Cultural Context." In *Critical Insights: Stephen King*, ed. G. Hoppenstand, 21–37. Pasadena, CA: Salem Press.

Pearson, R. 2005. "The Writer/Producer in American Television." In *The Contemporary Television Series*, ed. M. Hammond and L. Mazdon, 11–26. Edinburgh, UK: Edinburgh University Press.

Pezzotta, E. 2013. *Stanley Kubrick: Adapting the Sublime*. Jackson: University Press of Mississippi.

Prudom, L. 2016. "Stephen King's *The Mist* Gets Spike Pilot Order." *Variety* 25, February. http://variety.com/2016/tv/news/the-mist-series-pilot-spike-1201714903/.

Reuber, A. 2011. "More than Just Ghost Lore in a Bad Place: Mikael Hafstrom's Cinematic Translation of *1408*." In *Stephen King's Modern Macabre: Essays on the Later Works*, ed. P. McAleer and M. Perry, 136–149. Jefferson NC: McFarland.

Rodley, C., ed. 1992 *Cronenberg on Cronenberg*. London: Faber and Faber.

Rogak, L. 2009. *Haunted Heart: The Life and Times of Stephen King*. London: JR Books.

Saunders, M. 1998. "*Apt Pupil*." *Cinefantastique* 30:7/8, October, p. 117.

Scapperotti, D. 1998. "Stephen King's *Apt Pupil*." *Cinefantastique* 30:9/10, November, pp. 20–21.

———. 1999. "*Children of the Corn 666*." *Cinefantastique* 31:9, December, pp. 58–59.

Schuman, S. 1987. "Taking Stephen King Seriously: Reflections on a Decade of Best-Sellers." In *The Gothic World of Stephen King: Landscape of Nightmares*, ed. G. Hoppenstand and R. B. Browne, 107–114. Bowling Green, OH: Bowling Green State University Press.

Sederholm, C. 2015. "It Lurks Beneath the Fold: Stephen King, Adaptation and the Pop-Up Text of *The Girl Who Loved Tom Gordon*." In *Stephen King's Contempo-*

rary *Classics. Reflections on the Modern Master of Horror,* ed. P. Simpson and P. McAleer, 149–160. London: Rowman and Littlefield.

Segrave, K. 1999. *Movies at Home: How Hollywood Came to Television.* New York: McFarland.

Shannon, E. 2013. "An Interview with Tom Beauvais." www.filmonpaper.com /blog/an-interview-with-tom-beauvais/#Part4.

Shapiro, M. 1995. "*The Mangler*: Close Encounters of the Gory Kind." *Fangoria* 141, April, pp. 20–24.

Shary, T. 2005. *Teen Movies: American Youth on Screen.* London: Wallflower.

Silver, A., and J. Ursini. 1994. *More Things than Are Dreamt of: Masterpieces of Supernatural Horror—From Mary Shelley to Stephen King—in Literature and Film.* New York: Limelight.

Simkin, S. 2012. "Wake of the Flood: Key Issues in UK Censorship, 1970-1975." In *Behind the Scenes at the BBFC: Film Classification from the Silver Screen to the Digital Age,* ed. E. Lambertini, 72–86. London: BFI.

Simpson, P. 2011. "Stephen King's Critical Reception." In *Critical Insights: Stephen King,* ed. G. Hoppenstand, 38–60. Pasadena, CA: Salem Press.

Simpson, P., and P. McAleer, eds. 2015. *Stephen King's Contemporary Classics. Reflections on the Modern Master of Horror.* London: Rowman and Littlefield.

Skal, D. J. 1993. *The Monster Show: A Cultural History of Horror.* London: Plexus Publishing.

Stam, R. 2005. "Introduction: The Theory and Practice of Adaptation." In *Literature and Film: A Guide to the Theory and Practice of Film Adaptation,* ed. R. Stam and A. Raengo, 1–52. Oxford, UK: Blackwell.

Stein, R. 1984. Publicity flyer for the Criterion Collection.

Sterritt, D. 1995. "*The Mangler.*" *Christian Science Monitor,* 25 August, 14.

Straub, P. 2000. Introduction. In *Secret Window: Essays and Fiction on the Craft of Writing,* by S. King, vii-xxvi. New York: Book of the Month Club.

Strengell, H. 2007. *Stephen King: Monsters Live in Ordinary People.* London: Duckworth.

Strieber, W. 1986. "Thanks to the Crypt Keeper: Introduction." In *Kingdom of Fear: The World of Stephen King,* ed. T. Underwood and C. Miller, 39–44. London: New English Library.

Stump, D. 1985. "A Matter of Choice: King's *Cujo* and Malamud's *The Natural.*" In *Discovering Stephen King,* ed. D. Schweitzer, 131–140. Mercer Island, WA: Starmont House.

Syson, D. 1992. "King Cuts Ties to *The Lawnmower Man.*" *Screen International* 865, 10 July, p. 1.

Szebin, F. 1989a. "Mary Lambert on Directing Stephen King's *Pet Sematary.*" *Cinefantastique* 20:1–2, November, pp. 122–123.

———. 1989b. "*Pet Sematary*: Stephen King's Horror Bestseller Gets Filmed the Way He Wants." *Cinefantastique* 19:3, March, pp. 4–6.

———. 1997a. "Directing the Master." *Cinefantastique* 28:11, May, pp. 20–21.

————. 1997b. "Stephen King's *The Shining*." *Cinefantastique* 28:11, May, pp. 16–17, 19, 21, 23, 24, 27, 29, 30.

Timpone, A. 2005. "Dead Pet Misery." *Fangoria*, 239, January, pp. 66–69, 82.

Totaro, D. 2010. "Masters of Horror." In *The Cult TV Book*, ed. S. Abbott, 87–90. London: I. B Tauris.

Tremayne, P. 1988. "By Crouch End. In the Isles." In *Reign of Fear: The Fiction and Film of Stephen King (1982–1989)*, ed. D. Herron, 99–108. London: Pan Books.

Tucker, K. 1993. "Stephen King's *The Tommyknockers*." *Entertainment Weekly* 7 May. www.ew.com/article/1993/05/07/stephen-kings-tommyknockers.

Tudor, A. 2002. "From Paranoia to Postmodernism: The Horror Movie in Later Modern Society." In *Genre and Contemporary Hollywood*, ed. S. Neale, 105–116. London: BFI.

Venuti, L. 2012. "Adaptation, Translation, Critique." In *Film and Literature: An Introduction and Reader*, 2nd ed., ed. T. Corrigan, 89–103. London: Routledge.

Von Doviak, S. 2014. *Stephen King Films FAQ: All That's Left to Know about the King of Horror on Film*. Milwaukee, WI: Applause.

Walker, J. 2014. "Low Budgets, No Budgets and Digital-Video Nasties: Recent British Horror and Informal Distribution." In *Merchants of Menace: The Business of Horror Cinema*, ed. R. Nowell, 215–228. London: Bloomsbury.

Waller, G. 1986. *The Living and the Undead: From Stoker's Dracula to Romero's Dawn of the Dead*. Chicago: University of Illinois Press.

————. 1987a. "Introduction." In *American Horrors: Essays on the Modern American Horror Film*, ed. G. Waller, 1–13. Chicago: University of Illinois Press.

————. 1987b. "Made-for-Television Horror Films." In *American Horrors: Essays on the Modern American Horror Film*, ed. G. Waller, 145–161. Chicago: University of Illinois Press.

Warren, A. 1985. "Has Success Spoiled Stephen King?" In *Discovering Stephen King*, ed. D. Schweitzer, 15–25. Mercer Island, WA: Starmont House.

Warren, B. 1988. "The Movies and Mister King: Part II." In *Reign of Fear: The Fiction and Film of Stephen King (1982–1989)*, ed. D. Herron, 123–147. London: Pan Books.

Wasser, F. 2001. *Veni, Vidi, Video: The Hollywood Empire and the VCR*. Austin: University of Texas Press.

Watkins, T. 2015. "There's No Place Like Dome: An Assessment of the Adaptation of Stephen King's *Under the Dome* into a Prime-Time Drama." In *Stephen King's Contemporary Classics. Reflections on the Modern Master of Horror*, ed. P. Simpson and P. McAleer, 27–40. London: Rowman and Littlefield.

Wharton, D. M. 2007. "Coming Soon: *1408*." *Creative Screenwriting* 14:4 July/August, pp. 26–27.

Wiater, S., C. Golden, and H. Wagner. 2006. *The Complete Stephen King Universe: A Guide to the Worlds of Stephen King*. New York: St. Martin's Griffin.

Wickman, F. 2011. "Bond Beats Bronte: Who's the Most Adapted Author in Cinema?" www.slate.com/blogs/browbeat/2011/03/11/bond_beats_bront_who_s_the _most_adapted_author_in_cinema.html.

Wilcox, R. V. 2012. "The Darkness of 'Passion' Visuals and Voiceovers, Sound and Shadow." In *Joss Whedon: The Complete Companion*, ed. M. A. Money, 102–112. London: Titan Books.

Williams, S. 1997. "Ratings Aren't Even-Stephen for an Also-Ran *The Shining*." *New York Daily News*, 29 April. www.nydailynews.com/archives/entertainment /ratings-arent-even-stephen-also-ran-shining-article-1.766449.

Winter, D. 1989. *The Art of Darkness: The Life and Fiction of the Master of the Macabre, Stephen King*. London: New English Library.

Winter, S. 1980. "Stephen King and George Romero: Collaborators in Terror." *Fangoria* 6, June, pp. 26–27.

Wood, G. 1990a. "Stephen King's *Graveyard Shift*." *Cinefantastique* 21:3, December, p. 8.

———. 1990b. "Stephen King's *IT*." *Cinefantastique* 21:3, December, pp. 9–10.

———. 1991a. "*Misery*: Rob Reiner on Stephen King." *Cinefantastique* 21:4, February, p. 21.

———. 1991b. "*Misery*: To Splatter or Not to Splatter." *Cinefantastique* 21:4, February, pp. 16, 19–20, 22.

———. 1991c. "*Pet Sematary*." *Cinefantastique* 21:4, February, p. 39.

———. 1991d. "Stephen King and Hollywood." *Cinefantastique* 21:4, February, pp. 24, 27, 29–30, 35, 37, 40, 43–44, 46, 49, 51.

———. 1992a. "*The Lawnmower Man*." *Cinefantastique* 22:4, February, pp. 7, 60.

———. 1992b. "Stephen King: Computer Graphic." *Cinefantastique* 22:5, April, pp. 6–7.

———. 1992c. "Stephen King Strikes Again." *Cinefantastique* 22:4, February, pp. 4–7.

———. 1994. "In Development Hell." *Cinefantastique* 25:2, April, pp. 20–21.

Wood, R. 1986. *Hollywood from Vietnam to Reagan*. New York: Columbia University Press.

Wynorski, J. 1980. "*The Shining*." *Fangoria* 7, August, pp. 21–23.

BOOKS BY STEPHEN KING

This is not a complete list of King's books, but rather a list of those featured in this book. There are many editions of King's books, from countless paperback versions to signed and numbered limited editions. For the sake of consistency and simplicity (because these happen to be the editions that I own), all quotes in this book are taken from trade hardcover first editions. Since I am based in the United Kingdom, the majority of these are UK first editions, but a few are US first editions. For clarification, I have noted the publisher of each edition below, which identifies it as being UK or US.

1974. *Carrie*. New York: Doubleday.
1975. *Salem's Lot*. New York: Doubleday.
1977. *The Shining*. London: New English Library.

1978. *Night Shift*. New York: Doubleday.

1978. *The Stand*. London: New English Library.

1979. *The Dead Zone*. New York: Viking.

1980. *Firestarter*. London: Macdonald.

1980 [2000]. "On Becoming a Brand Name." In *Secret Window: Essays and Fiction on the Craft of Writing*, by S. King, pp. 39–70. New York: Book of the Month Club.

1981a. *Cujo*. New York: Viking.

1981b. *Danse Macabre*. New York: Everest House.

1982. *Cycle of the Werewolf*. Sevenoaks, UK: New English Library.

1982a. *The Dark Tower: The Gunslinger*. Hampton Falls, New Hampshire: Donald M. Grant.

1982b. *Different Seasons*. New York: Viking.

1982c. *The Running Man*. New York: Signet. (As Richard Bachman.)

1983a. *Christine*. New York: Viking.

1983b. *Pet Sematary*. London: Hodder and Stoughton.

1985. *Cycle of the Werewolf*. London: New English Library.

1985. *Skeleton Crew*. London: MacDonald.

1986a [2000]. "How *It* Happened." In *Secret Window: Essays and Fiction on the Craft of Writing*, by S. King, pp. 321–324. New York: Book of the Month Club.

1986b. *IT*. London: Hodder and Stoughton.

1986c. "Why I Was Bachman." In *The Bachman Books: Four Novels by Stephen King*, pp. iii-x. London: New English Library.

1987. *Misery*. New York: Viking.

1987. *The Tommyknockers*. New York: Putnam.

1987. *Eyes of the Dragon*. New York: Viking.

1989. *The Dark Half*. London: Hodder and Stoughton.

1990a. *Four Past Midnight*. London: Hodder and Stoughton.

1990b. *The Stand: Complete and Uncut*. New York: Doubleday.

1991. *Needful Things*. New York: Viking.

1992. *Gerald's Game*. London: Hodder and Stoughton.

1993. *Dolores Claiborne*. New York: Viking.

1994. *Insomnia*. London: Hodder and Stoughton.

1995. *Rose Madder*. London: Hodder and Stoughton.

1996. *Desperation*. London: Hodder and Stoughton.

1996. *The Green Mile 2: The Mouse on the Mile*. London: Penguin.

1997. "Before the Play." *TV Guide*, 26 April, pp. 22–25, 49–57.

1998. *Bag of Bones*. London: Hodder and Stoughton.

1999. *Hearts in Atlantis*. London: Hodder and Stoughton.

1999a. *The Girl Who Loved Tom Gordon*. London: Hodder and Stoughton.

1999b. *The Storm of the Century*. New York: Book of the Month Club.

2000a. *The Green Mile: The Complete Serial Novel*. New York: Scribner.

2000b. *On Writing: A Memoir of the Craft*. London: Hodder and Stoughton.

2000c. *Secret Windows: Essays and Fiction on the Craft of Writing*. New York: Book of the Month Club.

2005. *The Colorado Kid*. London: Titan.
2006. *Cell*. New York: Scribner.
2006. *Lisey's Story*. London: Hodder and Stoughton.
2008. *Duma Key*. London: Hodder and Stoughton.
2009. *Under the Dome*. London: Hodder and Stoughton.
2010. *Full Dark, No Stars*. London: Hodder and Stoughton.
2011. *11/22/63*. London: Hodder and Stoughton.
2013. *Doctor Sleep*. London: Hodder and Stoughton.
2013. *Joyland*. London: Titan.
2014. *Mr. Mercedes*. London: Hodder and Stoughton.
2014. *Revival*. London: Hodder and Stoughton.
2015. *Finders Keepers*. London: Hodder and Stoughton.
2016. *End of Watch*. London: Hodder and Stoughton.

ORIGINAL SCREENPLAYS

The Raymond H. Fogler Library of the University of Maine, Orono, is home to the Stephen King Collection, containing King's original manuscripts, which he donated to the university. Among the collection are four boxes of unpublished screenplays. The following were consulted for this book. Most are undated.

Dunaway, D. C. *Cujo*. Final draft. Box 2316.
King, S. *Cat's Eye*. 1st draft and 3rd draft. Box 2316.
King, S. *Children of the Corn*. 2nd draft. Box 2316.
King, S. *Creepshow*. 1st draft. Box 2316.
King, S. *Cujo*. 1st draft. Box 2316.
King, S. *Maximum Overdrive*. 1st draft. Box 2318a.
King, S. *Night Shift*. 1st draft. Box 2318.
King, S. *Pet Sematary*. 1st draft and revised draft. Box 2318.
King, S. *Silver Bullet*. 1st draft. Box 2318.
King, S. *The Dead Zone*. 1st revised and 2nd draft. Box 2317.
Leight, W. D., and S. Tippens. *Silver Bullet*. 1st draft. Box 2318.
Phillips, B. *Christine*. 2nd draft. Box 2316.
Turner, B. *Cujo*. 1st revised draft (dated 20 August 1982). Revised draft (dated 22 September 1982). Box 2316.

INDEX

Henriksen, Lance, 146, 147
Herbert, James, 25, 30, 54
Herzog, Werner, 153
Heston, Fraser C., 107
He Who Walks Behind the Rows (character), 81, 82, 139, 143, 147
Hicks, Scott, 19
Hill, Debra, 58
Hills, Matt, 24, 25, 131, 132, 171
Hitchcock, Alfred, 51, 53, 60
Holocaust, 111, 112, 116, 176
home-viewing market, 7, 55, 122–123, 125–134, 138–140, 142, 147; and Unrated cuts, 144–145. *See also* DVD; laserdisc; VHS
Hooper, Tobe, 12, 51, 62, 125; and *The Mangler*, 7, 20, 142–146, 149; and *Poltergeist*, 59; and *Salem's Lot*, 56, 152, 154–155, 161, 164; and *The Texas Chainsaw Massacre*, 29, 126, 154
Hopkins, Anthony, 19, 26, 49, 52, 103
horror: audience, 3, 20; body, 1, 54–55, 58–60, 74–78, 144, 159, 173–174, 184; cozy, 59–61, 82, 84, 86, 99–100, 131, 184; fandom, 4, 17, 25, 59, 64, 82, 91, 102, 109, 121, 126, 128–129, 131–132, 134, 138, 142, 145–146, 149, 171, 184; hybrid, 18–20, 26, 32–34, 36, 43–44, 46, 54, 59, 66, 68–70, 87–88, 91, 99, 103–107, 110–111, 115, 120–121, 130, 144, 149, 171–172, 175, 181–182; independent, 54, 58, 82, 109; literary, 27, 29, 48–49, 52–55, 58, 60–61, 73, 84, 86, 103–104, 106, 111, 131, 191; mainstream, 11, 18, 19, 23, 25–26, 27, 48–49, 51–53, 55, 58, 60, 76, 80, 84, 86, 91, 97, 100–101, 103–104, 106, 109, 116, 117, 119–121, 126–127, 130–131, 133–134, 138, 144, 145, 175, 184–185, 192; subculture, 127, 129, 130–133, 149. *See also* slasher film; splatter film; video nasties
horror comics, 62
Hostel II (2007 film), 118

Howard, Ron, 186, 187
Hulu (video streaming), 21, 185
Hunton, John (character), 143, 148

incest, 125, 160
Indian burial ground, 40, 43, 59, 96, 99, 137
Industrial Light and Magic, 59
Insidious (franchise), 119, 188
Insomnia (novel), 108, 109
Ironside, Michael, 147
IT (1990 TV), 21, 156–161, 162, 169, 170, 183; and *The Stand*, 162–163, 165, 167; and *The Tommyknockers*, 166–167
IT (2017 film), 21, 187–188, 190–192
IT (novel), 9, 14, 23, 91, 115, 156–158, 185

Jackson, Samuel L., 117, 120, 188
Jackson, Shirley, 26, 31
Jancovich, Mark: on adaptations of King's work, 4; on horror cinema, 27, 103, 104, 131, 148, 149; on King's fiction, 24, 39
Janus Films, 129
Johnson, Diane, 62
Jourdan, Louis, 153
Julia (novel), 30, 49, 50, 102. See also *Full Circle* (film)
Jurassic Park (1994 film), 104

Karaszewski, Larry, 118
Kasdan, Lawrence, 116, 117
Kelley, David E., 187
Kennedy, John F., 185, 186, 190
Kiersch, Fritz, 12, 58, 80–81, 82, 139
King, Stephen: as actor, 63, 84, 123, 125; as best-selling author, 3, 5, 10–11, 18, 23–26, 31–32, 48–50, 62, 65–66, 96–97, 102–103, 156, 167, 170–171, 182–183, 192; as blue-collar author, 8, 22; as cinematic/televisual brand, 13, 15–22, 26, 44–47, 52, 61–66, 71, 73, 80–

King, Stephen (*continued*)
85, 86–91, 94–96, 102, 107–112, 115,
117–121, 125–126, 133–139, 146–149,
167, 169–172, 182, 184–186, 188–192;
as director, 6, 16, 44, 45, 87, 123; as
executive producer, 150, 161; as literary brand, 3, 13–17, 18, 21, 26, 31, 44,
46–47, 61, 68, 96, 107, 115, 149, 151,
169, 185, 190, 192; as producer, 21;
as screenwriter (cinema), 6, 12, 16,
44–45, 62–63, 65–66, 83, 87, 97–98,
123–124, 134; as screenwriter (TV),
21, 161, 164, 168–170, 172, 183; as
screenwriter (unproduced scripts),
57, 64, 73–74, 76, 79, 81, 94, 98. *See
also individual King titles*
Kingdom Hospital (2004 TV), 3, 21,
170–172
Kobritz, Richard, 56, 151, 153–154, 156,
157
Korean War, 38
Krueger, Freddy (character), 3, 98, 99,
111
Kubrick, Stanley, 12, 62, 168; *The Shining* and creative control, 61, 68; *The
Shining* and critical prestige, 4–5, 21,
26, 111; *The Shining*, direction of, 32,
56, 97, 169, 182

Lachance, Gordie (character), 87, 88, 89
Lambert, Mary, 98, 100
Landis, John, 125
Langella, Frank, 53, 153
Langoliers, The (1995 TV), 167–168
Langoliers, The (novella), 167, 179
language, King's style of, 14, 41, 43, 44,
46, 115. *See also* swearing
laserdisc, 125, 129–131, 141, 144–145
Last House on the Left, The (1972 film),
29, 126
Last House on the Left, The (2009 film),
109
Laurel Productions, 57, 90, 97, 98, 135,
161

Laurie, Piper, 31, 49
Lawnmower Man, The (1992 film), 4,
19, 91, 95, 101, 120, 178; box-office
success of, 45, 120; King's lawsuit
against makers of, 96, 137
"Lawnmower Man, The" (short story),
94–95
LeBay, Roland D. (character), 37, 40, 41,
43, 77–78
Leonard, Brett, 95
Lester, Mark L., 12, 58, 70, 80
Levin, Ira, 27, 29
Levine, Ted, 145, 148, 149
Lewis, Geoffrey, 152
Lewton, Val, 49
Lifetime, 151, 187
Linder, George, 92
Linoge, Andre (character), 164, 165
Lisey's Story (novel), 14
Loncraine, Richard, 49
Lord of the Rings, The (novel), 33, 189
Lorimer Productions, 57, 58; Telepic-
tures, 156
Losers Club (characters), 157, 160, 185
Lovecraft, H.P., 3, 31
Lucas, George, 59
Lynch, David, 159, 170
Lyne, Adrian, 87, 103

Madder, Rose (character), 109
magical realism, 45, 112, 120, 188
Magistrale, Tony: on adaptations of
King's work, 2, 3, 6, 17; on *Carrie*, 29; on *Firestarter*, 67; interview
with King, 8, 123; on King's literary
style, 39, 41; on King's reputation as
popular writer, 4, 8; on *Salem's Lot*,
152–153
Maine Film Commission, 20, 135
Mangler, The (1995 film), 6, 7, 20, 142–
146, 147, 148
Mangler, The (franchise), 20, 145–148
"Mangler, The" (short story), 6, 142,
148